14-4

PELICAN BOOKS

A773

THE SYMPHONY

VOLUME 2

Born in 1921 at Leamington, Warwickshire, the composer
Robert Simpson was educated at Westminster City School
and began his career as a medical student. After two years he
decided to change to music and studied with Herbert Howells
until, in 1951, he obtained his D.Mus. at Durham. The same
year he joined the staff of the B.B.C. Music Division, where
he still works. He is well qualified to edit this book since,
amongst other works, he has written three symphonies himself,
of which No. 1 has been recorded. Dr Simpson is a frequent
broadcaster and, apart from B.B.C. publications on Sibelius
and Nielsen, Bruckner and the Symphony, he published a
book in 1952, *Carl Nielsen, Symphonist*. He holds the Carl
Nielsen Medal (Denmark) and the Kilenyi Bruckner Medal
of Honor (U.S.A.).

THE SYMPHONY

VOLUME TWO
Elgar to the Present Day

*

EDITED BY
ROBERT SIMPSON

PENGUIN BOOKS
BALTIMORE · MARYLAND

Penguin Books Ltd, Harmondsworth, Middlesex, England
Penguin Books Inc., 3300 Clipper Mill Road, Baltimore, Md 21211, U.S.A.
Penguin Books Australia Ltd, Ringwood, Victoria, Australia

—

First published 1967
Copyright © Robert Simpson, 1967

—

Made and Printed in Great Britain
by Hazell Watson & Viney Ltd, Aylesbury, Bucks
Set in Monotype Baskerville

CONTENTS

	Acknowledgements	7
	Introduction: Stravinsky, Hindemith, and Others *Robert Simpson*	9
16	Edward Elgar (1857–1934) *David Cox*	15
17	Gustav Mahler (1860–1911) *Harold Truscott*	29
18	Carl Nielsen (1865–1931) *Hugh Ottaway*	52
19	Jean Sibelius (1865–1957) *Harold Truscott*	80
20	Albert Roussel (1869–1937) *John Manduell*	104
21	Ralph Vaughan Williams (1872–1958) *David Cox*	114
22	Sergei Rachmaninoff (1873–1943) *Robert Simpson*	128
23	Franz Schmidt (1874–1939) *Harold Truscott*	132
24	Havergal Brian (b. 1877) *Harold Truscott*	140
25	Arnold Bax (1883–1953) *David Cox*	153
26	Serge Prokofiev (1891–1953) *Robert Layton*	166
27	Edmund Rubbra (b. 1901) and Michael Tippett (b. 1905) *Harold Truscott*	181
28	William Walton (b. 1902) *David Cox*	189
29	Dmitri Shostakovich (b. 1906) *Robert Layton*	197
30	Martinů and the Czech Tradition *Robert Layton*	218
31	Vagn Holmboe and the Later Scandinavians *Robert Layton*	230
32	The Symphony in America *Peter Jona Korn*	243
33	Prospect and Perspective *Hugh Ottaway*	268
	Index	279

ACKNOWLEDGEMENTS

The publishers of this book wish to acknowledge permission to use the following extracts from copyright music material:

Exs. 144, 151–8 and 174–88 to Anglo-Soviet Music Press; Exs. 220, 225 and 228–9 to Associated Music Publishers; Exs. 145–50, 191–8 and 218–19 to Boosey and Hawkes Music Publishers; Exs. 65–6, 68–83, 85–92, 189 and 190 to Breitkopf & Härtel; Exs. 132–43 and 221–3 to Chappell & Co.; Exs. 104–5 to J. Curwen and Sons; Exs. 93–101 to Durand & Cie, Paris (United Music Publishers, London); Exs. 39–51, 67, 84 and 211 to Wilhelm Hansen, Musik-Forlag; Exs. 159–64 to Alfred Lengnick & Co.; Exs. 1–10 to Novello & Co.; Exs. 106–11 and 169–73 to Oxford University Press; Ex. 212 to Southern Music Publishing Co., Inc.; Exs. 214–17 and 224, to G. Schirmer Inc., New York (Chappell & Co., London); Exs. 165–8 to Schott & Co.; Exs. 52–64 to Skandinavis Musikvorlag; Exs. 102 and 103 to Stainer & Bell; Exs. 112–21 to Universal Edition; and Exs. 199–210 to Viking Musikvorlag.

INTRODUCTION

STRAVINSKY, HINDEMITH, AND OTHERS

Robert Simpson

*

In the introduction to the first volume of *The Symphony*, I made an attempt to show the origins of symphony and tried briefly to define its essence. Now it is my task to indicate why some admirable composers have not found their way into the scheme of the book, even though they have published works called symphonies. Since some of these works are widely performed, their admirers will justly require some sort of *apologia* for my decisions. I must begin by reassuring my readers that none of these omissions is made with intent to disparage; so far as I am concerned, the matter is one of careful classification. No intelligent bat would take offence at the omission of his species from a book on birds; but he may well feel that his 'wings' entitle him to be mentioned, if only to show that he may deserve another book to himself. The title 'symphony' is in many cases even looser terminology than 'wings' in respect of a bat. To discuss this is valuable, so here goes.

Hans Keller's definition of symphonic music is 'the large-scale integration of contrasts'.* This is plausible enough, superficially, until one realizes that the word 'integration' begs a great many questions. The contrasts of *Le Sacre du printemps* or *Ibéria* may reasonably be thought integrated on a large scale in that their distribution produces a satisfactory balance (at any rate in the Debussy work). But such music is balletic, it is episodic, sectional. Why? Because all its elements are not functioning equally. When rhythm and melody are dominant, tonality marks time; when tonality changes, rhythm and melody wait. In a symphony the

* See Vol. 1, p. 52.

9

internal activity is fluid, organic; action is the dominant factor, through and through. At the end of a great symphony there is the sense that the music has grown by the interpenetrative activity of *all* its constituent elements. Nothing is ever allowed to lapse into aimlessness, or the kind of inactivity that needs artificially reviving. At times the activity of particular ingredients is abated – we can find passages in Beethoven's symphonies when nothing but rhythm is left, for instance – at such times, however, we always feel that the other things are merely latent. Often it is as if all the elements of the music have suddenly concentrated themselves into a rhythm or a harmonic progression, or a flash of pure tonality; but such moments are impossible in isolation. The great thing to keep constantly in mind is that no single element is ever abandoned, or deliberately excluded, that the composer must master them all and subordinate them to the demands of the whole. In this sense a symphony is profoundly *inclusive*. If a composer chooses deliberately to exclude, for example, a great natural resource like tonality, he at once excludes inclusiveness. He may bring off something expressive and individual, but he denies himself the kind of comprehensiveness that a symphony must have if we accept that it is to be the highest type of orchestral music (and, I think, history commands us to insist upon this).

If the term 'symphony' is to be the supreme challenge (and there does not seem to be any other accepted generic term of this sort), we must in composing symphonies ignore no basic response of the human mind, so far as elemental musical phenomena are concerned. The human sense of tonality has many times been modified, but cannot be abolished. To attempt to abolish it is to cease to be comprehensive, to be narrowly exclusive. If I appreciate the kind of expression Schoenberg achieved* my sense of tonality, though it may be deliberately anaesthetized for the time being, is by no means abolished. Since all my musical faculties are not being engaged, I cannot feel that such

* I happen to dislike it, but that is irrelevant to my appreciation of its accomplishment.

music is comprehensive. It is certainly concentrated, but that alone will not make it 'symphonic'; if you lose a leg, you have to concentrate in order to move about without it, but however hard you concentrate, you cannot escape the conclusion that it is better to have two legs. With these, you can forget problems of locomotion and concentrate on objects. With one leg you can hop about, but will find it difficult to invent new dance steps that have more than the temporary appeal of oddity.

This is taking the extreme case of the abandonment of tonality; but the fact that it is tonality that is the deepest current in the river of true symphony, means that the flow of the whole depends upon it. The composer cannot forget it while he gives over his senses to the enjoyment of rhythm and harmony. In a ballet he can let the tonality stick while he makes a dance; the tonality then becomes the floor of a stage rather than the current of a river. This happens in the brilliant and original works that Stravinsky calls symphonies. Anyone who believes these to be real symphonies cannot be aware of the nature of symphonic thought. If Stravinsky himself is aware of it, he clearly does not wish to develop it here, in works so vividly balletic in character. Within their own circumscribed terms they are highly organized, but the motion of symphony is absent. They are exclusively concerned with rhythm and texture rooted in primitive monolithic tonality; when one (or a combination) of these has transiently performed enough of its function, it is replaced, and the total effect, however internally agitated, is as static as a stage upon which dancers are gyrating. Because so famous a composer has made use of the title 'symphony' we need not be over-awed into a fundamental denial of principle. The more characteristic a work of Stravinsky, the further is it from the symphonic idea; if this is not obvious to his admirers, they must surely admire him for other than his best features. The Symphony in Three Movements, a consistent and highly individual work, reveals its virtues most readily if one listens to it as one would approach a ballet score like *Le Sacre du printemps*. It is no symphony; its episodic nature is disarmingly positive. It is interesting to compare Stravinsky's use of pedals with Sibelius's. The latter is very fond of long pedal-points, but they are in his mature symphonic works the background to an intense activity and create a vast slow motion of their own, like that of the sky as the earth rotates, while upon the planet's surface there is teeming human and animal movement. The pedals engender a new, larger dimension; they do not clog the symphonic flow, but throw it into relief against a sense of cosmic movement. In a slow majestic way, Sibelius's treatment of these pedals is as active as anything else in his music; they are drawn into the great current. Stravinsky, on the other hand, when he holds on to a pedal, allows the rest of the music to stick with it; a good example of this is the passage from Figs. 7 to 13 in the Symphony in Three Movements. The bass jogs in an *ostinato*, and the orchestra jogs with it; it is pure ballet music, and when the composer has had enough of this particular sort of jogging, he switches to another (see Figs. 13 to 21). These passages are not isolated examples, ripped from their context; they are entirely typical. The effect of the whole, though it is highly personal, is the opposite of comprehensive or symphonic.

Hindemith's is a different case. The basis of his art is nearer to that of Bach than to Beethoven's; his attitude to tonality is fundamentally like Bach's or Handel's, and he rarely treats it dramatically or dynamically. His splendid Symphony in E flat has the same kind of calm solidity as an early suite; the tonalities move round like the spokes of a wheel, rotating about a fixed centre that is never seriously in doubt. The so-called symphony based on the opera *Mathis der Maler* is another such work, not radically different from the magnificent ballet suite *Nobilissima Visione*. Although Hindemith can be sweeping and powerful, his action is more like that of a weight-lifter than that of a sprinter. He raises a massive object into the air, then puts it down again exactly as it was. This is impressive, but the music does not 'travel' like symphonic invention. His use of the term 'symphony' revives its ancient sense (as does Stravinsky in *Symphonies pour instruments à vent*), and these works have much in common with the *Turmmusik* of the seventeenth century; they are dramatic as wholes, dramatic as would be a great tower with trumpeters upon its turrets, not dramatic in their internal processes.

Omission of these composers from the book will also provoke questions about those actually included. A composer has been included if his prime intention, whether fully realized or not, is or has been to compose true symphonies; to omit him because of only partial success would have been really high-handed. We may argue for ever about the success of this or that symphonist as such (how about Shostakovich, for example?) but the fact remains that his main reputation may rest upon a body of such works, in which case we must include him. Neither Stravinsky nor Hindemith quite fit this category. Nor does Schoenberg, whose two tonal chamber symphonies would more than bear scrutiny. Here I hesitated longer, but finally decided that these are really chamber music; the full orchestration of No. 1, in my view, does no more than illuminate the chamber-musical sensitivity of the original. Again, Schoenberg's reputation can scarcely be held to rest upon these two compositions; further, they are adequately treated elsewhere. Some may aver that works like Benjamin Britten's *Sinfonia da Requiem* or his 'cello symphony should qualify; but this is music whose positive attributes do not depend upon the art of symphonic movement with all it implies – this composer's main achievement lies in other fields. His 'Spring' symphony shows this clearly, an enlarged song-cycle so unequivocal that it cannot be misunderstood as can some of Mahler's symphonies – similarly (but adversely) commented upon. The number of composers that could be dealt with has also been limited by space; here it has been necessary to stop somewhere in our own time. This unfortunately meant the exclusion of gifted figures. To mention only some British composers, the symphonies of Malcolm Arnold, Benjamin Frankel, Peter Racine Fricker, Daniel Jones, Alan

Rawsthorne, Humphrey Searle (a contributor to this publication) and William Wordsworth all deserve detailed consideration. The fact that there is still a notable body of music that, regrettably, has had to be crowded out is at least evidence that the idea of composing symphonies is far from dead. But I must leave the reader to speculate upon what he would have included here, or excluded; perhaps he will charitably observe that the two volumes cover a very wide range of music. If anything in them makes him cross, let us hope it will sharpen his enthusiasm as well as his temper.

16

EDWARD ELGAR
(1857 – 1934)

David Cox

*

How far does Elgar, in his best music, transcend his era (as all great composers do) and give us something of lasting value? Ernest Newman once said that besides the Edwardian side of Elgar there is also 'a personal element that derives its brilliant and eloquent energy from a constantly renewed inner struggle'. It is here that we must seek the lasting value.

Certain works of Elgar are now generally accepted as masterpieces by any reckoning – the *Enigma Variations*, *The Dream of Gerontius*, the *Introduction and Allegro*, the two concertos – and these receive regular performances. About the two symphonies, however, there is no general agreement. Hans Richter, at a London rehearsal in 1908, referred to No. 1 as 'the greatest symphony of modern times, written by the greatest modern composer – and not only in this country'; the critic, W. J. Turner, rejected both works contemptuously as 'Salvation Army symphonies'. Many people, whatever they feel about the music, find them too long. (B.B.C. records show that for No. 1, Elgar himself took 46 minutes in 1930, and Henry Wood 50¼ minutes in 1931. And for No. 2, Elgar took 51 minutes in 1930, and Hamilton Harty as much as 59¾ in 1940.) Like Mahler, Elgar is accused of writing at excessive length, using a great number of themes in what is formally too loose a manner. According to Mosco Carner, the basic weakness is that the works are rhapsodic rather than symphonic: 'the composer is inclined to string together the various structural sections in a more or less kaleidoscopic way'. I hope later to show that this is unfair.

Elgar's personality presented many contrasts, which are

reflected in his music. Exuberance and joyous acceptance were offset by nightmarish self-doubt. Crude patriotic feelings contrast with the sensitive, poetic, near-mystic side of him. Protected by a simply-held Roman Catholic faith, he was nevertheless a very 'insecure' person. Now emotional, generous, warm-hearted; now withdrawn, irritable, discontented. At times aggressive and abrupt, hiding a shy, extremely sensitive nature.

In a country of musical provincialism and amateurs, Elgar suddenly appeared on the scene – as completely professional as any musician could be; fully armed and with a clear sense of direction. It needed foreigners – Hans Richter, Richard Strauss – to convince us that he was a great composer. Courageously and persistently Elgar fought against difficulties and prejudices of all kinds. A late developer, success eventually came to him in middle life. He gladly accepted the honours that were showered upon him, but he remained humble enough to say, of Beethoven's Fifth symphony: 'When I look at it I feel like a travelling tinker looking at the Forth Bridge.' Elgar could never have written a *Heldenleben*: there was nothing of the megalomaniac about him. He could walk with kings, like the best of Kipling's *If*-men, and not lose the common touch.

The 'English' side of his music has been much argued about. Elgar disliked folk-songs and never used them in his work – though modality sometimes appears in the diatonic landscape, probably through the Roman Catholic influence of plainsong. His musical idiom was basically German – post-Wagnerian. Early influences included Mendelssohn, Spohr and Gounod; and he felt a special sympathy with Schumann, also with Berlioz and Liszt. In 1905 he said that Richard Strauss was the greatest living composer: he found him a cynical but a powerful genius. How, within this wholly foreign framework, could Elgar be 'the most English of composers'? The answer is in his own personality, which could use the alien idioms in such a way as to make of them a vital form of expression that was his and his alone. And the personality that comes through in the music is English and of his time. We may suppose that he felt at home in the England of his day. He was physically robust and enjoyed good health. He had an unsophisticated love of Edwardian England, with its superficial brilliance and splendour, its blatant imperialism, its ready-to-topple peace and prosperity; and this is reflected in his worst music. He looked like a military man and is reported to have said that he would have become a soldier had it not been for his musical destiny. The flair for pageantry which he showed, the gift for writing rousing patriotic tunes, the crude imperialism of a work like *Caractacus*, the English military band atmosphere of the *Pomp and Circumstance* marches – all this was more than superficial pot-boiling; it was a real part of the complete man, whether we like it or not.

There are also less crude forms of Englishness to be found in his music. Of great importance is the choral tradition, notably that of the Three Choirs Festival, with which the Worcestershire-born Elgar became so closely associated. The grandeur of this choral tradition – so unmistakably English – is reflected in much of Elgar's music, and not only in his choral works: the broad, confident themes, which Elgar rather indiscriminately labelled *nobilmente*, might all be aspiring towards the condition of a coronation anthem.

Above all, however, the Englishness is conveyed by a particular kind of restraint. It is a reserve which prefers to keep every emotion in strict control, however great the nervous energy. There is no exhibitionism, no morbid self-pity, no passionate love-music. (Perhaps the most passionate music Elgar wrote is Gerontius's declaration of faith, '*Sanctus fortis*'.) At his most mystical, at his most poetic, Elgar was still always clear and direct in his musical language. Violent utterance is never headlong: the spiritual conflict in the first movement of the First symphony, for example, is always well ordered. From the 'madness' of a Berlioz he seemed to be protected.

With all this went a technical brilliance, one aspect of which was his astonishing and original flair for orchestration. He had the example of Richard Strauss before him.

He said he learnt more about orchestration from Delibes than from Wagner; he also learnt much from Berlioz. In general, the Wagnerian richness (which included a preference for large forces) was leavened by French clarity. His early experiences with bands and amateur orchestras had made him extremely practical always in his scoring: all the possibilities of the different instruments are exploited with great virtuosity, but always within the bounds of the playable. Orchestral textures, however complex they may seem, are basically direct and invariably 'come off' in performance. Nothing is left to chance; expression marks, every minute detail of bowing, phrasing, and *tempo* are all indicated with scrupulous care.

The originality of the orchestration lies in the handling of colour and texture; the constant mixing of tone-colours for expressive, dynamic, and rhythmic purposes – a procedure which Elgar learnt from Meyerbeer, but made very much his own. The distribution and reinforcing of tone at the musical climaxes is as individual as the subtle handling of the instrumental strands in the quietest passages. As an example of typical Elgarian mixing of colours, take the beginning of the scherzo of the Second symphony.

The upper stave, to the first semiquaver of 6, is played by divided first violins, doubled by flutes from 2 to 3, emphasized by short doubled chords on the oboes at 4 and 6. The clarinets enter at 3 and continue to 10 reinforced by flutes from 6 to 7 and from 9 to 10. The note B at 9 is in the first violins (still divided) and all the violins take over from 11 to 15, reinforced by the flutes for two quavers at 12 and at 14, the lowest notes of the upper stave, from 10 to 15, being for second violins doubled by a clarinet. Oboes interject the quaver, G and E (in the lower stave) at 13. Bass clarinet and bassoons play the sustained chords in the bass stave from 1 to 10, while 'cellos and double-basses play the same chords, but *staccato*, not sustained. At 12 and 14 the chords in the bass are played by 'cellos and double-basses, reinforced by chords on the harps.

Other obvious characteristics of Elgar's style are the use of short motive-like phrases which are developed and treated contrapuntally in a manner stemming again from Wagner; a liking for wide, upward leaps of a fifth, sixth or seventh, to an accented note, and then dropping downwards; a characteristic use of sequence; well-balanced overall rising and falling of phrases; active and purposeful bass lines; a personal way of varying the rhythm by the insertion of triplets; and in general a feeling for broad, massive ideas.

Professor E. J. Dent, in a famous attack on Elgar, spoke of 'the chevaleresque rhetoric which badly covers up his essential vulgarity' – a criticism which could only be applied to his crudely patriotic works, such as *The Banner of St George* or *The Spirit of England*. But this is not the real Elgar. The composer-laureate, who was considered to be the musical mouthpiece of a nation, often spoke of the great loneliness of the creative artist. In the symphonies and concertos we are constantly aware of a wistful, contemplative, extremely sensitive side of the composer. The ceremonial mask is completely dropped, and his greatness appears clearly: many aspects and subtleties of a complex personality are revealed within a wide and powerful expressive range. The difference between *The Banner of St George* and the symphonies is as great as the difference between *Finlandia* of Sibelius and the symphonies of that composer. With both Elgar and Sibelius, the patriotic, community utterance contrasts strongly with the deeply-felt personal utterance.

Form in the Elgar symphonies is personal and intuitive, but symphonic in its processes. Elgar's practice of using a group of several short themes where one would normally serve has led to charges of formlessness. The development in a symphonic movement, however, is consistent but never obvious, because it explores relationships between aspects of the thematic material, often suggesting rather than stating. Many cyclic examples can be found, but the overall unity usually reveals itself only after many hearings.

The symphony No. 1 in A flat major, Op. 55, was composed in 1908, when Elgar was fifty-one years old and his reputation as an orchestral composer firmly established. The dedication is 'To Hans Richter, Mus. Doc., true artist and true friend', the great Wagnerian conductor who had done more than anybody to stimulate interest in Elgar's music. The work is in four movements and is scored for a large orchestra of triple woodwind, four horns, three trumpets, three trombones and tuba, timpani, two harps, and strings. It is just possible that the life and death of General Gordon had been to some extent responsible in the first place for its inspiration – in the same way that Beethoven's 'Eroica' was conceived 'in memory of a great man'. 'As to Gordon,' Elgar wrote to his friend A. J. Jaeger (Nimrod of the *Enigma Variations*) in 1899, 'the thing possesses me, but I can't write it down yet.' But time went by and Elgar's ideas about Gordon changed. There is no definite 'programme' to the symphony. The only clue to its interpretation, outside the music itself, was given by Elgar when he said that it represents 'a composer's outlook on life'. After its première in Manchester, in December 1908, with Richter and the Hallé Orchestra, this symphony achieved a record of nearly a hundred performances in its first year.

The introductory theme – one of the most memorable of Elgarian melodies – is a combination of nobility and simplicity.

This motto-theme sets the prevailing mood of the symphony, takes various forms, and eventually blazes forth magnificently at the end of the last movement in a *grandioso* apotheosis. After its introductory statement, it is brought into conflict when the first movement proper (*Allegro*) begins its restless struggle in the remote key of D minor (the distance of a tritone, *diabolus in musica*). Classical symphonic form is the basis of this movement, but there is a very long development – and the second subject is characteristically a group of four thematic ideas. The feeling of struggle is continued, with greater optimism, in the last movement. Several writers have pointed out the influence of Brahms's Third symphony, which Elgar so greatly admired – though not its scoring. (The impressive theme at figure 114, for example, is certainly Brahms seen through Elgarian eyes.)

The scherzo-like second movement (*Allegro molto*) is impetuous and electrifying, introducing in the trio a vigorous section in march rhythm, which may hark back to Elgar's original idea of a symphony in honour of General Gordon. The *Adagio*, which follows without a break, is one of the great slow movements of the symphonic repertoire

(Richter compared it to a Beethoven slow movement).
An example of the cyclic tendency of the work is a thematic
unity between the main theme of each of the two middle
movements: the same notes are used, but in different time
values.

Between the two symphonies came the tremendous experience of the violin concerto. The symphony No. 2, in E
flat major, Op. 63, is perhaps Elgar's most mature and
personal expression. How full of contradictions have been
the reactions to it! On the score we read: 'Dedicated to the
Memory of His late Majesty King Edward VII' – to which
is added the following note: 'This Symphony, designed
early in 1910 to be a loyal tribute, bears its present dedication with the gracious approval of His Majesty the King'
(i.e. George V) – followed by the date, 16 March 1911.
Here, surely, we should expect to find an 'imperialist' work;
and Basil Maine (in his well-known study of Elgar) calls it
'an epitome of the era which was quietly and gradually
fading away while it was being written'. But this is misleading. The key to the character of this very personal work
is more likely to be found in the quotation from Shelley's
Invocation which appears on the score:

> Rarely, rarely comest thou,
> Spirit of Delight!

The prevailing mood of Shelley's poem is despondency; the Spirit of Delight often appears in the symphony, but the joys are short-lived and always tempered by doubts and underlying sadness. In this connexion something which Elgar wrote to a friend is of interest. Canon Temple Gairdner found the work to be 'a passionate pilgrimage in which sorrow and extravagance lead finally to a haven of rest', and submitted this interpretation to the composer. Elgar wrote: 'It was absolutely correct to say the whole thing represents the "passionate pilgrimage" of a soul; that the last movement represents the final issue of his "passion" in noble action, and that the last two pages is the apotheosis and the eternal issue of the soul's pilgrimage.' He added that in the third movement the *fff* passage represented 'the madness that attends the excess or abuse of passion.'

Such may have been the composer's impressions in retrospect. But elsewhere he emphasized that there was no programme, that it was simply 'the frank expression of music bubbling from the spring within me'.

The scoring is for a large orchestra similar to that of the First symphony, with the addition of an E flat clarinet and some extra percussion. Of the first movement Elgar said: 'I have worked at fever heat and the thing is tremendous in energy.' This rich and complex movement (*Allegro vivace e nobilmente*) begins in 12/8, and compound rhythms are characteristic of the movement as a whole. The attention is immediately gripped by an exuberant theme, with leaps and syncopations typical of the composer.

The work has no motto-theme, but the descending four-note figure (marked A) recurs in many different forms throughout the symphony. The first subject consists of a group of four themes. After the one quoted there is an undulatory theme in the violins in parallel thirds and sixths; and another, again in thirds (a number of themes in this work run in thirds), this time with widely-spaced leaps. The final theme of the group energetically thrusts upwards sequentially by the interval of the fifth. (The short phrases that make up this thematic material are used together and also treated individually as the movement develops.) A climax is quickly reached, and subsides to give way to the second-subject group – beginning with a gracious melody in the violins, with harps, strings, woodwind, and horns accompanying. Here the tonality is constantly shifting in a very characteristic way. Note the marked relationship to A (above).

The second subject proper may well be the 'cello theme that follows shortly after, *dolce e delicato*, over a *pizzicato* bass. (This too bears a relationship to A.)

The above material is developed in Elgar's personal manner already described. A striking feature of the movement is a veiled, ghostly section with muted strings, against a tritone

figure in the bass, and introduced by eight bell-like strokes
on the harps: the effect is like a fearful, agonized cry. Then,
against *pizzicato* throbbing reiterated bass-notes, with which
the harmony comes into conflict, we hear muted suggestions
of the opening theme. The movement struggles to recover
its lost spirit and eventually ends in a tremendous burst of
energy. At its climax a version of A is thundered out *fff* by
the whole orchestra.

When making the original sketches for the symphony in
1910 in Venice, Elgar felt that the slow movement and
scherzo represented the contrast between the interior of St
Mark's Cathedral and the lively, sunlit Piazza outside. But a
great deal happened between that idea and the completion
of the symphony. The stately, sorrowful character of the
slow movement (*Larghetto*, in C minor) is appropriate to an
elegy inspired by the death of Edward VII. After a drum
roll and a soft chordal passage for the strings – flutes, clarinets,
a trumpet and a trombone play the first impressive theme,
against a slow march-like rhythm on the second and fourth
beats of the bar.

Three other important themes appear: a lamenting one (in
thirds) introduced by cor anglais and oboe, a tender
dolcissimo contemplation for the strings, and a strong passionate expression of grief, *nobilmente e semplice*, in the horns
and 'cellos. This material is used in the most varied way,
building to tremendous climaxes. At figure 79, the first
theme of the movement recurs in a remarkably orchestrated
section in which the first oboe has a counter-melody in
triplets – seemingly in complete independence from the rest

of the texture. Near the end, a version of A quietly steals in on two solo violas and then on the violins.

There is little sunlit gaiety about the third movement (*Presto*, in C major) which is basically a *rondo* in 3/8 time. Despite the brilliance and energy, the inner conflict and terror, apparent in the first movement, soon takes shapes as sinister as anything conceived by Liszt. The opening theme leaps forth, divided between strings and woodwind (see Ex. 1), and is developed sequentially with little regard for bar-lines. This first section is repeated. The episode that follows is a sonorous, swaying, *fortissimo* melody, in C minor, full of foreboding. Towards the end of this section the oboe has a counter-melody derived from A. Then the opening theme reappears in a different form, with some new thematic material (and again with references to A). A tremendous climax is built up. This is followed by a section of extraordinary uncanniness, and a new and enigmatic theme emerges:

which is brought into fierce conflict with the rhythmic force of the principal theme, and a relationship is seen between this episode and the uncanny section of the first movement. Elgar told Basil Maine that a true impression of the emotional significance of this episode is conveyed in the following lines from Tennyson's *Maud*:

> The hoofs of the horses beat,
> Beat into my scalp and my brain
> With never an end to the stream of passing feet.

A version of the swaying theme of the first episode leads to a brilliant final statement of the movement's principal idea.

The last movement (*Moderato e maestoso*), in sonata form, presents few problems, and is, for Elgar, remarkably concise in its use of material. The time-signature is 3/4, and we are back in the key of E flat. The opening four-bar theme is confident and easy-going; the rhythm of each bar is the same.

9

After several repetitions of this in various forms, another theme, *ff ma dolce*, majestic but more dramatic in character, is introduced and by repetition built up to a grandiose climax. This leads to the second subject proper – a typical Elgarian *nobilmente* theme:

10

A *più animato* section treats the second theme contrapuntally, with brilliant, flashing orchestration; then, *con fuoco*, the first and second themes are heard in combination. The tonality has now changed to B minor; the mood becomes tranquil. A new thematic figure in the violins, descending more than two octaves in three bars, is developed and reaches a climax; gradually it subsides, leading to a repeat of the opening theme – beginning quietly and gradually building up, bringing in all the main thematic material of the movement and presenting it forcefully and triumphantly. The end of the movement, like an epilogue, looks back peacefully: there are quiet versions of A and of the opening theme of the last movement. The mood is of acceptance and spiritual tranquillity.

When Elgar died in 1934 he left some sketches for a third symphony. They are in fact very sketchy indeed, and no kind of reconstruction is possible. The ideas had been in

Elgar's mind for years, and he had said that the work would be different from the previous symphonies – simpler in construction and design. The nebulous fragments are reproduced at the end of W. H. Reed's book, *Elgar As I Knew Him.*

17
GUSTAV MAHLER
(1860 – 1911)

Harold Truscott

*

MAHLER himself divided his symphonic work into three periods – symphonies I to IV, V to VIII, and a third period beginning with *Das Lied von der Erde* and the Ninth, and including what there is of the Tenth. In effect, this is not so much three periods as three symphonies – or four. The first four do form a complete work, so do Nos. V to VII; and *Das Lied*, the Ninth and unfinished Tenth also form part of a unity. In spite of its deep connexion with Nos. V, VI and VII, the Eighth stands quite alone.

Mahler, whose musical experiences reflected to an exceptional degree his experience of life, was (like Beethoven) the ordinary man with an extraordinary gift for expressing and analysing those experiences in musical language, both creative and recreative. His philosophy was real and genuine, though it often appeared factitious when he attempted the impossible task of putting it into words. Music was his language; even when he sets words, the music far transcends the power of the words, with one exception: the Eighth symphony. There, words and music are a match. At one end of the scale he saw humanity as mean and ignoble and human life as either cause or reflection of this nature; at the other he saw humanity as aspiring but doomed, and to be pitied. Sometimes the idea of redemption and final resurrection seemed to him an answer that made sense of both extremes; the Eighth symphony was the result of one such period. But only rarely did the whole of his being, intellectual, emotional and spiritual, really believe this answer, which at other times seemed too good to be true. The result is an inner struggle.

All this affected not only his choice of material but his actual technical means of using it. To say that he drew upon nature tells us very little. He did. Any collection of natural sounds could furnish him with a starting point. But such things never remained themselves alone. It was humanity and human reactions with which he was concerned, not nature as such. His awareness of the things that touch people most directly may explain his predominant use of the march and fanfare style – military music was always in his ears when he was a child. Such rhythm we find at the very outset of his earliest preserved large work, *Das Klagende Lied*:

This work, as symphonic as the First symphony and much more unified, is astonishingly mature; every page conveys a personal Mahlerian sound. In its atmosphere (and in its philosophical conclusion, so far as it has one), there is the embryo of another lamenting song, *Das Lied von der Erde*. The two works, at the beginning and near the end of his life, significantly frame most of this music. Both are laments for human frailty, yet both make the point that it is the very frailty of humanity and its capacity for folly, which makes its biggest claim to hope. In groping towards this, he is typically human, extracting the truly optimistic conclusion almost against his own will; this feeling is in the opening page of *Das Klagende Lied* as surely as it is in the closing page of the Ninth symphony. Mahler withdrew what programmes there were to his earlier symphonies, and vigorously denounced 'programme' as such in 1900. In the most superficial sense of the word he was not a programmatic composer. But his music has the programme or content of language, which is incoherent if it says nothing; Mahler is incoherent only when he is unsure of what he wants to say.

His music begins, after some youthful chamber and orchestral attempts, with *Das Klagende Lied*, and this has a definite literary programme. First designed as an opera, with a libretto by the composer based on the Grimm brothers' tale of 'The Singing Bone', it was reduced to a cantata in three parts and finished in 1880, when he was twenty. In 1888 he suppressed the first part, and the remainder is the shortest large work he ever wrote. All that is left of its origin is the outline of the story and the somewhat operatic nature of the orchestral introduction, where the themes follow each other more closely than is Mahler's usual custom. It is a beautifully balanced work and its only fault is a vindication of his later and freer expansion; at the end it seems unnaturally constricted, although all the implications of the libretto have been realized. Those who still maintain that Mahler was a long-winded composer should consider the meaning of this.

Practically every significant theme in this work is a march-type; Ex. 11 shows one, Ex. 12 gives another:

12

Even this early Mahler shows the wide range that can be expressed by a variety of themes of one predominant type.

Mahler wrote many songs, and this has led some critics to say that this genius was purely lyrical, that he was not naturally a symphonist, that his larger works are inflated lyrics. My impression is that the reverse is the case; although the songs contain a considerable range of music, delightful and profound, there is sometimes the sense that he needs space in which to breathe, to develop his thought in its natural element. The second song in the early cycle *Lieder eines fahrenden Gesellen* is nothing but a preview; it later received the space it needed – in the first movement of the First symphony. Another theme from the fourth song also grew to its proper stature in the slow movement of the same symphony. The point is that a feeling for the voice or chorus does not preclude a sense of the symphonic (any more than

fugue, originally a vocal style, is less pure when transferred
to instruments). The change of medium affects the nature of
the materials; Schubert, the song writer *par excellence*, has
shown how lyrical material can be the substance of dramatic
instrumental music and in fact be the cause of the drama
itself; Mahler, among others, has profited by Schubert's
example. (He did of course find it occasionally necessary to
use voices in his symphonies.)

The size of Mahler's symphonies can be the result of
near-perfect structure. Mahler frequently requires a large
orchestra, but rarely uses it for immense tuttis. His purpose
is rather to have at his disposal a number of *small* orchestras,
so that much of his large scale music is conveyed by a
chamber orchestra which can quickly change its composition
and colour. This requires great discipline.

Not every Mahler symphony is perfect, but each is a
medium valid for its subject matter; often its composer is
exercising a sense of discipline comparable to that of
Beethoven or Mozart. Mahler's symphonies from the Fifth
onwards show that, far from extravagance, there is a striking simplicity of outline. Few of the composers who
revolted against 'extravagance' could have discerned or
understood this kind of simplicity, very difficult to achieve,
demanding a courage which Mahler possessed. In spite of
partial failures, he brought it off with certainty and conviction in at least five out of nine or ten symphonies.

Besides the march-type of theme there is another factor in
many of Mahler's most characteristic themes. Whereas
his great contemporary, Sibelius, was fond of the interval
of a falling fifth, Mahler favoured a falling fourth. The prototype of many such examples occurs in *Das Klagende Lied*:

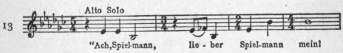

13

"Ach, Spiel-mann, lie - ber Spiel-mann mein!

Mahler's first acknowledged symphony, in D major,
first sketched in 1884, was composed between 1886 and
1888 and received its first performance under its composer

during his period as Director of the Royal Opera in Pesth on 20 November, 1889. As a work it contains fine things and unequal writing; considered as a complete work it is a lesser achievement than *Das Klagende Lied*. It is true that the latter work was revised before its first performance in 1901, but, according to Mahler, this mainly concerned the orchestration and texture.

The most successful complete movements of the symphony are the first three – nothing could be more effective than the introduction, with its gradually awakening sounds, and the size of the main movement is normal enough to cause no formal trouble. The original idea is naïve, the realization on Mahler's part fresh but subtle. I have already referred to the way in which the main theme of the movement proper:

14

reaches its full stature here from its cramped position in the second song of *Lieder eines fahrenden Gesellen*. The scherzo, too, youthful compared with the maturity of the Second symphony, is a complete achievement. The slow movement is justly famous for its mournful distortion of the French round *Frère Jacques* turned to the minor; it is one of the earliest glimpses of a somewhat bitter satirical trait that is to increase in Mahler's work. The weakest part of the symphony is also the most furious – the bulk of the finale; the stormy nature of the music seems an effect, not a necessity, as such music is in the later symphonies. Nonetheless, it projects a type of theme which is important and characteristic in its movement by broken and breathless phrases:

15

In 1888 Mahler also composed the first movement of his Second symphony, in C minor, completing it eventually in 1894; it is known as the 'Resurrection' because of the text of its choral finale. The first movement, large and mainly well balanced, takes over the march rhythms of *Das Klagende Lied* to make a huge funeral oration, or *Totenfeier*, as Mahler called it. Its form raises acutely one of Mahler's biggest problems, his handling of sonata form. Mahler continually attacked this stronghold; unlike Bruckner and some other nineteenth century composers he regarded it, and rightly, as the most essential vehicle for his large-scale thought. But there were other things which had to be reconciled with it, arising from his natural tendency to enlarge the scale. It is not merely that his 'subjects' are groups of themes; other composers from classical times had done this. The difficulty is that his themes are often melodic, long, with subsidiary groups of motives of their own. This is not incompatible with sonata form, but it presents a problem of balance, brought up by Mahler in an unusually severe form, and further complicated by the fact that the subsidiary groups of themes are not development in the wrong places; they are expository. This problem occupied Mahler throughout his work, although by the time he arrived at the Fifth symphony he had made a workable solution. Before then his success was variable; it is character that keeps the immense first movement of No. 3 going, for instance, in spite of large holes in the structure. The first movement of the Second is almost completely successful, but balanced a little precariously; the Fourth symphony, noticeably smaller than its two predecessors but no less tough in fibre, was the transitional work through which the right solution of the problem came to fruition. That solution is intimately connected with the overall simplicity of form emerging from the increased size of these works. It is a mistake to associate greater complexity and complication with such size; on the contrary, the lines stand out with the clarity, and at times the bald effrontery, of a pyramid. No classical symphony of Haydn, or Mozart, or Beethoven has this bareness of line in its structure, but Mahler, of necessity, approximates to the square-cut, departmental formula of the text-book; only on this scale can such simple lines be apt.

In the Second symphony the opening is an expansion and paraphrase of the beginning of *Das Klagende Lied*:

16

It is a phenomenally individual opening and there is a danger that a theme such as this, which goes rumbling on throughout much of the movement and is sensed in the background even when it is not played, could be overdone. Nevertheless, this theme gives off several pungent smaller ones, besides frequently changing its shape, and serves largely as a background for a whole new body of themes; here are four:

Notice the predominant march style and yet the diversity of atmosphere. Mahler makes a magical sudden change to the harmony of E major for this beautiful melody, replete with characteristic *appoggiature*:

This is usually referred to in analysis as his 'second subject'; it is not, although it is made part of the 'second subject' in Mahler's drastically compressed and reorganized recapitulation. The process is simpler and subtler than any textbook notion and a moment later we are back on the C minor tonic for more of Ex. 16. An *ostinato*, which has been heard already as a counterpoint:

leads to Ex. 18 in C major, and in a moment we are on E major:

Allowing for chromatic deviations and a fluctuation between major and minor, here we remain until the end of Mahler's exposition, which is as clearly marked as though he were drawing a map. With this E major-minor there is a whole new group of themes, intertwining as did those of the first group, as well as drawing on some of the earlier material. Again a great variety of march rhythms is evident.

Already we can begin to see that Mahler's solution to his large-scale problem is to make everything simpler in its foundations, however complex in its details. His E major is arrived at in the first instance simply as a plain harmonic move involving no real key-change at all, and it could move back to the tonic of C minor as easily as did the E major of Ex. 16. Instead, he goes back, not to the hey-day of the classical period but to its very beginnings: what we have here is Sammartini's process (a 'second subject' designed so that it works through chromatic harmonies to a fully established key)* on so large a scale that every significant point is clear because magnified.

The test of such a scheme, with so large an exposition, is what happens in the development, a test which the first movement of the Third symphony fails. In the Second the development is so concentrated (of the fifty-four pages of the score of this movement it occupies only twelve, whereas the exposition takes up twenty-eight) that the whole is drawn tight like a knot. It is this kind of terseness, which the

* See Vol. 1, p. 23.

mature Mahler could achieve in the largest movement, that often shows apparently sprawling lines to be as brief as possible with such material. And the material itself must be accepted as positively characteristic. In one way or another this happens in most of Mahler's symphonies; it is the essential clue, the fundamental simplifying of the whole process as a necessary condition of the increase of size. Details proliferate as a further condition of this overall simplicity.

Middle movements were never a problem to Mahler; their essentially lyrical nature came as easily to him as to Schubert or Mozart. In this symphony, as later, he makes them form a central group, which by running like an inner current against the main stream, creates a bivious effect which is employed with much more potent and cynical satire in the Seventh. The pastoral *Andante* has a main theme:

generating a powerful antithesis in the episode, which also suggests a connexion in Ex. 22 (*c*) with the *Andante* of Beethoven's Second symphony:

This movement is one aspect of a mainly pastoral contrast to the epic outer movements; here, also, is a dominant

pedal in the middle of the harmony which is Sibelian in its
persistence. The other aspect is the third movement, a
scherzo in which satire again figures. It is the full (and instrumental) interpretation of his song-setting of St Anthony
of Padua's sermon to the fishes, and Mahler makes it a
mock-serious and humorous commentary on many human
types, with a parody (conscious or not) of the trio from
Bruckner's Fourth symphony:

23

This is the first example of a type of scherzo which occurs
periodically, for different purposes; it is a kind of Mahlerian
Brandenburg Concerto.

With the other two movements, which are really one,
Mahler brings up all his forces to explode at us the Last Day
and the Resurrection; the contralto setting of the *Urlicht*
(from the collection of poems which furnished him with so
many of his songs, *Des Knaben Wunderhorn*) is superbly
beautiful; the rest, beginning on material from the scherzo
and first movement and using the *Dies Irae* motive, introduces a mixture of Klopstock's words and Mahler's own.
Impressive as it is, and in character apt to the rest of the
work, it betrays a certain uneasiness, a feeling that his will is
as yet beyond his capacity.

In the Second symphony, Mahler's maturing genius
settled so many vital structural questions that particular
problems connected with specific material were most likely
to arise. Despite this, the next symphony, though it contains some finer music than the Second, is structurally less
successful. The number of movements grows still further to
six, but even so the substance of the work is not properly
contained; the situation would have been worse if Mahler
had not removed a seventh movement and made it the
finale of the Fourth. The latter, composed 1899-1900, as
well as being the final transition to complete maturity, was

also a sort of shock-absorber for the three previous symphonies. Smaller, much more restrained, with a smaller orchestra, it is still the most frequently played of his symphonies in this country; most people find it immediately lovable, and although it is predominantly a happy work, it is happy in Mahler's own particular way; a way that keeps one eye on mischance, believing perfect human happiness to be not readily attainable; it lightly stresses (at the end) an innocent idea of heavenly happiness. Besides being originally extruded from the Third symphony, the finale also borrows from its fifth movement. Again prominent in the first movement of the Fourth is the Sammartini-like way of establishing the 'second subject' tonality, this time directly *on* the home dominant:

24

while the successively bigger chromatic climaxes of the tune gradually establish D major.

Soon after the Fourth, Mahler wrote the wonderful *Kindertotenlieder*, which suggests that a few of the many small orchestras he normally liked to use together had wandered off separately. The discoveries of these two very different works form a basis for the great symphonies of his maturity. The trilogy of the Fifth, Sixth and Seventh really forms one vast work. The Fifth symphony proceeds from the funereal first movement to a headlong triumph which is too forced to be completely convincing. It is followed by the tragedy of the Sixth, with its extremes of despair and hope, and the satirical, cavernously cynical pastoral burlesque of the Seventh. The great and resplendent Eighth is a thing apart, though it could not have been achieved without its predecessors. In them are the masks of death, love, tragedy and comedy, and after them the Eighth returns to the innocence of the Fourth, wiser, deeper and more certain – innocence with the blinkers off.

Since Mahler is, as any composer must be who makes the symphony his chief objective, a musical philosopher, it is not surprising to find him going through the same cycle a second and even a third time. His first group of symphonies attempts to trace the pattern, life, death, after-life (Mahler himself said that the first movement of his Second was the funeral rite for the hero of his First symphony), and the group of Fifth, Sixth and Seventh starts again from the beginning. What else can it do? There is no other path to tread; the alternative is to remain superficial and ineffective. A full life will know grief and it will know triumph, and so we have the Fifth; it will know tragedy and despair and hope, and so we have the Sixth; it will know the clash of a limpid love of beauty, natural and human, and the cynicism which sees beneath the beauty to the rottenness it believes to be its core, and so we have the Seventh. Without these things there would not be completeness. How strong is the evil pull on man? How strong the good? This is what Mahler probes, not doubting the good, but often doubting its power to prevail, and in this he is remarkably like a great contemporary of his in another field – Henry James. But having seen all this (with a depth of which he was not capable by the time of the Fourth symphony) he then went on to write a work which is the outcome of all this probing and yet is apart from it all; the Eighth symphony, with its gigantic affirmation of God and the drawing of all men to their Creator.

To understand Mahler's various achievements in expression it is necessary to perceive the variety of means he employed. Technically the three symphonies V–VII are tremendously contrasted. The Fifth is pre-eminently the contrapuntal symphony; all Mahler's work is contrapuntal, but none (apart from the Ninth) lives on counterpoint so much as the Fifth. This symphony is usually said to have five movements, but in fact the first two are one conception; like the Second symphony, it begins with a funeral march, or oration, and again, as it moves into the passionate A minor *Allegro* and on to the scherzo, it touches on the fundamentals of human life. The fourth and fifth movements, again one conception, blaze out to a triumph that is somewhat forced. At the very end of the work, the last triumphant statement is not only a theme connected with the main material, but also a quotation from the inexorably tragic first movement of Beethoven's Ninth symphony:

25

Once more we find Mahler using the sonata principle in both the A minor second movement and the scherzo, as well as the sonata-rondo finale; again with deepening subtlety, he simplifies the outlines. Now, however, there is an added complexity arising from the attempt to reconcile so much counterpoint (much of it fugal) with sonata. It is vital that this symphony should be understood as a whole; the pernicious practice, for instance, of playing the fourth movement (the *Adagietto*) by itself has prevented its function from being understood. In the symphony this 'sentimental little *Adagietto*', as it has often been called when heard separately, becomes a major point of irony and lights up the whole finale, to which it is an introduction; the point of its main melody becomes clear only in the last movement.

The Fifth, Seventh and Ninth bring up a problem in tonality already indicated earlier in Mahler's work. This is the habit of seeming to end in a key other than the initial one. Various terms have been applied to this, such as 'progressive tonality', but none explains what really happens. My own view is that the 'progression' is only apparent. Like all other elements in these symphonies, tonalities are expanded in size, and Mahler expects the tonal sense to be perceptive of a large scale. The clearest example is the Fifth symphony where, while the struggle is working itself out, the five movements, adding key to key, C sharp minor, A minor, D major, F major, D major, are, in fact, outlining the solution to the whole – a huge perfect cadence, covering the entire work.

The Seventh takes some of its material from the Sixth (to be treated in some detail later in this chapter) and twists it to its own cynical purposes. Here is the main theme of the Seventh's first movement; notice again the characteristic falling fourth:

26

The connexion with the Sixth is shown by Ex. 28 (a). Ex. 26 (b) shows how the Eighth begins with this germ, evidence of the great range and variety Mahler extracts from basically similar beginnings. The cavernously cynical sound of the Seventh is intensified by the tenor horn, and cowbells create an atmosphere totally unlike that produced by them in the Sixth. The five movements of the Seventh are arranged so that the two outer ones complement each other, the three middle ones seeming to flow against the main stream. The second and fourth are different types of nocturne, the former not a little like a ghostly army on the march, the latter both sentimental and sarcastic, with twang of mandoline and guitar. In between them the scherzo slithers like a snake, in opposition not only to the outer movements but also to the two nocturnes. The work has been reproached for a lack of unity because of this difference between the middle and outer movements; but this *is* Mahler's unity, the sarcastic affirmation of evil doubt just as man is preparing to stand firm. To accuse such a work of disunity on such grounds is like accusing the Devil of not being a Christian.

The tendency of these works is to greater and greater

compression, and I always have the feeling that they are ready to burst at the seams. The Eighth, inevitably, is a result of this, for it shows, besides its panoply, a new and intimate note in the chamber-musical treatment of the largest forces Mahler ever used. Again we have the simplification of sonata; the *Veni, Creator Spiritus* that forms the first part is, perhaps, the greatest sonata movement he wrote, though the first movement of the Sixth almost rivals it. The more one hears the Eighth, the quicker the exalted end seems to come; the whole thing seems to grow shorter.*

Had Mahler stopped at this superb climax, his work would have appeared complete; but Nature can rarely bring herself to avoid loose ends, and so Mahler the unquenchable must go on exploring and questioning in a new kind of music. Disturbed tranquillity, passive yearning, active fare-well – these make up the spirit of resignation that gleams through his last works. *Das Lied von der Erde*, which he super-stitiously avoided calling the Ninth, is really no more a symphony than Sibelius's *Tapiola*; in it he reverted to an old love, the song, with a new free rhythmic treatment of the voice. Here the song-cycle is expanded to symphonic propor-tions. The closing 'Ewig' of *Das Lied* reaches towards the Ninth; the old saga is being followed anew, and perhaps this *is* his end, to fight and question on level after level until . . . The unfulfilled Tenth takes us only so far; the last phase was cut short, perhaps with the answer he had sought all his life. One can have nothing but praise for the superb artistry with which Deryck Cooke has brought to genuinely Mah-lerian life the taut fragments of the Tenth; he has made an experience I would not willingly have missed, which merits the closest attention and gratitude of all who love Mahler's music. As it stands, it points to another positive conclusion, expressed in still more rarefied language. But the last com-plete utterance is the purely instrumental Ninth, and of this I will say only that the great and unearthly Rondo-song

* The Eighth symphony has become exaggeratedly known as 'The Symphony of a Thousand', because of the unusually large number of performers required.

44

which forms its first movement is a rare example of music
influenced by Beethoven's last period.

To close this study let us examine in some detail the Sixth
symphony, the key work of the central phase. This has almost the tautest of Mahler's first movements; its compression is profound, moving ever more and more towards bare
statement. Here Mahler and the Sibelius of the Fourth
symphony, opposites though they may seem, are closely
connected. The amount of basic material is not large; first a
march rhythm:

27

This leads to:

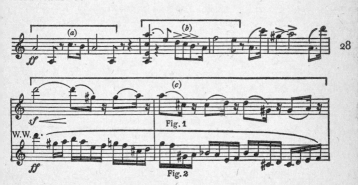

28

Each of these themes is a generator, and Ex. 28 (c) is an
instance of a feature which grows, a double theme (each is
going to be used separately) in which one is a variation of

45

the other. Ex. 27 adds the subsidiary shown in Ex. 29 (*a*) and leads to another important theme, Ex. 29 (*b*):

This and further developments of Ex. 28 (*c*) are really Mahler's first group, which completes itself dutifully on the home dominant. It brings in its train a short but pregnant transition passage, which consists of three themes:

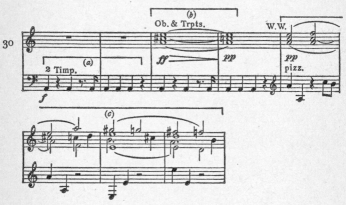

The first of these, Ex. 30 (*a*), brings up a point we must consider briefly – Mahler's use of 'banal' themes, for which he has been much criticized. He himself said that he must use everything, but there is more that can be said: nothing is banal in itself, there is nothing which is not interesting, and the banality may well be our own weariness and failure of imagination. We hear not the thing itself, but associations. Mahler uses such things for the latent mystery in them. He is not the only one; there is Nielsen's side-drum rhythm in

the first movement of his Fifth symphony, and Alkan's* use
of almost exactly the same rhythm as Ex. 30 (*a*) in his piece
Le tambour bat aux champs, Op. 50, No. 2. Alkan, indeed, is
the only earlier composer to show a real affinity with
Mahler.

Ex. 30 (*c*) is accompanied by Ex. 28 (*b*) played *pizzicato*
in the strings. This leads straight from the still prevailing A
minor on to F major for Mahler's 'second subject', a tune
developed from Ex. 28 (*b*):

31

The continuation, with all its internal contrasts and apparent impulsiveness of detail, is so close-knit in thematic
tissue as to bear the severest examination and it carries out
with complete certitude the Sammartini-like process already
found in the Second symphony. The music subsides on to a
cadential passage with a tonic (F) pedal, built on the opening of Ex. 31.

Mahler directs that the exposition be repeated, and this is
the one movement in his mature symphonies where such a
procedure is not only necessary but possible without over-
balancing the piece as a whole. His development, large in
proportion to the brief exposition (notice the opposite proportions in the corresponding movement of the Second),
expands and combines in ever new forms most of the material already heard, combining Ex. 27 with Ex. 29 (*b*); the

* Alkan (a pen-name for Charles-Valentin Henri Morhange) was one
of the greatest pianists of all time and an outstanding composer of unusual piano works (1813–1888).

latter grows tremendously throughout this development until, with Ex. 30 (undergoing a similar process) it dominates everything. One outburst on E minor looks ahead to the first movement of the Seventh. Gradually the last three notes of Ex. 30 (*a*) are separated and snarl over everything, while the three quavers beginning Ex. 31 take on the jerky rhythm of Ex. 27. The themes remain always recognizable but their characters and forms are being constantly changed by their reactions to and against each other; something in the process reminds one of chemistry. This is a classical development such as Beethoven would have understood.

In true tragic manner the recapitulation begins in A major and abruptly changes to the minor, echoing on a large scale the similar change of Ex. 30 (*b*), which is by stages becoming more dominant. As before in Mahler, the recapitulation is much curtailed; the second group is reached at almost its original final climax from a much enlarged version of Ex. 30 (*c*), newly scored. To offset this shortening there is a large coda, nearly a second development, with a wonderful combination of Ex. 30 (*c*) and Ex. 31. Towards the end there is an astonishing reminiscence of the finale of Bruckner's Seventh symphony. The end is overwhelmingly major, in Ex. 31.

This piece has the clarity and impact of a great classical sonata movement. The slow movement is one of his two finest, its opening paragraph broad and beautiful:

Its phrasing is as subtle as its melody is direct; note the way in which the cadence in bar 5 is switched to carry on the opening. Fig. 1 of Ex. 28 (*c*) is in evidence and is, indeed, the most important single motif in the movement, as Ex. 33 will show:

33

It generates most of the other themes, some of which also hark back to the first movement:

34

This idea, emerging naturally,

35

becomes important in the first episode (the whole is a slow rondo) and, as usual with Mahler, tension mounts as themes show more and more relationship with each other and are combined. Mahler's control is perfect, and despite the in-

tensification of feeling, the predominant atmosphere is one
of profound calm.

The differing scherzo movements of the Second and
Fourth symphonies are part-humorous, part-sarcastic
statements of a similar type. That in the Sixth is the tragic
culmination of this kind of movement; there are no more
like it. Like its precursors, it seems inexhaustible in its
prodigal use of a few thematic ideas. Here are its main
themes:

On these the movement proceeds as inevitably as a Greek
tragedy, and there is also the drum-rhythm derived from
bar 2 of Ex. 30 (a). The trio, not separable, is lithe, cat-like:

Its subtle expanding and contracting rhythms leaven the
heavily accented character of most of the scherzo.

The finale, huge and yet with proportions apt to the rest,

derives much from the first movement, bringing some of its tragic elements to a culmination. The courage that enables Mahler to face despair so realistically is itself suggestive of hope. Such hope is no delusion, and despite its grim aspect, this gigantic finale is a kind of vindication. The 'second subject' of the first movement is also pressed into service:

38

Material from the scherzo, too, is used. Nothing is wasted. All Mahler's works are personal documents, but the Sixth, notwithstanding its intensity, has something of Bruckner's objectivity. In it he puts his 'romanticism' to the test.

18

CARL NIELSEN

(1865 – 1931)

Hugh Ottaway

*

To write about the six symphonies of Carl Nielsen is to
write about the man himself, for they reflect the development of his mind with an uncommon truthfulness and
completeness. Nielsen cannot be slickly categorized. Born in
the middle of the Romantic era – in the same year as
Sibelius, incidentally – he was neither a 'romanticist' nor an
'anti-romanticist': the intense subjectivism which, in one
form or another, characterized so many of his contemporaries was simply foreign to his temperament. While he
learnt from Brahms in matters of large-scale musical
structure, Nielsen was unaffected by the Brahmsian melancholy. Again, though his music has a quality that is specifically Danish, he was not a 'nationalist' in the sense that
Borodin, Smetana, or even Dvořák were nationalists. Far
from being contradictions, these facts are evidence of a
truly independent outlook.

Independence, generosity, and a capacity for growth –
these are the qualities that impress themselves repeatedly as
one gets to know Nielsen's work. From early childhood he
was fascinated by the inexhaustible variety of living things,
human beings in particular. 'In every man and woman,'
he wrote, 'there is something we would wish to know, something which, in spite of all defects and imperfections, we will
like once we look into it; and the mere fact that when in
reading about a person's life we often have to say "Yes, I
too would have done that!" or "He ought not to have done
that!" is valuable because it is life-giving and fructifying.'*
This is typical of Nielsen's outward-looking attitude to life

* *My Childhood* (Hutchinson, 1953).

and tells us in a sentence why his music is expansive, inclusive and free from stultifying mannerisms. He was not concerned with projecting his own personality but with creating what he knew to be true to experience. Though full of personal 'fingerprints', his music is entirely innocent of egocentric melodrama and exaggeration.

Nothing reveals more of Nielsen's musical thinking and power as a symphonist than his use of tonality – 'progressive tonality'. This is not a dogma or a magic formula. The term refers to the evolution of one tonality from another, by a process of *sustained key-conflict*. (The italics are important, because any muddle-minded dabbler can end in a key other than the one he started in!) For example, in the two movements of the Fifth symphony, Nielsen 'progresses' from F to E flat: the first movement is built on three great tonal planes, F, C and G; the second begins in B major-minor – tonally, the remotest point from F – and eventually arrives at E flat. Each step in the tonal argument plays a vital part in the changing 'current' of the music (see the analysis, below). Among Nielsen's contemporaries, only Mahler used progressive tonality as a conscious principle of construction* – and to very different effect. With Mahler the treatment is poetic rather than dynamic, and less concentrated.

It is sometimes objected that only trained musicians can follow the long-term key-relationships which Nielsen establishes. If by 'follow' we mean the ability to describe technically what is happening, then the point is obviously true. But it is equally true in respect of Beethoven, Mozart, or Haydn. Such an approach is curiously narrow and academic. Where vital processes are at work, the perceptive listener gains an imaginative grasp, an insight, of far greater import than the mere naming of keys; and as we know, perceptive listening is not the prerogative of trained musicians. Millions have experienced, say, the depression in tonality at the beginning of the development in the first movement of Mozart's G minor symphony (K. 550), or the

* Harold Truscott takes a different view – see p. 42. (Ed.)

twist into F sharp minor, and back again to F major, in the finale of Beethoven's symphony No. 8 – millions have *experienced* these events without being able to describe them. If it is felt that Nielsen makes somewhat stiffer demands, this is because, for him, a change of key is not an excursion before returning 'home' but an active step in an evolutionary process.

Along with this dynamic view of tonality, Nielsen had a fine command of counterpoint, especially counterpoint of the rhythmic, energizing sort. His alert rhythmic sense was one of his greatest assets; it gave his music a characteristic springiness and tautness which is hard to define in the abstract but essential to the staying power of many a big symphonic paragraph. Examples will be cited in the analyses below.

Melodically one soon notices and values Nielsen's feeling for the basic diatonic intervals, thirds especially: the minor third, both rising and falling, is perhaps his most revealing 'fingerprint' and is very marked as early as the First symphony. His views on intervals were given forcefully in an essay on 'Musical Problems'.* Commenting on the Brünnhilde motif from *The Ring*, he wrote: 'It is the taste ... in Wagner's theme that is intolerable. The only cure for this sort of taste lies in studying the basic intervals. The glutted must be taught to regard a melodic third as a gift of God, a fourth as an experience, and a fifth as the supreme bliss. Reckless gorging undermines the health. We thus see how necessary it is to preserve contact with the simple original.' And again: ' ... we must first reverence and respect the simple intervals; dwell on them, listen to them, learn from them, and love them. The composer for the intervals' sake alone, the singer for his singing, and the instrumentalist perhaps more than any of these because his technical skill alone carries with it the risk of losing the feeling for expressive simplicity.'

I have quoted this at length because the emphasis on the 'simple original' and 'expressive simplicity' takes us far

* In *Living Music* (Hutchinson, 1953).

beyond the purely melodic aspect of Nielsen's music. At a time when the general trend was towards an ever greater complication of harmony and texture, Nielsen's reappraisal of the basic things in music gave him an importance which has seldom been adequately recognized. Perhaps this is because his work began within a broadly conservative (Brahmsian) convention and developed in a way that was outwardly unspectacular compared with much that was happening in the music of his time. To those who scent progress whenever they are titillated by newness of idiom – by appearances, in fact – Nielsen is doubtless 'unprogressive'; and yet, ironically enough, his work reveals a sense of progress far deeper than that of many of his more 'radical' contemporaries. Even if he had not composed anything after the *Sinfonia espansiva* (No. 3), the Brahmsian label would still be inept; for quite apart from Nielsen's own strongly marked individuality, the spirit of his work is Beethovenian rather than Brahmsian. As Wilfrid Mellors has remarked, 'both Beethoven and Nielsen are preoccupied with the experience of 'becoming'; Nielsen's themes change their identity through conflict just as Beethoven's do, and the victory his symphonies achieve is a triumph of humanism won, not in the interests of the self, but of civilization.'* In other words, Nielsen was a man of the Enlightenment, and his symphonies are real conflict-symphonies in which a positive outcome is not only possible but is actually achieved. To pursue such a course in the early twentieth century was to go 'against the wind' with a vengeance. Still less is it acceptable today – acceptable, that is, to the artistic intelligentsia. While those who set the pace in cultural matters remain, at bottom, nihilist rather than humanist in outlook, Nielsen will continue to be underrated. And not only Nielsen; the present devaluation of Sibelius is a symptom of the same disease. It says much for Nielsen's toughness and integrity, as well as his creative gifts, that he not only kept his independence but expressed himself sym-

* *Man and his Music*, Vol. 4; *Romanticism and the Twentieth Century* Barrie and Rockliff, 1957).

phonically with an increasing clarity and directness. Which brings us back to the 'simple original' and 'expressive simplicity': the opening movement of his last symphony (No. 6) is in conception far simpler than that of No. 1 (though it is, of course, subtler in execution).

Nielsen's First symphony, completed in 1892, is a confident assertion of his powers: one readily agrees with Robert Simpson that it is 'probably the most highly organized first symphony ever written by a young man of twenty-seven'.* The framework is traditional, and in three of the four movements there is even a repeated exposition. Those exclaiming 'What! In 1892?' had better turn directly to the recapitulations, for the way in which the material is recast is far more significant than any aspect of the ground-plan. Here already is something of that sense of 'becoming', and the key-structure is likewise prophetic. This symphony 'in G minor' in fact begins with a chord of C major, and at the end of the finale – also 'in G minor' – the key of C is triumphantly established. This treatment of tonality, matched by an equally dynamic use of rhythm, is unmistakably Nielsen. But so is the work as a whole, despite the scattered reminiscences of Brahms and Dvořák. That Nielsen never belittled his First symphony is in no way surprising; it is a strong, clear-headed piece of writing, and the more one gets to know it, the more profoundly its individuality emerges.

Symphony No. 2 ('The Four Temperaments') was composed just ten years later. Prompted by a group of comic paintings of the same name, which Nielsen had seen in a village pub in Zealand, this reflects both his growing mastery as a symphonist and his deepening interest in human character. Each temperament – the choleric, phlegmatic, melancholic and sanguine – is explored with an insight and a sympathy far removed from the rough caricature of the pictures: a good example, this, of the way in which some

* *Carl Nielsen, Symphonist* (Dent, 1952) – a most valuable book, highly illuminating on Nielsen and challenging in general. My own indebtedness is gratefully acknowledged.

trifling incident will sometimes 'trigger-off' the creative imagination in all its richness and variety. Nielsen's awareness that the temperaments interpenetrate to form a mobile and complex unity is revealed in many facets of the work, not least in tonality. The symphony progresses from B minor to A major in what was clearly conceived as a continuous scheme.

In strength of style and range of expression, the Second symphony marks a considerable advance. The Third (*Sinfonia espansiva*) both opens up this new territory – with tremendous vigour and assurance: see, for instance, the opening paragraph of the first movement! – and points the way to further developments. In the words of Dr Simpson, '*espansiva* means the outward growth of the mind's scope and the expansion of life that comes from it'. Here, in fact, is the key to Nielsen's personality, and for those who like to strike directly at the root of the matter, the *Espansiva* makes an excellent introduction to his art. It is precisely in this generous, outward-looking aspect, and in the optimism springing from it, that Nielsen stands apart from so many of his contemporaries. As his thought develops, so the contrasted movements of a work become more closely bound together and the relevance of traditional formal patterns, notably sonata form, begins to fade away. Without a doubt, Nielsen's first movement (*Allegro espansivo*) was composed against the background of sonata form, but this is not the most important fact about it; the way in which it thrusts outwards from D minor to A major, the ultimate key of the whole symphony, gives it a character decidedly its own – a mobile, evolving character – and only to a limited extent can it be thought of as complete in itself. In his Fourth symphony (*L'Inestinguibile*) Nielsen took a further step, actually linking the four movements, which are played without a break.

The *Espansiva* dates from 1911, the Fourth from 1916. Again the 'mind's scope' has been extended, this time to include a deep awareness of the vitality, variety and, above all, tenacity of life itself. 'Music is life,' wrote Nielsen, 'and, like life, inextinguishable.' In a sense, this is what he had been saying all along, but in his new symphony it became a conscious (and specific) motivating force. In part, it seems, this symphony was a protest against the madness of the First World War – a far more creative protest than any mere outburst of anger – but fundamentally it was a product of Nielsen's own inner development. The *Espansiva* had celebrated the joy of living; though the element of conflict was scarcely absent, one wonders whether energy or excitement are not better words for it. In *L'Inestinguibile*, conflict comes to the fore: an elemental opposition of forces which expresses itself rhythmically and tonally in some of the most inspired passages Nielsen ever wrote. Where the conflict is fiercest, there the music is at its most original – especially after Figure 59 in the finale – and the world of the Fifth symphony comes within earshot.

The Fifth, which is unnamed, is Nielsen's most penetrating masterpiece. Completed in 1922, it is the work of a man in his middle fifties and has nothing in common with the fashionable evasions of the 'bright young things' of its time. Nielsen, in fact, was acutely aware of the negative, evasive character of much that was happening in music after the first World War. He was seriously worried by what he heard and saw; for the scramble to find new styles, new means of expression, new musical creeds seemed to him misconceived and misdirected. 'Joy howls,' he wrote, 'Cupid squirms and writhes, mirth is stylized on stilts, and sorrow and grief look like the mask of some sphinx with great hollow eyes.'* This is not the voice of blind reaction. On the contrary, Nielsen saw with considerable clarity the nature of the crisis through which he was living; and he was quick to realize that the so-called 'revolutionaries' of art were reacting superficially to a human situation which could not be interpreted, less still understood, purely in terms of artistic techniques – of experimentation versus old-fogeydom.

* 'The Fullness of Time' – from *Living Music*.

While many of the younger generation became fiercely involved in the battle of the styles, Nielsen was deepening his insight into the wider human struggle of which the commotion in the arts was but a partial and distorted reflection.

The Fifth symphony is very much about that struggle. As Dr Simpson puts it, 'here is man's conflict, in which his progressive, constructive instincts are at war with other elements (also human) that face him with indifference or downright hostility'. It is a powerful, heroic work in which the 'tragic' vein – the urge to pity, compassion, even despair – never obscures the issues involved. There are two movements, neither of which has anything to do with sonata form: the first embodies the conflict itself; the second is a big regenerative piece, an expression of tempered optimism all the stronger for the setbacks it encounters and overcomes. Music is said to be 'the art of thinking in sound without concepts'; but Nielsen, especially in this symphony (and again in subsequent works), is a striking, possibly unique, example of a composer who thinks in sound *with* concepts: not the colourful, picturesque 'concepts' of, say, a Strauss narrative, but ideas and forces abstracted from life. Nielsen would have firmly denied that No. 5, or any other of his symphonies, was programme music – and with ample justification. The dramatic 'programme' is tonal and thematic and is therefore self-explanatory, self-contained; yet each musical step in some way reflects the underlying (human) idea. Perhaps this is just another way of saying that Nielsen achieved a remarkable unity of form and content. The result was a directness, even literalness, of expression peculiarly his own.

One can readily grasp that the Fifth is the climax of a long period of development, both musically and philosophically, and also that it contains the germ of much that is new. But its successor – Nielsen's last symphony—is curiously difficult to grasp, in all senses. When as old a hand as Leopold Stokowski says of a work that he understands it 'technically, but not spiritually, psychologically, emotionally',* we should beware of coming up with facile explanations. All the same, the problem must be grappled with, and we need not add to it by trying to discover in the Sixth the kind of musical-conceptual unity that is basic to the Fifth. This is indeed tempting, for a number of reasons, but is bound to cause confusion: in the Sixth *no such unity exists*.

After the immensely concentrated thought of the Fifth, Nielsen relaxed in the 'pure sound' of the wind quintet (1922), and he approached his Sixth symphony (*Sinfonia semplice*, 1925) in much the same spirit. Between these two works, however, he was struck down by the heart disease which was eventually to kill him, and this affected the 'completely idyllic character' of the symphony at more than one level. Precisely *because* the intention was relaxed, the notes that Nielsen set down were bound to reflect his depressed state of mind, even when, as in the finale, he 'tried to make the symphony as lively and gay as possible'. This gaiety has a sardonic edge to it and sounds sadly forced after the pathos of the first and third movements. The *Humoreske* (second movement) is also hard to reconcile; it explores the 'characters' of individual instruments in a way that obviates all serious invention. Nielsen's search for new ways of using instruments is very marked in movements two and four, but it lacks the sense of purpose so compelling in, say, the clarinet concerto (1928). On the other hand, the tragic opening movement is among his finest achievements and one returns to it again and again. In the end, though, the work must be considered as a whole, and as a whole it is deeply disturbing: Carl Nielsen, that exceptionally well-integrated man, is here in disarray, the victim of his own physical collapse, and this is expressed – unconsciously, no doubt – in a way that brings home to us one colossal aspect of our human precariousness. At the same time we are aware of Nielsen's active, exploring mind; for the Sixth, like the Fifth, contains the germ of many new

* In a broadcast discussion, 12 September 1965 (B.B.C. Music Programme).

possibilities, especially in its use of the orchestra. These are taken further in the two wind concertos, works which show that Nielsen recovered his creative vision, despite the fact that his health was permanently undermined.

Looking through this outline, I find the word Danish occurs only once. To Nielsen's compatriots, conscious of his dominant place in their country's music – and even more, perhaps, of the countless Danish inflections in his musical speech – this may seem extraordinary. To the outsider, though, it is character rather than 'national character' that looms so large in Nielsen's symphonies. True, his sense of kinship with his fellows, particularly the country folk from whom he sprang, played a vital part in his growth as a man; and likewise his love of Danish song was a continual source of inspiration in his work. But in general Nielsen took his nationality for granted. As the Danish critic, Frede Schandorf Petersen, has remarked, 'the value of his message is that he embraces the great European traditions and epitomizes them in music of profoundly human implications'.

Something more of the 'human implications' will, I hope, emerge from an analysis of the Fourth and Fifth symphonies. Though reference is made to the scores, these analyses are intended to be intelligible on their own – or rather, in conjunction with the music: the method is a narrative one, with a minimum of cross-reference, so the reader who wishes to 'trace out' the music in performance should not find the text too exasperating.

In the Fourth symphony the evolution of a key (E major) is basic to the musical expression and continues throughout the work. We shall find that all the really important points of arrival are in this key, or its close relative, A major; but not until the end of the finale is E completely triumphant – along with the theme *first associated with such a prospect*.

The symphony begins with a fearsome burst of energy, more or less in D minor – another key to bear in mind. The essence of it is a propulsive two-part counterpoint (woodwind and strings):

This generates the whole of the opening paragraph (some thirty-five bars) and is highly characteristic. Especially notable is the rhythmic freedom and variety: the interaction of even quavers, triplets and dotted rhythms gives the music an immense vitality. The passage subsides on the dominant of A, and after quiet references to Ex. 39 (*b*) by the 'cellos, in sails a gloriously spacious theme in A major (clarinets, accompanied at first only by bassoon and violas):

40

This expands so naturally and continuously that it is hard to decide where to end the quotation. With its warm thirds and ordered sense of flow, here is the perfect counter to the opening. Taken up by the strings, the theme at once begins to alter course (Fig. 6, miniature score) and the tonality drifts away towards A flat minor, in which key (Fig. 8) the clarinets quietly attempt to reintroduce Ex. 40. This, however, is entirely alien to the nature of the theme and its role in the work, and the attempt is decisively cut off by a sudden onset of most of the orchestra:

41

And so E major makes a dramatic first appearance! Thematically, Ex. 41 is a white-hot fusion of Ex. 40 (*a*) and a prominent figure from the opening *tutti*. When this impulsive music lands on the dominant of C, the heavy brass seize on Ex. 40 (at Fig. 10) and with the rest of the wind lead the whole orchestra into a massive peroration on Ex. 40 (*a*) in A major (*pesante ma glorioso*). A *diminuendo* marks the end of the exposition.

The development begins quietly and sparsely: a subdued agitation (violins, preceded by flute), an isolated pedal note played by the timpanist, and that is all. The pedal note is D; and D minor, we remember, was the scene of the symphony's opening. Further portents begin to appear. First, the violas cut in incisively on D with a pattern of repeated notes already heard (at Fig. 8) just before the strenuous E major passage. This happens again, and then a third time, when a rumbling reply ('cellos and basses) comes in the form of Ex. 39 (*a*) and (*b*):

42

Apart from the stab of the violas, the atmosphere is still subdued and remote, with the violins keeping up their weird, impotent commentary on nothing in particular. But even in this static world, Ex. 39 is a source of energy, and the 'cellos and basses succeed in heaving the tonality upwards, semitone by semitone. When the violas have been forced up through E flat to E, the violins become enraged. Clearly, something is about to explode. The tumult that follows is without parallel in Nielsen's music, a unique example of ordered, calculated confusion (from Fig. 17, *con fuoco*). Derivatives of Ex. 39 (*a*) are held to by all the bass instruments, and (*b*) is shrilled out by the piccolo, but the essence of the passage is its chaotic brilliance. After the dim light of the previous sixty bars or so, the listener is blinded by the sudden glare.

Order begins to re-emerge, with yet another derivative of 39 (a):

Soon the renewed triplet pattern becomes all-important in a succession of great buffeting descents by the whole orchestra, interspersed with brave attempts at Ex. 40 by pairs of wood-wind instruments. As the buffeting spends itself with re-peated shifts of key, Ex. 40 strengthens its hold, but nothing like a complete statement of it is given, either here or in the recapitulation. (That is to come at the end of the finale.) Instead there is one of the loveliest passages to be found any-where in Nielsen's symphonies. For me, this music always brings to mind some words by A. E. Housman:

> On the idle hill of summer,
> Sleepy with the flow of streams . . .

The 'streams' are literally there in Nielsen's score; streams of thirds (woodwind) that enter and re-enter and flow together in a hazy, warmly-lit texture – a truly magical effect. Meanwhile, on the violins and violas the triplets continue, but now *pianissimo* and gently floating. The bass part is motionless, underlining the deep calm of the whole passage. The key? C major.

The way in which this summer-seeming pastoral is evolved from the middle of the development is a fine example of Nielsen's 'follow-through'. Notice especially how a transi-tion is made through G major, with one last disturbance of tonality (Fig. 22) before the tender lift into C. What could be more natural, and yet so unforeseen? As for the passage itself, this is as typically Nielsen as the symphony's opening: readers may like to compare it with parts of the *Andante pastorale* from the *Sinfonia espansiva*.

Suddenly Ex. 39 (b) erupts in the bass, there is a rapid

crescendo and the recapitulation surges in, very much in D
(minor-major). What follows is far more compressed, and
more strenuous, than the exposition. As the tension increases,
a reminder of Ex. 40 is heard twice on the horns:

44

This is quickly taken up by the violins and with a last
mighty effort the music reaches E major and a big *diminuendo* in terms of Ex. 40 (*a*). At this stage E is 'provisional'; it
lacks the peroration with which A was given emphasis at the
end of the exposition. And so the movement dies away,
leaving only a distant drum-beat and muted violins – a
link passage that holds the listener in suspense.

Whatever will emerge from this tentative groping? The
answer is a *Poco allegretto* scored mainly for woodwind – a
quite unpredictable turn of events. Here is a different world
(G major) and the writing has a simple, archaic charm
completely free from self-consciousness. All its 'subtleties'
are delightfully spontaneous: for example, the rhythmic
waywardness of the melody quoted below. Like the C major
'pastoral' in the previous movement – but very different
in mood – this music seems to come directly from the Danish
countryside:

45

This opening section is followed by another, in D flat major (Fig. 28), a third, in C major (*pizzicato* violins), and finally by a modified version of itself, again in G major – a clearly-defined four-part scheme.

As the movement flickers out – with a quiet orgy of flattened sevenths! – the violins begin a long, impassioned line that has something both of lyricism and declamation:

Once again Nielsen's fine sense of flow makes it difficult to quote anything less than the complete musical sentence. At the last half-bar of Ex. 46, the violas and 'cellos enter, *above the violins*, their high pitch giving an added tension to the line. The texture is severe, with only the barest of accompaniments. What is the key? It is striving to be E major. This, you remember, was established 'provisionally' at the end of the first movement. After the relaxation of the *Poco allegretto* – an *intermezzo* in all respects – the main endeavour of the symphony is now resumed, but on a different plane. The *Poco adagio quasi andante* has an inwardness, a quality of intense deliberation, very different from the dramatic conflict of the outer movements. It is the difference between thought and action.

At the end of the opening passage, already described, a solo violin discovers the serenest E major:

47

The texture of five solo strings, with little touches of wood-wind colour, has a chamber-musical intimacy. All the strings take up the theme (*pianissimo*), but this dream-like vision quietly wafts away towards a remote C major. An urgent summons from the woodwind brings the movement back to earth:

48

This important motive – an extension of Ex. 46 (*a*) – provides the energy which will enable E major to become a reality. After making a further interjection, Ex. 48 establishes control by means of a *fugato*. From here onwards the course is continuous and unfaltering, though each step has to be striven for. The once serene, visionary theme (Ex. 47) is now a heavy, baleful utterance (horns and trombones, Fig. 38), a drag on the progress of the music. The remainder of Ex. 47 – the little figure marked (*a*) – also changes its character, becoming the means by which the final climax is both heralded and acclaimed by all the strings and woodwind.

The climax itself – a great blaze of sound, firm and unequivocal – gives more weight to E major than any other passage so far. The fact that it is virtually non-thematic is the only limitation. (A romantic composer would probably have crowned this movement with an apotheosis of Ex. 47.) Perhaps the absence of a theme is Nielsen's way of recognizing that thought alone, however purposeful and intense, is not enough; it must be translated into action. This principle is splendidly applied in the final *Allegro*.

But we are not quite there yet. As at the end of the first movement, the E major climax is followed by a *diminuendo*; and then comes a marvellously poetic piece of writing in which the movement's origins (Ex. 47 and the beginning of Ex. 46) are deeply pondered. With Ex. 46 (*a*) sounding distantly on an oboe and the air full of trills, reflection gives way to expectancy and suspense. There is a rapid *crescendo*, tremendous preparations break out in the strings, and the finale is duly launched:

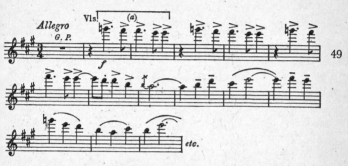

49

To say 'duly launched' does less than justice to Nielsen's mastery at this point. By means of the 'general pause' and the rhythmic shape of (*a*), the tension of the preparation is carried over into the finale itself; only at the eighth bar or so is this resolved in a swinging 3/4. A splendid line then emerges, in A major, but as soon as its expansiveness has been revealed, it runs into trouble (Fig. 44). Fierce dissonances tear the texture apart, and a new, disruptive theme dominates the scene:

50

The upshot of this affray is a savage onslaught by two pairs of timpani.* The creative forces, epitomized in the

* The second pair, used only in the finale, is placed at the side of the orchestra. A menacing tone is asked for explicitly, from both players.

movement's principal theme (Ex. 49), strive to reassert themselves, in F sharp minor (Fig. 48), but again the tumult breaks out. This time the counter-stroke is overwhelming: the 'anarchic' tritones of the timpani are *literally* countered by perfect fourths, and the swinging stride of Ex. 49 brings the music to a triumphant climax in A major.

Another big *diminuendo* – the last – leads into a passage full of quiet suspense. With repeated notes and subtle hints of the principal theme, Nielsen prepares the ground for the final contest. After many changes of key, B major is reached and the theme itself appears in canon on the strings (Fig. 54). The atmosphere is still hushed and expectant. Intimations of the big first-movement theme (Ex. 40) are sounded by flutes and clarinets (Fig. 57). Surely the end must be in sight!

The way in which Nielsen builds up the dramatic tension through all these events, the dynamics remaining low, even very low, is immensely intriguing. Now, with a slight quickening of pace, the key darkens to B minor, and the two timpanists are once more let loose. They are hammering a chord of *D minor*. (This, it will be remembered, was the key of the symphony's opening conflict.) If E major is to be achieved, such a challenge must be powerfully resisted. The violins and woodwind defiantly insist on the note B (the dominant of E), and Ex. 40 (*a*) is pressed forward by the horns and trumpets:

When the timpani admit defeat, Ex. 50 goes careering through the strings and woodwind – and then a full, exultant treatment of Ex. 40 opens out, in E major.

Something of the general character of the Fifth symphony has already been given. It is in two vast movements, the 'form' of which is entirely governed by the work's expressive idea. As in the last two movements of *L'Inestinguibile*, no useful distinction between form and content can be made.

The basic tonal structure is not difficult to grasp, and its main features should be kept in mind. Throughout, the key of F is treated as a negative, inert region in which nothing creative can develop. This is where the symphony begins. Subsequent events bring forward C and then G as new tonal centres in the first movement – a rise of a perfect fifth in each case. The second movement begins in the key furthest removed from F, which is B. Nothing could be more appropriate to this energetic, purposeful *Allegro*, for in the cycle of keys F and B are *literally* at opposite points. Nielsen not only *feels* them as opposites, but associates opposing qualities with the two keys: F, inertia; B, energy.* Put like this, without reference to the expressive detail, something stiff and mechanistic may be suggested – yet another 'system', in fact! The best corrective to such a view is, of

* This is quite different from the association of a certain mood or character with a key *per se* – e.g., Mozart's intense, tragic view of G minor, or Beethoven's judgement that F minor was 'barbarous'. Nielsen's repeated use of G major as a key of diatonic warmth and well-being might also be cited. The two approaches are not incompatible.

course, the music itself. Another 'opposition' used by Nielsen in this work is that of A flat and D; and here there is an added significance in that F – the fatal F – lies midway between them.

Inseparable from this treatment of tonality is an increasingly literal mode of expression. The finale of *L'Inestinguibile*, particularly the final crisis (from Fig. 59 in the score), has already given a vivid illustration of this trend. In the Fifth it is revealed in many subtle ways, as well as in the passage where the side-drummer is urged to do his damnedest – 'as if at all costs he wants to stop the progress of the orchestra'. One immediate result is the directness and clarity of the music's emotional impact. In this respect the symphony is easy to follow, despite its profound originality.

Consider the opening stages. We know that Nielsen wished to express indifference, lack of purpose, inertia. The first sound we hear is a quiet oscillation on the violas – a kind of static presence, entirely 'neutral' in its implications. Bassoons make a dismal attempt at a theme, pottering about in D minor, then settling uncertainly in F:

Why the key of F? The answer seems to be that this is the easiest way of accommodating the violas' C-A. But the effort peters out, and with a loud, disgruntled gesture the bassoons give up. Horns try the key of D, flutes that of C. For a moment the violas hint at C minor, then resume their oscillation:

53

Muted violins play a more extended theme whose various ups and downs seem so much purposeless meandering:

54

Meanwhile the 'cellos tell us that the key is really F (Fig. 4). But it is an F that has no mastery whatever: the Mixolydian, C majorish tonality of Ex. 54 achieves a virtually independent existence.

Here indeed is lack of purpose! Tonally, the music is full of contradictions and uncertainties, and each attempt at melody fails. Soon the side-drum makes its first appearance, tapping out the most commonplace of rhythms, and the minor third characteristic of Ex. 54 becomes a strutting *ostinato* on the timpani and lower strings:

Thus impotence begins to turn belligerent. When a clarinet breaks loose with wild, anarchic cries (Fig. 12), the mood becomes still more destructive. What about tonality? The endless repetition of Ex. 55 emphasizes F in a way that is almost meaningless, and the violins continue to seek a melody centred on the note G (cf. Ex. 54):

Tonality through pitches – the simultaneous assertion of F and G – is all that we are left with here: as we shall see the emphasis on G has far-reaching implications.

A new figure now appears in the woodwind:

This quickly forms itself into another *ostinato*, which brings about a change in atmosphere. After a last savage climax, Ex. 55 ceases and a firmly-held C is set down in the bass. Bassoons and horns revive the thematic groping of Ex. 52. All things considered, it seems that we are virtually back where we started. But the new bass persists, and the 'groping', though still precisely that, is at least more active. As soon as the bass attempts to rise from C to G – it eventually succeeds in reaching G flat – the hostility of the percussion to all constructive effort once again declares itself. Ex. 56

CARL NIELSEN

reappears, at a different pitch, and the sense of struggling
over the same old ground becomes still more acute. At
length the passage fades out indeterminately, leaving an
oboe playing Ex. 53, *centred on F*, and a mysterious repeated
D sounding on the celesta (Fig. 21). The bass falls back to C,
but this note is now revealed as the mediant of A flat. (At
Fig. 24 an A flat *arpeggio* rises expressively on the 'cellos.)

The scene is hushed; the mutual antagonism of A flat
(horns and timpani) and D (violins) quietly fills the air.
Will this lead to a fatal return to F? The suspense is height-
ened. Then D alone is heard. Suddenly this is shown to be
the dominant of G major – cf. the role of B (dominant of E
major) in the final crisis of *L'Inestinguibile* – and a new
theme is gloriously unfolded:

58

This is expanded contrapuntally, with a climax *in B major*
(Fig. 29) – one of the most exalted passages Nielsen ever
wrote. Ex. 58 is not simply a memorable theme; in the
context it is felt as the embodiment of all that is generous
and creative in mankind, and its treatment is as *literal* an
expression of well-directed purpose as is that of inertia
and hostility to effort in the earlier part of the movement.

Here is the dawning of a new consciousness; not a victory,
but a sudden revelation.* The crucial struggle lies ahead.
The first portent is the reappearance of Ex. 53 (woodwind),
and at once the scene begins to darken. The brass build a
stretto on the first eight notes of Ex. 58, but in G minor, and
Ex. 53 becomes a frenzied agitation, kept up alternately by
woodwind and strings (Fig. 33). Next the side-drum returns,
fortissimo and openly hostile to the flow of the music. So

* As is the way with revelations, there is a good deal of unconscious
groping in the background: for instance, Ex. 54 with its warm melodic
thirds, and the seemingly 'blind' insistence on G. Those who criticize
Nielsen for introducing Ex. 58 'from out of the blue' should re-examine
the wider context.

75

depressing is its influence that the horns and trombones, still trying to sustain Ex. 58, fall back into the key of F (Fig. 35). The side-drum increases in ferocity, and the trumpets imitate its rhythm, *on the dominant of G*. The same note (D) is firmly held by the timpani. Soon the side-drum runs amok in a completely free cadenza, but the dominant of G is not to be dislodged. Through all this din the horns and trombones manage to stagger on, and eventually they heave the music into a great blaze of G major.

This triumphant climax has a power that cannot readily be described; it is one of music's really big moments of fulfilment and affirmation. Even the side-drum is engulfed and then immobilized. As the great spread of sound dies away to a quietly-held G major chord, memories of the struggle are recalled. A solo clarinet plays a mournful cadenza in terms of Exs. 53 and 54, and the side-drum makes a last defiant gesture.

The *Allegro*, which follows, is truly a finale – and in Nielsen's toughest, most exhilarating vein. Striding out in B major-minor, this movement at once conveys a sense of strenuous activity, with immense reserves of energy:

As already noted, B is the key remotest from F. It was entered in the first part of the symphony, at a very significant stage: the most exalted moment (Fig. 29) in the initial expansion of Ex. 58. There it was visionary, the peak of aspiration. Here it is a reality, and a none too stable one at that. Embedded in the harmony is a sustained E; after a mere eighteen bars, E springs out as the dominant of A major, and in this key the music sweeps on:

After further shifts of key, the tension is relaxed and a new theme appears:

By comparison, this is almost sanguine, but as (*a*) becomes predominant (Fig. 48), there is renewed excitement – in expectation of a forceful E major. This key does not materialize; instead comes a 'general pause', and then a passage in which breadth and a shifting of key are combined:

If 'sonata' terms were appropriate, the next great paragraph might be described as the beginning of the development. In fact, of course, the music has been developing all the time, without reference to any external framework. Even so, the heightening of tension which the term suggests may help in placing the events that now occur.

Against a background of scurrying quavers on the strings, the woodwind make various shots at Ex. 61. At first it seems that B major is going to be re-established (before Fig. 54), but the moment passes and the quavers become increasingly restless. A long *crescendo* gradually involves the whole orchestra; the strings remain active with their quavers all the time, and the heavy brass take up Ex. 59 (*a*). The climax is suddenly cut off, leaving only the strings, now tremendously agitated (Fig. 59). The tonality is dangerously confused – a chord of D major was the last we heard – and the strings make heroic efforts to find a rallying-point. Rising higher and higher, they eventually reach the note B. This they hold triumphantly aloft, while below it Ex. 59 (*a*) enters on the wind (Fig. 60). B, however, only succeeds in functioning as a dominant. Disillusionment sets in, and the long 'running-down' that follows is one of the most dispiriting of musical experiences. Once again Nielsen's literalness is peculiarly telling: all thematicism disappears; the strings resume their former scurrying, gradually drifting into the region of *A flat major*, and the wind play nothing but repeated chords of *D major* (*sempre diminuendo*). The opposition of these two keys has already been encountered, at a crucial stage in the first movement. But the present situation is more desperate, because a perfect equilibrium is established (from Fig. 67). A deadly sense of inertia is the result.

Clearly, the great constructive purpose with which this *Allegro* began has been disastrously undermined. The only thing to do is to accept an *inevitable* F – the mean between A flat and D – and try to build anew. Such is the thinking behind the *presto* fugue, in F minor, which now begins:

Though 'worked out' at length, this fugue completely fails to achieve its object. That is precisely its dramatic point; the more it struggles the more frenzied it becomes, and still F minor pins it to the ground.

This situation demands a far more thoughtful approach

Another fugue begins, *Andante un poco tranquillo*, and again the muted first violins introduce the subject:

Scored mainly for strings, this marvellous slow fugue literally thinks its way out of F (now major-minor), and it does so with the deepest poetry and tenderness. Rooted in Ex. 59, and embracing Ex. 61, it has a thematic relevance such as the F minor fugue never even attempted.

Eventually the *Allegro* is able to return – in its original B major-minor, complete with pitfalls. This time, however, in a very free recapitulation, the music drives exultantly into E flat major, a key that counters both the relaxation into A (opposite again) and the drift towards F* – the two main threats to the movement's stability. The brightening of key and the vehement preparation – the repeated B flat, with octave leaps, on horns and trumpets – bring a sense of achievement unrivalled in Nielsen's work.

* In relation to E flat, F can behave only as an 'enhanced dominant' i.e. the dominant of the dominant. Thus if it is to exist at all, its original inertia must be transformed into hyper-activity. (Ed.)

19
JEAN SIBELIUS
(1865 – 1957)

Harold Truscott

*

SIBELIUS is a strongly tonal composer with roots in late romanticism, who nevertheless is a genuine twentieth century phenomenon. Everything moves in cycles, and even the serialist's world has roots in the past; but nothing comes round again in the same way as before. Consider a few passages that express a new view of musical language, such as this from *En Saga*:

or this from the first movement of the Fourth symphony:

or this from the first movement of the Sixth:

None of these extracts is foreseeable from the music of the nineteenth century as a whole; and yet each grows from the past. It is not the dissonance that is remarkable in Ex. 1, although it has more point than most dissonances one can hear thrown about with the freedom of the newly rich on a spending spree. What is remarkable about it is that it is a new treatment of a foundational part of musical speech and that this possibility was latent in tonal music from the beginning; but no one found it until Sibelius did. Once found, it enlarges the whole musical horizon.

If we pass on to Exs. 66 and 67, we have two more facts of immense importance. The first is again an enlargement of normal speech, this time arrived at, as often with this composer, by an excision. One chord grows into another in a way that enlarges our vision and, incidentally, teaches us a good deal about earlier forms of speech, by omitting connecting chords that earlier composers would certainly have used. By thus bringing close together the two extremes Sibelius has taught us more than we knew before about what he is leaving out. He is simply seeing the new in the old, and he points forward as well as back. Ex. 67 looks still further into the past, but no less surely ahead. The guiding light here, as in much of the music written at the time of this Sixth symphony, is the polyphony of Palestrina; such a passage as Ex. 67, growing out of the string polyphony with which the work opens, recalls the logically-placed clashing of parts common in sixteenth century music, and yet is part of a forward-looking twentieth century style. Insisting without heat on the clear Dorian mode of the movement as a whole, Sibelius achieves a view of tonality possible only in this century, while others were searching for ways to avoid it altogether.

I have mentioned his interest in Palestrinian polyphony, but it is worth noting that in 1936 he could say this: 'The error of our day has long been its faith in polyphony. It has seemed as if people imagined that the whole had become better by placing nonentities on top of each other. Polyphony is, of course, a force when there is good reason for it, but for a long time it has seemed as if an illness had been raging among composers.'* One cannot hear such an opening as that of the Sixth symphony without wishing Sibelius had allowed himself to think contrapuntally more often, but the fact is that his music avoids counterpoint to a greater extent than that of any other great composer. Since counterpoint is one of the most natural means of creating musical movement, and since Sibelius's music moves with rare consistency and mastery, it is worthwhile and necessary to discover his secret. He frequently denies himself even the moving bass of the homophonic classical composer, so that sometimes the impression of swift movement is an illusion – but a successful illusion, and that, after all, is art.

His methods should become clearer if we examine the tone-poem *En Saga*, Op. 9. This grew out of an octet for strings, flute and clarinet, written during his student days in Vienna. From this he gathered the material for the orchestral work which was composed in 1892 and revised in 1901:

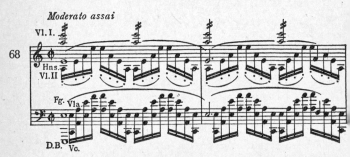

* *Jean Sibelius: his life and personality* by Karl Ekman (1936).

Its opening, Ex. 68, together with Ex. 65, prepares the way
for the first of the three main themes, in the bass:

69

It is a rarity among Sibelius's themes, for it is a really long
tune, albeit with a fair amount of cumulative repetition in
it; as a rule, his 'long' tunes are made of one or two self-
repeating phrases, again with cumulative effect. The harmony shifts and the tune comes again, a semitone higher.
While these two statements of the tune are proceeding, the
harmony about each is static, moving unobtrusively and
quickly only between them. The harmony moves again,
equally quickly, with a diminished version of Ex. 69, and
remains poised about the dominant of C major; a new derivative of Ex. 69 appears:

70

The speed, at first *moderato* in a lowering atmosphere, increases to that of a real classical *Allegro*. All this is preparation and transition; we approach the real harmonic goal as
the key signature changes to three flats and the music arrives
at the second main theme:

71

This fascinating theme is already typical of the mature Sibelius in that its matter is contained in the first four bars, plus Ex. 71 (*b*) (diminished version of Ex. 69), which develops an important function as a hinge. The tune itself has no end; it is self-repeating and could go on indefinitely.

So far there appears to be a first subject, Ex. 69 (in a rather indeterminate key) with a transition passage leading to the second subject, Ex. 71, in E flat major. But this impression is deceptive if one uses the eye rather than the ear. I have read an analysis attempting to relate this piece to sonata form; at the end I was not sure which had suffered more, the music or the writer. The music is making its own form and, like most of Sibelius's characteristic forms, it is a very simple one – much simpler than that of a sonata movement.

Harmonically and tonally, the music is stabilized by its arrival at E flat major. From here to the end of the piece, with only one or two excursions elsewhere, the music hovers between E flat major and C minor, treating each as part of the other; if one is emphasized more than the other, it is C minor, but it is E flat (minor) which has the last word. As well as the material already noted, the piece contains another derivative of Ex. 71 (*b*):

which is also connected with the third main theme:

This, at its initial appearance, follows directly on the heels of Ex. 71 (*b*). This may seem a fair amount of material but, in fact, it is none too much for a movement of this size. Sibelius's structure in *En Saga* depends on the proportioned alternation of its themes at varying levels of expressive power, dynamics and, most important, speed. There is also one other unifying factor – the consistent and persistent use of pedal basses, very long ones indeed.

This last is perhaps the most obvious of all Sibelius's habits, and the most imitated. Unlike his imitators, Sibelius has the secret of suggesting great speed even in passages which are harmonically rooted – the illusion I have already referred to. In this Op. 9 the impression of symphonic movement is maintained by two chief means: (1) by the sparing use of crude counterpoint (the crudity is intentional, not involuntary, expressing rugged strength – the passage from *Allegro molto* following letter Q in the score is one example) and (2) by the solid persistence of E flat-C minor throughout most of the work, offset by occasional divergences from this dual harmony (to such *apparently* faraway harmonic regions as G sharp minor and, in one poignant short slow passage, F minor and D flat).* These devices enliven the daring insistence upon long mediant pedals: out of the 810 bars in the piece, 285 are over a pedal E flat, and for much of this time the harmony is that of C minor.

Here are some of Sibelius's most prominent characteristics, already clearly marked in an early work. We need add but one more figure (from the passage after letter Q):

74

This, at the most turbulent part of the work, foreshadows much of his later writing even though all of this is not the kind of tense music that is generated here.

* G sharp minor in this context is really A flat minor.

Sibelius could not fail to be aware that many critics looked askance at him because he pursued the symphonic ideal at a time when musical tendencies were in totally different directions. But a genuine artist cannot alter the nature of his thought at the behest of fashion. His first full-scale symphonic work is the five-movement *Kullervo* for a large orchestra, soloists and choir. This had been begun in Vienna and was completed and first performed in 1892, and so dates from the same period as *En Saga*. It extends Sibelius's feeling for the power of natural forces, for native Finnish folklore, and was a tremendous success. It was acclaimed as so true an expression of the soul of the Finnish people that many asserted that in it Sibelius had made direct use of folk melodies. This he had not done, and indeed he never did in his music. He has explained that it was only *after* writing *Kullervo* that he visited Karelia and heard for the first time the Kalevala runes from the people.

Kullervo, in spite of its first success, is a strangely inhibited work with but a glimmer of its composer's real power; it is a looser, less impressive work than the terse *En Saga*. It is significant that Sibelius never published it, and that after the first flush of its success it was not performed. But it is an interesting glimpse of his development towards his first real symphony, the E minor, Op. 39. This arrived in 1899, and with it we encounter mastery of means, though not always applied to the highest content. There is the solid satisfaction of feeling a form expanding to its natural size as if taking control of its composer; this fits with what Sibelius has said about his being always the slave of his themes. It is a fruitful slavery.

This First symphony, especially in its first movement, shows a complete mastery of the classical sonata form so successfully avoided in *En Saga*. There is a simple but individual introduction, for solo clarinet with part drum accompaniment, and the *Allegro energico* opens with an ambiguously poised theme:

The second half of the theme is on a full G major harmony:

The exciting *crescendo* that results in the climactic statement of Ex. 75, and the neat sidestep on to the dominant of B minor, creates a new world. Yet everything in this musical language has been used a thousand times before; Sibelius feels it with an intensity that enables him to make new use of it, and with remarkable certainty of touch. The greatness of his later music is unmistakably foreshadowed here, and there is a controlled force surpassing that in *En Saga*. Not a note is wasted.

From *En Saga* (and used here with greater mastery) comes the pedal-note bass. As in the earlier piece, but here with a far stronger assurance, the music moves as on a series of tiers, staying at one level, moving quickly up (or down) and remaining still again. At the same time there is perfect command of a wide range of movement. After a fundamental G, sometimes a mediant pedal (as in *En Saga*), sometimes root of a G major chord, the dominant of B major brings with it an inverted pedal C sharp, as the harp quietly gives definition to the soft fuzziness of the string *tremolandi*:

Then, in the main stage of this second group, a deep pedal F sharp:

This pedal note is unbroken for forty-four bars; astonishingly, the large second group is in suspension throughout, and the device is incalculably potent – an enormously elongated perfect cadence of B minor. The tonic of this key, sensed plainly throughout, is fixed for the first time only at the end of the exposition (*Tempo I*, before letter I in the score). This fact, whether the listener realizes it or not, has much to do with the tremendous excitement imparted to this essentially simple music. Much of Sibelius's originality of thought is in his technique.

For a while the development, taking up the first four violin notes in Ex. 75, tosses them about harmonically, but a mediant pedal-note intervenes for a few bars with Ex. 78. This exhibits a kinship with both the introduction and Ex. 75, and the final stage settles again on F sharp. Ex. 75 is heard in a long series of overlapping entries, extremely chromatic in texture. This shifts upwards, and out of this texture Ex. 76 struggles to emerge, broadening out successfully on to G major. Then comes the whole exciting *crescendo* and climax as at the beginning of the movement, so that the recapitulation begins with the original counter-statement, a short cut justified by the extensive treatment of Ex. 75 in the development. No classical symphonist could have brought it off better. To balance this approach the first part of the 'second subject' is omitted and replaced by an eloquent string passage leading to Ex. 78. The coda is short, the movement ending with a powerful suggestion of the equally powerful ending of one of Beethoven's most characteristic middle-period movements, the first in his D minor piano sonata, Op. 31, No. 2.

The slow movement shows more pedal-notes (the main tune is over an E flat throughout its length) and, as well as some fine melodic invention and scoring, a relapse – in that its presentation of material is rather scrappy. There are distinctive moments, as for instance the merging of the repeated chords and the droop of the theme just before letter F into the accompaniment to the new horn theme, and the use of the chord marked (x) in Ex. 79. This chord is fresh here in spite of its use at high tension in the first movement, but it does become one of the few overworked devices in Sibelius's music:

Andante (*ma non troppo lento*)

79

There is one passage, just before and at letter O, which glances prophetically at the Seventh symphony.

The scherzo, a magnificent movement, has been compared with Beethoven; for power, yes; in any other way, no. It has more connexion with Bruckner – a Bruckner whose music is moving faster than usual. Many harmonic gambits suggest the Austrian master; only the energy is Beethovenian. The trio, whether by accident or design, takes Ex. 79 as a starting point and is one of the most fine-drawn passages in the symphony or, for that matter, in Sibelius's work in general for some time afterwards. In both scherzo and trio pedal-notes are very much in evidence.

With the finale we come to the one movement which is not commensurate with the rest. It is patchy, a fact that Sibelius has recognized but not rectified by calling it *Quasi una fantasia*. It nevertheless introduces a formal practice that becomes important in his music in specimens more successful than this one: his use of the sectional rondo in a finale, often of Dussek's type with one episode. The finest example is undoubtedly the finale of the Fifth symphony; this one is the least felicitous. There are admirable strokes, but the real mistake is that the material is the wrong type for such treatment. The beautiful tune which forms the episode is (apart from its full-blown treatment towards the end of the movement) splendid and almost the last such tune we shall find in the symphonies. The thing of most importance to a study of Sibelius's symphonies which emerges from this movement is the intractable tritone, which, as Ex. 80 (*b*) shows, is also present in the first movement:

80

The Second symphony (1901) has been much discussed. Its first movement has caused many Sibelians to discover a new way of dealing with symphonic form, reversing 'orthodox' procedure. This is an optical illusion and I am not going to refute it further here* except for two points. Firstly, attempts to decide where a second subject occurs would be more successful if analysts would remember that tonality has something to do with it. Secondly, many writers have belaboured the point that whereas a classical exposition is 'complete', Sibelius's statement achieves 'completion' only in the final pages of his first movement. The curious thing is that those final pages are exactly the same as those of the exposition. In fact, most of Sibelius's recapitulation is identical with his exposition, the only departure being a beginning, in *D major* (the key of the symphony) with themes originally heard in a different order – a classical process. Even the combining in the recapitulation of two themes from the same group has a precedent in Brahms's Second symphony.

What the first movement of No. 2 does show is an advance on the formal mastery of that in the E minor, again with a classically proportioned return to the recapitulation that yet arises from the contemporary nature of Sibelius's thought. In movements such as these no composer has done more than Sibelius to refute the ridiculous notion that sonata can ever be played out. A composer who can handle tonality with such mastery and truth gives the lie to those 'progressives' whose only way of learning from failures is to throw the language away.

*I have done so fully in the *Chesterian*, Autumn 1957.

The Second symphony is in its slow movement much tauter and more convincing than the E minor. The scherzo and its wonderful repeated-note trio, the connecting passage which heaves and surges its way into the finale,* and the finale itself, all show a finer accomplishment. Yet the whole is more transitional in nature than its precursor; knowledge of the later symphonies can therefore tempt one to underestimate it. It is true that its finale is again the weakest feature; it exhibits certain characteristics of Sibelius's mature style, but as yet not fully formed. The obviousness of the main theme is no difficulty (it is the most readily acceptable part of the movement) but the most obviously 'original' passage, the long, repetitive 'second subject' (and its even longer restatement) becomes insupportable in its disproportion, fascinating though it is. Nonetheless, this kind of thought is later to prove a source of strength. The finale problem has bothered more composers than have solved it, and Sibelius failed but twice.

The first two symphonies are much more than preliminaries; yet they are a preparation. One still has the impression that complete mastery really begins with the Third symphony, in C, Op. 52, composed 1904–7. There are fumblings and hesitations in the first two, as well as some confusion over content. But from No. 3 onward, all this has disappeared. Sibelius knows exactly what he is doing and why. The Third symphony is a positive achievement and the key to all that followed it. One could draw up a sort of genealogical tree, thus:

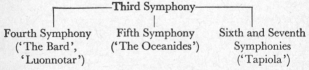

Third Symphony		
Fourth Symphony ('The Bard', 'Luonnotar')	Fifth Symphony ('The Oceanides')	Sixth and Seventh Symphonies ('Tapiola')

I have not included all the smaller works that should go into the various categories; the reader may like to extend the tree for himself.

* To suggest an influence from Beethoven's Fifth is to misunderstand both works.

Neither of the first two symphonies is slow in getting under
way, but they appear to fumble beside the inevitability and
force with which the Third is propelled from its first bar.
There is a spareness about the whole of this symphony which
is the reverse of starved; on the contrary, its leanness is that
of an athlete with immense reserves of energy. The magnificent opening theme is followed by the swinging phrases of
Ex. 81:

81

Notice the tritone, which has already appeared in Ex. 80,
and the figure shown first in Ex. 74; they are marked (a) and
(b) respectively here. The tritone has always been regarded
as an intractable interval, but both Sibelius and Nielsen
have disproved this. With Sibelius, so far from disrupting a
tonal sense, it establishes and reaffirms it – still more in the
superb move to the dominant of B minor for the 'second
subject', another self-repeating theme which dissolves into a
cloudy figure that becomes the basis of the development.
The whole first movement, connected though it may be with
fog banks rolling along the English coast,* is one of his
clearest.

It is useful to compare the development of this movement
with its counterpart in the E minor. Both are classical in
their handling of material; in No. 1 Sibelius is to some extent
poising himself experimentally, but in No. 3 he is definitely
past any line of hesitation. The problem is resolved, there is
a decided advance, yet the process is the more fundamentally
classical in its freedom because of this. Such freedom is one

* Sibelius told Sir Granville Bantock that he intended the frequent
semiquavers to convey this impression.

of the legacies this symphony confers upon its successors, with diverse results. This particular movement is crowned by a coda on quite new material (a Schumannesque trait), with but one echo of the main subject-matter; this coda includes something that looks ahead to the Seventh symphony (in the same key):

82

There is in fact a certain kinship binding all the music Sibelius wrote in C major – embracing even the Sixth (where, although ostensibly in a Dorian D minor, the greater part of the first movement is poised about a pentatonic C major). This is no superficial impression but involves considerable subtleties.

The middle movement of the Third draws attention to the pedal-point in a new way – it is mainly in the centre of the harmony, a pedal dominant, and the music proceeds as a series of simple variations, attempting at times to leave the fundamental G sharp minor but always being firmly pulled back again. There is a clear counterpart in the corresponding movement of the Fifth. Such uses of a pedal-note as we have in these two movements bring to mind Sibelius's remarks to Bengt de Törne about creating a sustaining pedal for the orchestra. Such music has a very real though indefinable attractiveness.

The finale of No. 3 has a remarkable structure; writers have often treated it as a stereotype of Sibelius's individual 'method', whereas it is here entirely peculiar – it occurs nowhere else in his work! It begins with a number of scraps of themes, tossed about from harmony to harmony for about half the movement (evoking briefly the middle movement on the way and beginning with a striking though probably accidental echo of the opening of the *Leonora No. 3* overture). Then there emerges one of the most positive tunes Sibelius

ever wrote. This tune has no thematic connexion with the
first part of the movement, except for one interval; but the
'scraps' are developed, not vaguely improvised, as some
writers have inferred; the music they form is at times almost
fugal, and it emphasizes again the tritone. The big tune of
the second half has a rhythm of ♩ ♩ | ♫ ♩ ♩ continu-
ally repeating itself. It pounds on and on, accumulating
orchestral weight, until it is stopped suddenly and violently
by a C major triad played downwards note by note. In its
course it unleashes more of the power of the tritone, and at
one point very nearly gives us one of the most pregnant
motives drawn from the tritone in the finale of the Fourth
symphony:

83

At the same point (Fig. 16 in the score) in the finale of the
Third symphony, Ex. 81 (b) begins to appear in the woodwind to make a persistent atmosphere against which the
tune pursues its way (see Ex. 74).

The Fifth, in its final version, wherein the original four
movements are telescoped into three, explores the mysterious
elements of No. 3, especially in the first movement, which in
structure, however, is closer to *En Saga* than to anything else.
It is certainly no sonata form, in spite of a likely candidate
for a 'second subject' – Sibelius's tonality here has no interest in the key-antagonism of sonata. He is much more intent

on a fascinatingly Schubertian use of the Neapolitan sixth
(especially in the wonderful deviation on to B major); still
more Schubertian is his creation of two speeds simultaneously in operation. Below the surface movement (from
extreme *moderato* to *presto*) lies another slower momentum
that swings round a central point. Here is one of the finest
examples of Sibelius's skill in suggesting the illusion of great
speed. The movement is fundamentally a continuous assertion of E flat; it proliferates, yet nearly all arises from the
first theme, harmonically as well as thematically. The theme
is only another version of Ex. 81 (*b*):

84

Eventually the notes of Ex. 84 are simply pressed together
into one persistent chord.

The middle movement, strong and delicate, often of
Mozartian simplicity, is intensely characteristic. Tonally it
emphasizes the G major already prominent in the first
movement, and its one excursion is to the fundamental E
flat. It is a set of simple variations on a rhythm. The finale is
brief and uncomplicated but huge in its effect, the impression of size being created by a vast tonal swing from one side
of the fundamental E flat (C major) to the other (G flat
major). The clashing coda is a *locus classicus* for diatonic
dissonance, at once a commentary on the past and an augur
for future sanity. The movement makes convincing the kind
of thought attempted without proper basis in the finale of
the Second symphony. The four chords and two unisons at
the very end carry without effort the weight of the whole
work.

Many characteristics of the Third symphony help to form
the Sixth, so totally different, again (like No. 5) avoiding
sonata. Here Sibelius evolves a thematic growth which might
almost be said to replace normal tonal processes. The first

movement is enclosed between two fundamental Ds, but most of it is in a pentatonic C major. To speak of main and subsidiary themes is purposeless, since the only theme which could be called the principal is no more than a quaver rhythm whose shape is inconstant while yet remaining recognizable (compare the first movement of Schubert's Second symphony). But the mood is the important thing, and this is predominantly contemplative. This is true of the whole symphony, except for the extraordinary third movement, a scherzo-type which, with as little as possible in the way of themes and harmonies, shivers and shudders neurotically, but with periodical squaring of the shoulders. There is nothing like this work anywhere else in Sibelius, although it leads directly to the Seventh. The latter is more obviously a positive statement, but I have found that it is the shadowy Sixth which has at length left the stronger impression.

For a long time I had doubts about the genre of No. 7, and it was no surprise to learn that Sibelius did not plan it as a symphony, but as a *Fantasia Sinfonica*, under which title it received its first performance. I am sure that its one-movement plan is a contrivance rather than a growth; in the first place it was 'in three movements – the last a "Hellenic" rondo'. It is no more a one-movement symphony than is Schumann's Fourth, but if one leaves aside any such bothersome questions, however, the work is convincing. I cannot readily explain why *Tapiola*, symphonic as it is in some ways, could never begin to be a symphony, while the first movement of the Fifth just as obviously is part of a symphony. It certainly has nothing to do with the monothematic basis of *Tapiola;* if this were so, many of Haydn's finest and most indubitable symphonies would be tone-poems, not symphonies at all. On the other hand, it is my firm belief that another work, which Sibelius also called *Symphonic Fantasia* (and did not alter the title for publication), *Pohjola's Daughter*, really *is* a genuine one-movement symphony.

The conviction behind the massive root polyphony of the Seventh, the wonderful growth of theme to theme in its

opening portion, the great climax and ending, all these make
it, with the equally great *Tapiola*, a fitting end to the work of
this composer (and it seems certain that his large-scale work
did end here). But I am doubtful if they contain the most
lasting part of his message, or even the most optimistic. The
most potent kind of optimism is founded on the fullest realization of the frailty of humanity, coupled with belief in
humanity's power to overcome its own most powerful faults.
Sibelius expresses this in what is, for me, the greatest thing
he ever did – the Fourth symphony.

This work, begun in 1910 and completed in 1911, is full of
a foreboding which is probably the unconscious result of a
concern over his own country's difficulties with Russia and
the sensing of an atmosphere which was to explode in 1914
into a world war. But a profound optimism may also be felt.
The work absorbed him completely, and one is reminded of
Conrad, for two years or more simply a vessel for the conveying of *Nostromo* to paper. The symphony consists of two
slow movements (first and third), a scherzo, and a rapid
finale. In it the tritone is used in two opposite ways, and to
an extent not found elsewhere in Sibelius's work. It is used
to establish and sustain a tonality, and to express antagonism and disintegration. It begins the symphony:

85

As we have found in other works, there is a strong tendency
here to identify what are called relative major and minor as
essential parts of the same tonality, much as Schubert does.
The music at first sounds like C major, but the stubborn F

sharp actually helps to establish A minor as the fundamental.
At the end of Ex. 85 occurs what is usually referred to as the
main theme, although Cecil Gray calls it the 'second subject'; in fact the tritone figure (x) is really the main theme.
The 'cello tune is the main melodic idea of the exposition
proper, for this slow movement is in a perfect sonata form,
and Ex. 85 is outside the normal exposition. The music
achieves dissonances of a markedly Sibelian diatonic order,
as the quavers of the 'cello tune climb and the phrases catch
at each other as they overlap; there is a slow but dogged
determination to arrive at F sharp major. This is reached
via Ex. 66, and a transition passage in which the brass, with
menacing chords, drive home the tritone:

The figure marked (a) is of special importance. From a
warm B major chord, a rare splash of sunshine with muted
horns, the music subsides, again by means of the brass, to a
fully-established F sharp major for the 'second subject'.

So far the progress of the music is like nothing else. The
short ejaculations should produce a disjointed result, one
would think, but the continuity is complete. This is because
the 'fragments' are complete ideas of a weight not often
attained by melodic lines of normal length and shape. The
'second subject' is simply the 'cello tune, now built into a
magnificent paragraph, of a deep beauty beyond the power
of words to describe. The 'cello theme itself, using the
tritone, sets off the development, concerned throughout with
this interval in a variety of forms:

Notice the rhythm of Ex. 87. The whispered, misty sound of the string *tremolandi* gives a sense of wraithlike unreality to the music, while the other versions of the figure press home the fact that all this is only too real. The development, without a break, culminates in the original transition passage and the 'second subject', now in A major. Then, in a few bars of coda, the tritone figure rises and vanishes. It is worth noting that in all but one particular (the short cut to the 'second subject' after the development) this movement follows the individual form of the first movement of Schubert's B minor symphony and, on the evidence of the music, for the same purpose of tragic expression.

The second movement is in two parts. The first is rapid, the tritone again prominent, as well as other characteristics already noted:

This could be self-repeating and needs to be drastically interrupted, as it is by the second part of the movement. The speed is halved and the music emphasizes the heavy, leaden tragedy latent in the tritone by involving it in grinding diatonic clashes:

89

The final drum notes, quietly but curtly forbidding a reprise, could be regarded as the most meaningful in the movement.

The third movement wanders like a lost soul looking for a final home. There are a number of figures, four being quoted here:

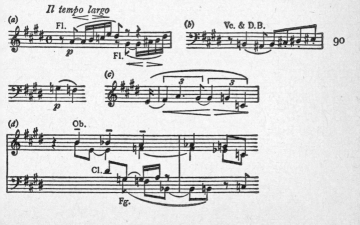

90

Gradually, at intervals, a stronger idea tries to emerge, and it eventually achieves the final form of Ex. 91:

The movement ends with a mixture of anguished desolation and well-founded hope (strikingly anticipated by Alkan in the first movement of his vast concerto for piano solo).

The finale at last vents the pent-up feelings and meets the tragedy with a savage explosion of energy. But direction is given to it as Ex. 83 (*b*) is extracted from the opening theme, and sonata is again replaced, to new purpose, by Sibelius's essentially simpler harmony-alternation. The real meaning emerges as the music rushes to a head-on collision between A major and E flat major – the inescapable tritone. This and what comes from it make one of the profoundest passages in all music:

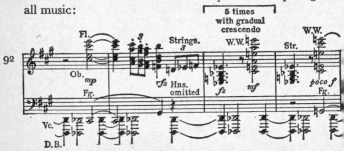

Everything in this movement, every theme and derivative, lives on the tritone; rarely can so much have been extracted (to a positive end) from this interval as in this finale. Every step is certain – the ennobled triumph on a blazing C major, the descent into the depths following it, the building of a kind of recapitulation on the E flat extreme of the interval, the final extracting of two notes, a D and an F, from one of its figures, and the answer of a knife-edged major seventh hurled downwards. All this, to the last sombre repeated A minor chords, convinces in a musical form that springs organically from the nature of the thought. And the final and lasting word is hope. All the composer's most characteristic gestures are here; but this language he had never used before, and except for one strange echo in *The Bard* he never needed it again.

Health and sanity will always demand such music as Sibelius's. It would be idle to maintain that he is the only great symphonist of his time, but there can be no doubt that his work is one of the most encouraging signposts in a weary and war-torn world, and that perception of and therefore growth towards some finer end can only flourish in his presence.

20

ALBERT ROUSSEL
(1869 – 1937)

John Manduell

*

THE history of the symphony in France is quickly told, for there are remarkably few notable symphonies by Frenchmen. This is not altogether surprising when one remembers the strong pull towards pictorial music which nearly all the great French composers have felt. The symphonies of Berlioz are really giant tone-poems,* while composers such as Fauré (apart from an unpublished one), Debussy, and Ravel have left us no symphonies. Other French composers who did write symphonies were either too heavily influenced by models from across the Rhine or simply lacked the essential qualities for the task. This certainly applies to Chausson, Dukas, Lalo and Saint-Saëns, to the young Bizet and, in a lesser degree, to Franck and d'Indy.

Viewed against this background, the four symphonies of Roussel acquire an added significance. Roussel is on record as believing that it is only in music which does not try to tell a story or paint a picture that the composer can achieve the fullest expression of power and beauty. This contention his Second, Third and Fourth symphonies certainly do much to substantiate.

It is not that Roussel eschewed pictorial music. He wrote a great many descriptive works, and among them is the First symphony (1904–6), *Le poème de la forêt*, with its four movements entitled *Forêt d'hiver*, *Renouveau*, *Soir d'été* and *Faunes et dryades*. But already here in this relatively early work the importance which Roussel attached to classical principles is very evident, for in this symphony we find sonata form, a ternary *Adagio* and a rondo last movement.

* David Cairns thinks otherwise, and I agree with him. (Ed.)

Roussel's natural classical style really asserts itself positively immediately after the war, starting with the appearance of two closely related works, *Pour une fête de printemps*, written early in 1920 and initially planned as a movement of the Second symphony, and the Second symphony itself, which occupied him off and on from the summer of 1919 to the summer of 1921. The Second symphony may really be said to usher in the full development of Roussel's classical style from which his music never significantly departed for the remainder of his life. But although this symphony is thus representative of much of the best of Roussel and is a considerable work, it is rarely played. The listener, certainly in Britain, is far more likely to have opportunities of hearing the Third and Fourth symphonies, and for this reason this study will concentrate on these. They do in any case represent in many respects the most significant heights of Roussel's achievement.

In them are to be found all those qualities which are Roussel's strength as a symphonic writer: his clear-cut adherence to classical forms, his always consistent harmonic language with its own highly personal tang of asperity, never forsaking tonality but frequently exploring possibilities such as bitonality, his incisive and no less personal orchestration, his highly individual and well-contrasted melodies, the tremendous vitality of his music – such are the salient features which immediately stamp the post-war works of Roussel. A late starter, he was fifty before his music may be said to have reached its full maturity. It is works such as the Third and Fourth symphonies which display all those qualities of strength and style, discipline and elegance that collectively make Roussel's contribution to music, and French music in particular, such a fundamentally sane and satisfying one.

Roussel wrote his Third symphony, in G minor, in 1929 and 1930 at the invitation of Koussevitsky for the special celebrations arranged to mark the fiftieth anniversary of the Boston Symphony Orchestra. Three years earlier this orchestra had given the first performance of Roussel's Suite in F, and it is an indication of the respect in which Roussel was by this time held that he should have been asked to contribute to the occasion in this way. The symphony was first played at a concert in Boston in October 1930, and Roussel himself went over to America for this first performance.

The symphony is in the four traditional movements, but it is, I think, reasonable, before charting its course in detail, to draw attention to one short phrase in particular:

93

When this first appears it is at the climax to the development section of the first movement, and at a first hearing one might not pay any special attention to it. But as the symphony progresses it becomes clear that this is a very potent germ, a motto germ if you like, and in a sense a small hangover from the cyclic theory which Roussel inherited from d'Indy at the Schola Cantorum. Increasingly important use is made of it. The main melody in the slow movement grows out of a slightly altered form of it. Later it serves as the whole basis for the extended violin solo in the *Andante* section of the last movement. And, finally, it is used as the climax to the whole work in the coda to the finale. Its growth and increasing prominence are thus an important feature of the symphony as a whole.

The first movement, in rondo-sonata form, has great vitality. Its harmonies have that astringent crunch which is typical of Roussel and its distinctive melodies are admirably contrasted. Above all, perhaps, the strength of this movement lies in its lucid construction.

After three bars which set a rhythmic stamp on the whole movement, the first violins, doubled by oboes and clarinets, present the first subject which begins:

94

This kind of leaping figure is very typical of the composer as are, to take a more detailed point, the jumps of an augmented fourth in the first bar, for Roussel always showed a particular fondness for this interval of the tritone, both melodically and harmonically, as indeed he did for the major seventh.

Towards the end of the statement of the first subject comes a particularly graceful phrase heard on violins and flutes while most of the rest of the orchestra maintain the impetus with dancing staccato quavers, and then the way is prepared for the introduction of the gentle and lyrical second subject by the first flute:

95

Though somewhat angular (it will be seen that this tune also embarks by way of a tritone), it has an elegance which Roussel could always command without softening his melodic contours. The cadence in B flat, following the G minor opening, is another reflection of Roussel's fundamental classicism.

This is admirably demonstrated by the form of the movement as it now progresses. The first subject is heard again and then comes the development, full of delightful invention but admirably unified, at the climax to which occurs the first allusion to the germ motto (Ex. 93). The recapitulation is again completely logical and orthodox, and the movement ends as it began with a precise rhythmic energy which is most exhilarating.

The finely-woven slow movement is by dint of its breadth the most considerable in the symphony. It is in a straightforward ternary form with an *Andante* in the middle, flanked by two spacious *Adagio* sections. The main melody of the *Adagio*, heard on the violins, has a long, weaving and highly expressive line. The *Andante* possesses that lithe, almost lazy buoyancy often found in Roussel's slower movements. It is centred around a very fine fugue, a twentieth-century model of its kind and particularly stimulating to the ear on account of the bitonal relationship between subject and counter-subject. Here are the first six bars of this fugue:

96

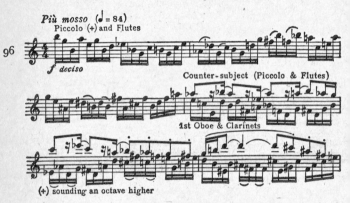

After the climax to which this fugue progresses, the opening *Adagio* returns. In due course its pace, too, is quickened and the main tune loses something of its gentleness and becomes much more strongly accented. Then in the last bars the pace slackens again to the opening tempo, and this simply-shaped but profoundly beautiful movement ends with a solo violin echoing the opening melody as the music settles finally on a chord of E flat major.

The third movement is of the kind which hardly calls for detailed analysis. It is all over in three minutes or so, but what sparkling fun it is while it lasts! A quick, vivacious waltz with no pretensions to do anything more than entertain, it is full of an athletic gaiety which is wholly delightful. It has an essentially French quality and were it not for its slightly rustic character the rollicking world of the French musical theatre might not seem far away. But it is all carried through with such perfectly calculated sophistication that the obvious dangers inherent in setting a piece of this kind in the context of a symphony are never more than remote. Melodically it contains a number of diverting short strands, each of them diatonic and simple in shape, but all threaded into the general picture with just enough cunning, a scintillating orchestration and sufficiently chromatic harmony to ensure that this scherzo is the complete and expertly balanced success it is.

The one serious regret which one may reasonably entertain about this symphony is that the finale is rather too lightweight to follow the bustling scherzo and, more important perhaps, it does not really come near enough to matching the substance of the first two movements. This is not to suggest that it is flimsy, and it is all put together in an unerringly deft way, but the ideas themselves are unusually slender and no real attempt is made to develop them. Here, for example, is the first rather fragmentary idea, heard at the outset on the flute:

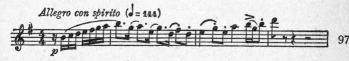

97

This simple little melody, meticulously marked as always, is supported by Roussel's usual harmonic piquancy, bright orchestration, considerable rhythmic verve and a few discreet metrical manoeuvres in the form of an occasional pair of 3/4 bars. A rather more sustained tune is introduced by the violins, and then by way, for instance, of a short snatch of a march for the brass Roussel proceeds in his usual forthright way until an *Andante* section is reached. This consists exclusively of a bitter-sweet reflective violin solo based on the motto germ. Then follows a return to the *Allegro* which in due course moves into a considerably quicker *Allegro molto* by which Roussel approaches the broad but brief coda, dominated by a heavily accented final statement of the germ motto.

The Fourth symphony followed the Third after five years at the end of 1934, and was actually written in the relatively short space of four and a half months. At this time, despite a severe bout of pneumonia the previous winter, Roussel was at the height of his powers, writing with great fluency and energy; in fact, it seems that he embarked on this symphony only four days after completing the *Sinfonietta* for string orchestra. The first performance, in October 1935, was conducted by Albert Wolff, to whom the symphony is dedicated.

To anyone who has followed the Third symphony in detail, the plan of the Fourth will cause no surprises. Again it is in four movements, with the slow second movement followed by a spirited scherzo.

The opening movement, like that of the Second symphony, does however begin with a slow introduction. In it, it is possible to argue, are the last traces of cyclic influence on Roussel in that he alludes here to two themes which play important parts later in the symphony. It would, however, be a mistake to exaggerate the importance of their inclusion in this introduction, for, as in many an operatic overture, they do little more than give us a foretaste of things to come. The first is a short motif, rocking to and fro on Roussel's favoured interval of a tritone, introduced by the cor anglais at the third bar:

It is to appear later in the slow movement. The second is a leaping upward figure which, slightly contracted, Roussel uses as the first subject to launch the *Allegro con brio*. It is heard on violins and violas, supported by cor anglais and clarinets:

How typical of Roussel is this theme with its restless bounding energy, and also how typical of his extrovert vitality that for the first eighteen bars each note on every instrument except the timpani and percussion should be deliberately accented.

This movement follows strict sonata form and the second subject, heard on the violins after the way has been prepared by a slackening of the pulse, provides a warm and gentle contrast to the first subject. The development, which primarily makes use only of the first subject, is compact and economical, the recapitulation is no less terse and to the point, whilst the short coda recaptures all the drive of the opening.

Once again, as in the Third symphony, the slow movement is the most extended and profound. Although there is no highly-organized counterpart to the fugue in the Third symphony, there is much elaborate but always fluent counterpoint, as in the beautifully woven opening for the strings, a good example of Roussel's capacity for sustained partwriting, expertly handled and full of genuine melodic interest. There is a great sense of continuity about this movement, of the kind which is the hallmark of the really mature composer, and, though it passes through a number of tempo changes and ranges in mood from the reflective repose of the opening and the end to the declamatory character of the climaxes, it never loses its complete sense of unity. Once again there is an admirable contrast between the two main themes and once again one is constantly fascinated by the subtle variations in the general orchestral texture. The orchestration in this movement is by Roussel's own rather spare standards almost lush. He gives greater emphasis to the luxuriantly long melody lines by entrusting them so often to the strings and the flute in the lower part of its range, and even at the climaxes when everyone is engaged the general texture is far more compact than we usually find in Roussel's music. In short, this movement, despite such features as the bitonality at the first appearance of Ex. 98, is essentially warm-hearted music and to this extent rather different from the general image of Roussel's writing which immediately comes to most people's minds.

Sophistication returns again in the scherzo. The slightly bucolic waltz of the Third symphony gives way here to a jaunty frolic in 6/8 but with at all times that element of polished style and taste with which Roussel invariably endows his music. The first tune, heard on the violins after a few crisp introductory chords, is another optimistic wide-stepping affair not unlike the first main tune in the opening movement of the Third symphony (Ex. 93). The second subject, first given to the violins and flute, has a more sinuous character, but the buoyancy is cleverly maintained by the simple accompaniment it receives. This scherzo is a perfectly proportioned short movement, full of sparkle and wit and with many intriguing and wholly delightful touches of orchestration.

Roussel reserved to the last one of his finest symphonic movements, for the concluding *Allegro molto* is undoubtedly a masterpiece of fertile compression. It is all over in under four minutes, but during this time we have a free rondo of such concise, powerful invention that the result is quite breathtaking. The movement opens in A major with this main theme heard on the oboe:

As the first section builds to a climax we already have the first suggestion of a syncopation which is to play such an important part later in the movement. After this climax the

way is quickly prepared for this second idea introduced by
cor anglais, bassoons and 'cellos, a perky little affair of which
Roussel later makes most ingenious play:

101

What follows is a fine example of Roussel's incisive clarity
of thought both as regards form and orchestration. It all
passes by at great speed, but among the many interesting
turns the music takes there are a few which are particularly
striking. One is the whole passage in which first a flute and
later the other woodwind and the trumpets have a short
flirtation with a syncopated figure while tambourine, tri-
angle and cymbals achieve with a mere handful of perfectly
calculated notes, an effect which either Bartók or Stravinsky
might well have envied. The return to A major which follows when the whole orchestra now swings into Ex. 100 is no
less interesting for the ingenious way in which this formerly
flowing and graceful tune is now broken up to great effect as
Roussel allows the syncopation to carry on into this passage.
And this in turn is followed by another passage which will
certainly delight the listener as it might Stravinsky; it is a
last, slightly grotesque, reference to Ex. 101 lying fairly high
on the bassoon with just three muted trumpets impishly
dancing attendance. Then the full orchestra gathers itself for
a final triumphant return to Ex. 100 as it literally hammers
its way to the final A major chord with every note on the last
two pages deliberately accented like the start of the *Allegro*
in the first movement. Roussel may at the time have been a
sick man, but from first to last in this symphony it is clear
that his music had lost none of its natural fertility and
vitality.

21

RALPH VAUGHAN WILLIAMS
(1872 – 1958)

David Cox

*

DURING the last decade of the nineteenth century, Erik
Satie was telling Debussy that he must free himself from 'the
Wagnerian adventure' and write a French music without
Sauerkraut. In England at the same time, Ralph Vaughan
Williams was considering how to write an English music
without *Sauerkraut* – not for narrow nationalistic reasons,
but because the accepted German-dominated musical
language was actually repugnant to him and did not enable
him to say what he wanted to say. Believing that everything
of real value in our spiritual and cultural life springs from
our own soil, and believing that art should express the whole
inner life of a community, he turned to his own country's
musical heritage. Like Bartók and Kodály, Vaughan Williams went into the country, lived among the people, and
collected folk-music material. Through folk-music he found
a natural means of self-realization. To this was added the
rich influence of Tudor music; and sometimes, like Holst, he
went back further – to medieval influences. In Purcell, also,
he found a rhythmic and declamatory strength, and in
Parry a choral mastery which he greatly admired. It took
him some time to digest all these influences, and it was not
until his late thirties that his musical personality reached
maturity.

Behind the directness, the sincerity and humanity, was a
complex personality, a combination of mystic and realist,
finding complete musical expression through a polyphonic
style which could be contemplative, stormy, gentle, passionate, often sharp-edged with dissonance, often rich in
humour and satire.

Vaughan Williams's last two symphonies were published as No. 8 and No. 9, but the composer did not attach numbers to the others – though this has been done later for convenience. His first work bearing the title 'symphony' was composed between 1905 and 1910: *A Sea Symphony*, rooted in the English choral tradition, reflecting the composer's admiration for Parry. Also, it reflects his sympathy with the unconventionally direct utterance of the American poet Walt Whitman. The work is symphonic in that its structure was suggested by the orchestral symphony. It is choral-and-orchestral throughout, in four movements – settings of poems by Whitman about the sea – and there is no independent section for the orchestra alone. The shape of the first movement ('A Song for all Seas, all Ships') is governed by the words, but is recognizably in sonata form, with first and second subjects, development and recapitulation. Similarly, the slow movement is in ternary form. Two traditional sea-songs are woven into the scherzo, 'The Waves' – which is in the usual binary form, with trio. Only the form of the last movement ('The Explorers') is free and unsymphonic, following the Whitmanesque journey of the soul into the unknown. . . . Already, in this 'early' work, many fingerprints of the composer are apparent: the frequent juxtaposition of major and minor triads, for example, and a particular way of contrasting triplets and duplets.

The descriptive titles of the next two symphonies 'London' and 'Pastoral' must not mislead the listener into expecting descriptive music. About the 'London' symphony the composer wrote: 'A better title would perhaps be *Symphony by a Londoner*; that is to say, the life of London (including possibly its various sights and sounds) has suggested to the composer an attempt at musical expression; but it would be no help to the hearer to describe these in words. The music is intended to be self-impressive, and must stand or fall as "absolute" music.' That a subjective intention should be combined with objective details, such as Westminster chimes, a 'Lavender' cry, sounds of mouth-organ and the jingle of hansom bells, is natural when one remembers that the composer also said: 'Have not we all about us forms of musical expression which we can take and purify and raise to the level of great art?' We might be reminded also of Tennyson's words (in *Idylls of the King*):

> ... the city is built
> To music, therefore never built at all,
> And therefore built for ever.

This work was first heard in 1914, when Vaughan Williams was forty-two, and was drastically revised by 1920. It is dedicated to the 'pastoral' composer George Butterworth (killed in the First World War at the age of thirty-one). The range of mood is immense – from raucousness to quiet brooding, from bright pageantry to sinister undertones – and the musical ideas are as copious as in Elgar. There is dramatic contrast between musical ideas, but little formal cohesion. This came later.

The opening pentatonic phrase is a generating figure – a very characteristic one – pervading the whole work:

102

The slow movement of the 'London' symphony – a hushed, deeply-felt meditation – foreshadows the later Vaughan Williams, with its bare harmonies and its gentle flowing melodies, such as the following for solo viola, quietly springing from the London street-cry 'Sweet Lavender!':

103

In 1922 came the 'Pastoral' symphony, described by the composer as 'almost entirely quiet and contemplative'. It was quite unlike any other symphony that had ever appeared before. Despite the general lack of outward movement, there is any amount of contrast, variety, and spiritual excitement throughout the work. Chordal 'blocks' shift against each other regardless of dissonance. There are suggestive contrapuntal movements below the surface, and contrasted textures – such as the combination of triple and duple rhythms at the beginning of the third movement (which is in the nature of a slow dance):

104

It is the expression of moods, not scene-painting. There are no babbling brooks, no rustles of spring. The prevailing mood is of deep stillness, remoteness, an impersonal union with nature, which finds perfect lyrical expression in the wordless vocal solo of the last movement – recitative-like, pentatonic, over a soft drum-roll. Melodic shapes proliferate, grow out of each other with perfect naturalness and a strong sense of unity in diversity. No outside laws of form govern the treatment of themes. Shape and formal balance grow logically from the nature of the material. A symphonic movement (in the composer's own words) 'is not merely a set of melodies neatly fitted into a pattern; it is a living growth, not a mechanical arrangement. One thought grows out of another, one idea develops out of a previous hint, so that, as in a tree, the topmost leaf and the deepest root are parts of one complete whole.'

At the very opening of the 'Pastoral' symphony we are at once aware of the composer's individual voice – the reticence, the liking for parallel fifths, the personal use of common chords, the modality and folk-song character of the theme (which is harmonized in chords following the contours of the melody in a manner reminiscent of Debussy):

The 'Pastoral' is scored for large orchestra – but (as was the composer's practice) 'cueing' is provided so that the work can be played by a normal-sized orchestral body. Usually in Vaughan Williams's music, the scoring is realistic and appropriate, calculated in terms of polyphonic blend, colour, and direct statement. He knew the capabilities of the instruments, but avoided virtuosity, just as he avoided vagueness. In general, one is not specially aware of the orchestration in a work by Vaughan Williams; it takes its place naturally and inevitably in the musical conception as a whole.

Twelve years separate the 'Pastoral' from the F minor symphony (the Fourth) which appeared in 1934. Meanwhile, in 1931 Vaughan Williams's great stage work *Job* (a 'masque for dancing', after Blake's *Illustrations to the Book of Job*) had been produced. In this, the opposing forces of good and evil are vividly portrayed in symbolic form and brought into violent conflict. In the F minor symphony and the one which followed, this fundamental conflict and its reconciliation are developed in purely musical terms. The F minor was sketched as early as 1931 and 1932, and its tension was inevitable at this stage of the composer's musical development. To those who remembered the quiet and contemplative 'Pastoral' symphony, this work may have come as a rude awakening; but it was not unexpected after *Job*.

The work is held together by two motives:

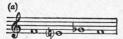 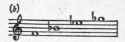

106

which are the basis for themes in all the four movements. Everything is concise, clear, and uncompromisingly uttered. The powerful, strident opening at once proclaims its kinship with Satan's music in *Job* (but we must beware of any misleading, extra-musical interpretations):

107

The form of the first movement is without precedent. The bitter violence of the opening material is brought into contrast with a long, passionate *cantilena* in the upper strings and an equally passionate syncopated theme in D major – interrupted by the opening theme. The development section is very short, and concerned only with the first theme. It merges into the recapitulation, where the *cantilena* is put in the bass (with a counter-melody above it), and the movement comes to a conclusion with a quiet version of the D major theme, now in the key of D flat.

The slow movement is in a binary form, each half ending with a cadence for flute. The texture is contrapuntal, arabesque-like; the mood of restlessness and anxiety rises to emphatic statement and quickly subsides. The scherzo breaks forth and hurtles along in a satirical version of Ex. 106 (*a*) (with strident shouts of Ex. 106 (*b*) from brass and woodwind) followed by a lighter, more expressive theme against a pounding accompaniment. The trio is a mock-jovial *fugato*-like section begun by a solo tuba with a theme again based on the rising fourths of Ex. 106 (*b*). This leads to a condensed reprise of the scherzo, and a long *crescendo*, over a pedal note, leading directly into the three emphatic chords at the beginning of the finale. (No doubt the composer would have self-disparagingly called this a cribbing from Beethoven's Fifth!) In spite of cynical swagger and what the composer describes as an 'oom-pah' bass, the finale is stern and aggressive in character. An energetic version of the cadence figure from the slow movement, a sustained melody for wind instruments (based on Ex. 106 (*b*)), a further theme whose *scherzando* quality has a sinister ring – such is the material of this movement. Then, the 'fugal epilogue' is a tremendous summing-up for the whole work. In a programme note Vaughan Williams described it in plain language as follows: 'The subject of the fugal epilogue [Ex. 106 (*a*)] is played first on the trombones and then heard both in its original form and inverted, combined with the other subjects of the Finale. The work ends with a reference to the opening bars of the first movement [Ex. 107]'.

After the violence of the F minor symphony came the peace and serenity of the symphony in D major (the Fifth), completed during the war years and first heard in 1943. Here Vaughan Williams admitted an outside association with his then-unfinished stage work *The Pilgrim's Progress*, and some of the material of the symphony originated there. The third movement, *Romanza*, originally bore the following quotation from Bunyan: 'Upon this place stood a cross, and a little below a sepulchre. Then he said: "He hath given me rest by his sorrow, and life by his death."' The fact that the quotation was omitted from the printed score emphasizes the composer's wish that the work should be regarded as a purely musical argument. The previous symphony was dedicated to Arnold Bax; this one to Sibelius – originally in the following words: 'Dedicated without permission and with the sincerest flattery to Jean Sibelius, whose great example is worthy of imitation.' (But the imitation is not found in Vaughan Williams.)

When this symphony appeared the composer was seventy. He conducted the first performance of it at a Promenade Concert in 1943. To many it seemed then like his final testament and farewell, 'calm of mind, all passion spent'. (Who could have foreseen the apocalyptic fury of the Sixth symphony that was to break forth in five years' time?)

With this serene symphony in D major we are back in the modal-polyphonic contemplative world of the 'Pastoral' symphony. It is only in the last movement that the key of D major is clearly established. The *Preludio* sets out in tonal ambiguity. The rhythm of the opening figure in the horns is to become an important feature of the movement as a whole:

108

Both these ideas (*a*) and (*b*) develop at once, by extension; the key changes to C minor, leading to a brighter but serious second theme, in E major, rhythmically akin to the opening horn phrase. Again the key changes to C minor, and the tempo quickens to *allegro*. Now against a very quiet background of quickly-moving strings, the woodwind and horns have a foreboding three-note descending figure. This builds up to a powerful climax, and subsides. There follows a restatement of the opening material, leading to the culminating statement of the whole movement:

The movement ends very quietly, the opening horn figure persisting against a conflicting modality.

The scherzo (*Presto*) is a mysterious, fleeting vision. It is built mainly on two ideas. The first is a pentatonic figure in the strings, softly rising and falling in an irregular wave-like motion in which the interval of the fourth is predominant, with duple and triple rhythms in juxtaposition. Then, against this, a smooth dance-like tune, a ghostly folk-melody, is played on flute and bassoon, then imitated and developed by other instruments. A more directly sinister figure in oboe and cor anglais has echoes of Satan's music in *Job*, and a quasi-liturgical contrasted idea further emphasizes the unearthly atmosphere.

Why Vaughan Williams called the third movement *Romanza* is not clear. In character, it is a profound meditation on the three main musical elements presented at the outset. The opening progression of triads and the main theme (played by cor anglais) are taken from the opera *The Pilgrim's Progress*. Other material seems to be related to the first part of the scherzo. Further relationships are suggested, and an underlying unity of the different elements is felt, as the movement proceeds.

The finale, in the form of a *passacaglia*, brings the symphony to an impressive and satisfying conclusion. Again, the theme comes from *The Pilgrim's Progress* – from the music for the House Beautiful (Act I, Scene 2). The working-out of the *passacaglia* idea is not at all strict: the theme (Ex. 110 (*a*)) and the counter-melody (Ex. 110 (*b*)) are equally important in the construction:

110

When the theme (with its variations) has been repeated ten times, it is interrupted by an episode in three sections, dominated by the counter-melody; then begins another series of variations with the theme in a different rhythm. There is a contrapuntal section resembling a development, which builds to a climax and leads to a *fortissimo* statement of the opening horn figure of the first movement, scored now for the full orchestra. This is subtly combined with the *passacaglia* theme. But the final quiet summing-up is based mainly on the counter-melody (Ex. 110 (*b*)).

A performance of the Sixth symphony in E minor leaves an impression of compulsive strangeness rather than profundity. Begun before the war was over, it was finished in 1947, when the composer was well into his seventies. *The Times* declared that it represented the composer's feelings about war: the composer roundly denied this, insisting that his only concern was to produce sounds that are good to hear for their own sake.

It may be tempting to imagine that in 1934 the F minor symphony foretold the Second World War ('He saw the whole thing,' declared Sir Adrian Boult), that in 1943 the Fifth spoke of profound faith in the ultimate triumph of good over evil, and that the Sixth expressed numbed horror at the reality of atomic destruction. Such interpretations have often been suggested, but they are crude and misleading. Throughout more than half a century of symphonic writing Vaughan Williams consistently increased his powers of expression – the technique, the personal language, and the range of feelings – to include everything from the most violent tensions to profound tranquillity. In music these feelings find universalized expression. A musical idea may be suggested by something specific in the outside world, but to tie its interpretation to this is to impose an undue limitation.

With the E minor symphony (in four linked movements) we find Vaughan Williams expanding still further his technique and his expressive range. At the opening, the clash of ninths which we found at the beginning of the Fourth symphony becomes here the more violent clash of two keys a semitone apart (E minor and F minor). The rhythmic range is extended to include jazz-like syncopations and many kinds of conflicting textures. Contrasts of mood are extreme. The saxophone has an important part. 'Intellectual' devices are frequent. The ominous power of the second movement leads to an unusually obsessive repetition: ninety-four times a three-note rhythm is repeated by trumpets, timpani and side-drum. The scherzo is more 'diabolic' than ever before; instead of the rising fourths that we found in the two previous symphonies, we have a combination of tritones and semitones in the following pattern:

The *Epilogue* has been described as one of the strangest journeys ever undertaken in music. (The only comparable movement is by Holst – 'Saturn, the Bringer of Old Age' from *The Planets*.) Vaughan Williams gives us a kind of ghostly fugue. The only dynamic mark is *pianissimo*, and repeated again and again is the injunction *senza crescendo*. For some, this movement may suggest a dead continent, or an impotent searching, or the final mystery of death. Thematically, it is related to music from the opening scene of *The Pilgrim's Progress* – to Pilgrim's question 'How can I rid me of this burden?' But the composer (in his own programme notes on the symphony) mentions no outside association: 'The music drifts about contrapuntally with occasional whiffs of themes and with one or two short episodes on the horns.'

The *Sinfonia Antartica* (1953) was the direct outcome of the incidental music that Vaughan Williams wrote for the film *Scott of the Antarctic*, and some of the thematic material is common to both. The composer's wish seems to have been to express in extended symphonic shape and in a universalized form the prevailing emotions of the film. Each movement is headed with an appropriate quotation relating to heroism and love, to man's struggle against the menacing and impersonal world of nature. A large orchestra is used, which includes organ, vibraphone, a wind-machine, a soprano soloist and female chorus used orchestrally. In five movements, and lasting about forty minutes, the work is too long for the nature of its material, and the reliance on colour and crudely realistic devices only emphasizes its unsymphonic origin. This antarctic adventure, however, introduced a new element into the composer's music – an interest in the possibilities of unusual instrumental colour. Not only did this lead to such works as the *Romance* for mouth-organ and orchestra, and the concerto for tuba, but it also suggested new musical imagery, a new attitude to the reconciling of contrasted material.

For the light-hearted and exuberant symphony No. 8 in D minor (1956), the orchestra is a Schubertian one, plus harp, plus 'all the 'phones and 'spiels known to the composer', including three tuned gongs (as used in Puccini's *Turandot*). Especially in the last movement, there is a naïve enjoyment in sound for sound's sake. The first movement, however, beginning with chords on the vibraphone and runs on the celesta and called *Fantasia* (*Variazioni senza tema*), is a fairly substantial structure of unusual sonorities and unusual form. After this, a very short *Scherzo alla marcia* – for wind instruments only – is a clever and high-spirited piece of contrapuntal intoxication making pawky fun of Prokofiev and Shostakovich. In the beautiful *Cantilena* movement for strings alone, the composer reverts to his most characteristic contemplative style. And it is spontaneous enjoyment rather than serious summing-up that characterizes the rondo-like finale, called *Toccata*, which 'commandeers all the available hitting instruments which can make definite notes'.

New sonorities and textures are also found in the symphony No. 9 in E minor (composed 1956–7). The large orchestra includes important parts for a trio of saxophones and a flügel-horn (a valved bugle used in brass bands – 'a beautiful and neglected instrument', said the composer). At eighty-five the serene but vital flow of ideas continued unabated. The Ninth is a far more serious work than its predecessor, with close integration of diverse material, culminating in a last movement which is a true summing-up, transforming earlier themes of the work into a form that is strong and purposeful.

Like Elgar, Vaughan Williams was a great national figure, important musically and historically. From the Tallis

Fantasia onwards his voice is unmistakable and the warmth and depth of the personality clearly apparent. He was rooted in tradition; he was also vigorously forward-looking, but caring nothing for musical fashions; always completely himself, whether he was writing for the concert hall, the stage, the cinema, the church, or the women's institute. A stubborn extrovert, a mystic dreamer. In the Fourth and Fifth symphonies, contrasted and complementary, we find his most complete and satisfying musical expression. Vaughan Williams once described genius as 'the right person in the right place at the right time'. This applies very aptly to his own achievement. His contribution to the revival of world interest in English music is of immense importance. Is the idiom too redolent of his native soil, too circumscribed to be widely appreciated in other countries? As one would expect, the Fourth and Sixth symphonies have proved on occasions quite readily exportable; the others less so. But unexpected things have happened. The 'Pastoral' symphony – the most personal, the most idiomatically restricted of all his works – was enthusiastically received at the Prague Festival of 1925. In New York, the slightest of the symphonies, the Eighth, was voted by the Music Critics' Circle the best new symphonic work performed there in 1956. And back in 1932, a well-known Italian music critic, Guido Pannain, wrote about Vaughan Williams in these terms: 'All that is traditional in music speaks to him of what is eternal in man; he senses, in its simplicity, a universal religion.' Sympathetic responses as far-flung as these suggest that, beneath the superficial aspects of the music, Vaughan Williams's original aim has been realized. In an essay he once put this aim into words: 'Our national art must not be a backwater – but in the stream we must preserve our own current, not become an indistinguishable part of the general flow.'

22

SERGEI RACHMANINOFF
(1873 – 1943)

Robert Simpson

*

ALTHOUGH Rachmaninoff was included in the earlier
Pelican book on the symphony, it was not at first obvious
that he really belonged in this present publication. Despite
certain fine things in his Second and Third symphonies, he
could scarcely be considered an outstanding figure in
Russian symphonic music – his reputation rested securely
upon his piano works and songs. At the time when Ralph
Hill's symposium appeared, the First symphony was still
unknown, and it was this work that finally settled the matter
of whether or no there should be something about Rachmaninoff here. Its history is now tolerably well known,
though the work itself is not. It was written in 1895, when
the composer was twenty-two; he was at that time teaching
in Moscow. His brilliance was already notable, especially
as a pianist; the first performance of a symphony by him
was already something of an event. But it was a disaster;
the work was badly played, the critics damned it (it is
easy to blame the composer), and Rachmaninoff, overcome
with grief, tore up the score. It does not seem to have
been heard of again in his lifetime, and there can be no
doubt that the traumatic experience of its first performance had a permanent effect on his creative work. In the
early nineteen-forties the orchestral parts of this D minor
symphony were found in the Conservatory at Leningrad; a
new score was made from them, and performances in the
Soviet Union and America quickly followed.

Despite this, the work has still not had its due. Most
critics treated it (at a time when Rachmaninoff's stock was
not in any case high) with *de haut en bas* indulgence. The

music shows few of the obvious characteristics of the later composer; there is, for example, very little trace of the languishing sequential descents that have made his romantic concertos so popular and such an anathema to many critical listeners, a fact which should have commended the symphony at once. But the very critics who would normally have looked askance at yet another typical piece of Rachmaninoff complained that this was atypical. This is true if the rest of his work is regarded as the fulfilment of his true capabilities; but the symphony can also be seen as the prototype of what might have been if it had been a success at the outset, or had the sensitive composer been able to withstand the shock of its failure. Close acquaintance with it, moreover, reveals that to call it a prototype is to do it an injustice. It is a powerful work in its own right, stemming from Tchaikovsky and Borodin, but convinced, individual, finely constructed, and achieving a genuinely tragic and heroic expression that stands far above the pathos of his later music.

As a piece of symphonic composition the D minor is much superior to the other two: as an artistic whole, created naturally and without strain, it leaves little to be desired. It does not, like the E minor symphony (No. 2) and the piano concertos, try to inflate a lyrical theme into a forced final climax, and the *dénouement* of its finale is as overwhelmingly powerful as it is economical. It never lapses into facile sentiment as does the slow movement of No. 2; its *Larghetto* is spare and original, and intensely felt. The structure of the work as a whole cannot be faulted; in the E minor Rachmaninoff had to resort to cuts in order to prevent the work's collapse under its own weight; even then it is less well set up than its predecessor. Where the older Rachmaninoff tends to fall resistlessly into the hoary old romantic habit of a slow and succulent 'second subject' in the course of a stormy *allegro*, the twenty-two-year-old composer, though he does relax into a slower tempo at this point in his first movement, keeps a firm grip on the music and allows nothing to get out of hand. And at no time is it ever less than intensely personal, strongly compelling. All four movements are thematically genuinely integrated.

The opening of Rachmaninoff's First symphony recalls Borodin's Second, especially in the shape of its 'motto' theme. Here, however, Rachmaninoff is writing an introduction, whereas Borodin's is a proper beginning. Rachmaninoff's introduction is short and leads to a supple and very Russian *Allegro ma non troppo* which shows the influence of Tchaikovsky's Sixth (*Pathétique*), especially in the way its development starts (that is the word!) with a crash, followed by strenuous fugal writing. But the music itself is not imitation Borodin or Tchaikovsky; obviously Russian, it shows a genius of its own, and a force that proclaims the advent of a new master. The second movement (*Allegro animato*) is certainly the most subtle and original scherzo Rachmaninoff ever wrote, and loses nothing from comparison with the best by any of his compatriots. It is all half-lights and mysterious hush, beautifully and cunningly scored, superbly composed, a ghostly piece of great refinement, a civilized piece, unsensational but softly insistent. The slow movement (*Larghetto*) is equally restrained, very intense and fine-drawn and quite free from intemperance, its two climaxes disciplined. The D major finale (*Allegro con fuoco*), with its vivid fanfares, is outwardly festive, yet it leaves the hearer with an underlying sense of tragedy. Like the other three movements it is composed with genuine control of motion, and it is an impressive culmination to a symphony that might still come to be regarded as the strongest by a Russian since Tchaikovsky. I don't think such a claim is too high; at any rate, one is left with the feeling that here is a grand master, that if Rachmaninoff had followed this work with advancing successors, he would have been one of the great symphonists of the first half of the twentieth century.

The Second symphony (1907), diffuse though it is in many ways, has much fire and depth of feeling. The fire is fiercest in the brilliant and vigorous scherzo, perhaps the most completely satisfactory part of the work. Despite the weaknesses, the tendency to take the romantic easy way out of a problem, the drift towards inflation, the E minor symphony has many strong qualities, most important of which is its haunting atmosphere, familiar enough in its characteristic gloom but here intensified and often potent. Far less compelling is the A minor symphony (No. 3) of 1936, neatly and economically composed, showing a refined taste, but without spur, written when the composer's creative urge was at last leaving him. If a symphony by Rachmaninoff is to be remembered, it is likely to be No. 1; it would be unjust were it not so. Sad though we may be at the thought that its disastrous *début* may have dimmed a great flame just springing into life in Rachmaninoff's brain, we ought at least to be thankful that the brief blaze produced one large-scale masterpiece.

23

FRANZ SCHMIDT

(1874 – 1939)

Harold Truscott

*

In Austria (and especially Vienna), Franz Schmidt has a position something like that of Vaughan Williams in England. There has been a sort of minor civil war in Vienna over criticism of Franz Schmidt. I do not know if Vaughan Williams's many admirers would go to quite this length, but to defend what you believe in is a good thing; that is to say, so long as it *is* what you believe in and is not merely allowed to become a matter of faction, with consequent derogation of other artists to bolster up your cause. In that case the object of the defence pays an unjust penalty. We read a lot about music which does not 'travel'. I think much of what is said is nonsense. It is more often true that natives are less than reliable guides; they tend to take too much for granted. Those who come fresh and without extraneous influence to such music can more often penetrate the more deeply to its *musical* core. This has its bearing on the music of Franz Schmidt, who like Bruckner has been cited as a composer whose music does not 'travel'; possibly because it does not possess the necessary permit. It 'travels' very well, when allowed to do so, and I will go so far as to say that anyone who claims a love and understanding of Beethoven, Brahms, or Sibelius, should have no difficulty with Schmidt.

Born in 1874, one year after Reger, Schmidt developed slowly; Reger developed very quickly, and this is why Schmidt was as much influenced by Reger as by Bruckner. But the result is rather like that of mixing blue and yellow – a new colour. His published output is not large but covers most fields – organ, chamber and piano music, orchestral, opera and oratorio. His organ music is important, comparable with Reger's (no mean feat); the four short chorale preludes are a good introduction to his work, while two very large works such as the *Fantasy and Fugue in D* and the *Chaconne* (later orchestrated) show completely different aspects of the majestic instrument. His work in general progresses slowly but inevitably from frank imitation to complete individuality; it displays four clearly defined periods, and each of the four symphonies is the culmination of a period. There is really a fifth period represented by one work – the huge setting of the Book of Revelation, *Das Buch mit sieben Siegeln*, his last composition.

His First symphony, in E major, was composed in 1898–1899, and won him a prize from the Society of the Friends of Music. It is a curious mixture; the romantic outlook is reflected in the shape and size of the work (large but not abnormally long) yet the material is classical, even baroque in nature. It begins almost like a French overture; an introduction proceeds with majestic dotted rhythms and a sustained trumpet theme. The main movement opens with a fanfare for four horns and is a stream of material that is classical despite its somewhat opulent orchestral setting. Yet the result is successful. In this symphony the composer resolved many doubts, producing some fine symphonic music, of which the scherzo is outstanding. Schmidt shows himself in this type of movement to be the only real successor to Bruckner – in so far as there is one at all.

Twelve years elapsed before Schmidt began work on his Second symphony, in E flat; this was completed in 1913. He has grown in the interval and his approach is different; his tendency is to break new ground in each succeeding work, and it is nearly impossible to find 'fingerprints' in his music. The Second symphony is scored for a larger orchestra than the first, but it conveys the impression of comparative restraint. It begins with a theme not unlike some of Bach's most characteristic keyboard writing:

This grows into a great first movement, with a natural (and now mature) feeling for symphonic growth. Here, more is said with less effort than in the First symphony. The middle movement is a set of ten expanding variations on a gentle *Allegretto* theme, arriving at a beautifully proportioned slow movement with No. 8 and a very large scherzo in No. 9, of which No. 10 is the trio. The finale is a slow fugue-cum-rondo, beginning with some intensely moving wind polyphony.

The Third symphony, in A, is in some respects the most difficult of the four to grasp. Written in 1928, it won Schmidt the first prize in the Austrian zone of the Schubert Centenary competition organized in that year by the Columbia Gramophone Company. In some ways it leads to the Fourth; until one really knows it, it seems indeterminate, and perhaps it cannot be fully understood except in the light of its successor. There could scarcely be a more positive work than No. 4, whose confidence is complete and without bombast. It was composed in 1933 and is the fitting climax to Schmidt's symphonic thought. It is in C major, which is the stronger for the dark Neapolitan harmonies which beset so much of its progress.

The three previous symphonies have separate movements (except for the joined slow movement and scherzo in the variations of the Second). Each movement is a self-contained design reacting on the others, as in most classical and romantic symphonies. The Fourth, however, is continuous. It begins with a theme for solo trumpet, in itself a triumph of composition:

113

I have quoted the whole of this theme because it is literally the foundation of the work, and no one but a natural symphonist could have achieved it. The end of Ex. 113 shows the strings entering and the oscillation of the last three notes of the theme turning the C to the leading-note of a local D flat major. This oscillation is very important in the argument of the symphony. Schmidt now harmonizes the trumpet theme, with the D flat gently booming in the bass; this time the oscillation turns the D flat to C sharp and the dominant of another local harmony – F sharp minor. The slow, purposeful movement of the music leads on to a pedal G, dominant of C, which lasts for sixteen bars, climbing to a great climax before resolving resoundingly on to the tonic C. This tonality emerges the stronger for the chromatic battering it has hitherto received, a first indication of the resolute determination expressed in this symphony. The device of establishing a tonic by approach through its chromatic environs rather than by direct assertion is derived from Reger, but is here carried out in a way fascinatingly characteristic of Schmidt.

The falling fourth which is so prevalent in Ex. 113 now makes a transition passage, forming two combining themes:

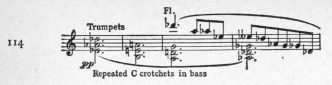

114

The music moves almost imperceptibly on to the dominant of F sharp major with sixteen bars of dominant preparation for the 'second subject'. This, in contrast to the comprehensive length of Ex. 113, is one short phrase on strings with an answer:

115

The whole of the large group, in F sharp minor and major, is built from this phrase and its answer, plus a diminished version of the opening of Ex. 113. As the music dies down on the tonic of F sharp, the development ensues without a break, the horn beginning Ex. 113 and passing it to the cor anglais. The first half of the development treats the main theme as the basis of a sort of *passacaglia*, the oscillating notes being constantly used to give new direction. It builds a climax on a chord of B major; here Ex. 115 takes over and brings the second part of the development to a furious climax. The music subsides into the *Adagio*.

The slow movement is a ternary structure. The first part is built on a beautiful and profound 'cello melody:

116

The tempo is slow and firm, and very different from the deliberate but dramatic Schubertian progress of the first movement. A calm climax descends into tenebrous depths and the middle part is also based on a 'cello theme:

117

The funereal dotted rhythm of the lower instruments produces the biggest climax in the work so far, with typical diatonic chromaticism:

118

The first part returns with flowing new counterpoint and moves to the scherzo. The slow movement has been in B flat major; the scherzo is in B flat minor, and begins by trying to convince us that it is a fugue:

It is not long, however, before its initial falling fourth remembers its connexion with Ex. 113, and the whole of this
theme is played with the *staccato* quaver counterpoint. Ex. 119
has many guises but its relationship with Ex. 113 is always
clear. Later Ex. 115 appears in the prevailing six-eight rhythm
and creates the effect of a trio. The tonality gradually veers
round to F minor and eventually a climax brings the searing
descending chromaticism of the first movement; again the
music descends into the depths. Then Ex. 115 arises on a horn,
in F major, and begins one of the most wonderful passages
in the work, the original single line burgeoning into three-,
then four-horn harmony:

This brings us to a very subdued suggestion of the original
opening climax; Ex. 114 follows and the whole of the second
group. But at its end this passes through a whole series of
slowly moving harmonies and begins to build up the initial
climax that so firmly established the tonic C. It comes now
in all its glory, except that its final chord is deflected on to
another chromatic exploration based on Ex. 115. This reaches
a firmly rooted C major with a prominent A flat; the A flat
becomes natural and the trumpet plays the whole of Ex. 113
with accompanying harmony and a firm bass fifth of C and

G. The D flat of the final oscillation is drawn out and the
final C is unsupported:

121

A more unmistakable Q.E.D. could not be imagined.

24

HAVERGAL BRIAN

(b. 1877)

Harold Truscott

*

RELATED as fiction, it would seem to stretch the limits of the credible that a man could compose, among other large works, twenty-six symphonies, displaying perhaps his most active and individual period of composition in his seventies and early eighties, and yet remain unknown as the major force he undoubtedly is. But this has been the lot of Havergal Brian. I am not going to recount here the tragi-comedy of errors that caused this neglect in spite of vigorous championship by many outstanding musicians, among them Sir Donald Tovey and Sir Henry Wood; it seems more to the point to anticipate the recognition that must surely come and give some positive account of his very positive art.

Brian was born in 1877 in Dresden, in the Staffordshire potteries. He was practically self-taught; this fact, coupled with the extreme independence of mind and outlook he has always displayed, while it certainly helped to shape him and make him what he is, may also have had something to do with his failure to take a lasting hold on the musical world of his early maturity – the early years of this century. The public does not take kindly to rapid changes of style from work to work, and it is difficult to find, even in his earlier orchestral works, such as *For Valour, Fantastic Variations on an Old Rhyme, Dr Merryheart* and the first three *English Suites*, much community of expression. But they do have in common a tremendous adventurousness, with a strong touch of satirical humour.

Musical journalists, casting about for something to keep the pot boiling, periodically alight on a sort of requiem for the septuagenarians or octogenarians of English music.

Not so long ago we had once more a lament for the music of Holbrooke, Rutland Boughton and Sir Granville Bantock, which, representing a period past and done with, had had its chance and lost it – or so it was said. Whenever these composers are mentioned, Brian is brought in at the tail. And it is true that he did grow up in the musical world represented by these admirable men, as well as that of the older Parry, Stanford and Elgar. Now I confess to liking some of the music of Holbrooke and Boughton, while I believe Bantock to be an unjustly neglected important figure. They are not really alike though they do share a certain feeling (leavened in Bantock by his great interest in things of the East) for a type of restrained and somewhat characterless beauty which can be called English only because it is not definitely anything else. Holbrooke, it is true, had a touch of the Brahms brush, but not enough to offset the predominant English quality. But Brian, with them in time, was never remotely with them in thought. His earliest work has a forthright and at times breezy insouciance and a streak of defiance which is his own very personal mark. As a contemporary he was apart from them. He is a contemporary still, he still goes his own way, and he is still apart from his present active contemporaries; but the Brian of the nineteen-sixties is a very different Brian from the composer of before the First World War.

He has changed as he has expanded mentally, but never within the limits of any one school. One might be tempted to find a link with Richard Strauss. He has a tremendous admiration for the composer of *Der Rosenkavalier*. He once talked to me for nearly an hour about *Elektra* and his knowledge of this work was phenomenal. His Second symphony, the 'Gothic', is dedicated to Strauss. But there is no other connexion. It would be difficult to find any music less like Strauss's and, indeed, less German than this symphony. Its one apparent connexion, a superficial one, is due to its great size, and this aligns it more with Mahler or even Berlioz than with Strauss. But, in fact, it is individual. Outward similarity with anything else disappears as one begins to know this enormous work and to realize that it stands

alone, its size a merely incidental though necessary aspect of
it. It is true that the 'Gothic', which now stands as Brian's
first symphony since the actual first was broken up (the two
pieces *Festal Dance* and *Fantastic Variations on an Old Rhyme*
are all that is left of it), resulted from a conversation with
Sir Henry Wood, who suggested that it would be a good
idea for some composer to write a work reviving all the old
and obsolete instruments. This was the result – the instruments had become the necessary means of conveying what
could be conveyed in no other way. The 'Gothic', with its
unique setting of the *Te Deum* for finale, was completed in
1919, and had its first performance in June 1961!

As with Mahler (and this is the only connexion between
the two) Brian has found necessary a spacious treatment of
the orchestra, as well as the use of voices at times. He has
written other music: a great many part songs, solo songs,
choral music, operas (where again this sense of space is
evident) and some piano music. The songs alone would
justify a full-scale study of one aspect of his many-sided
mind, and the piano music, although not so extensive, is
fascinating – a Prelude and Fugue in D minor and a Double
Fugue in E flat show new resources in grouping piano sonorities structurally, rather than dwelling on them for the sake
of the individual sound. It is to be regretted that he has not
pursued these possibilities even further; a piano sonata in
this style would be a most exciting work. Some of his short
piano pieces show him dabbling in a type of impressionism
totally different from that of Debussy. His real fulfilment,
however, comes in his operas, his huge choral setting of
Shelley's *Prometheus Unbound*, and especially in the symphonies (in addition to the numbered ones there is also a *Sinfonia tragica*, based on Synge's *Deirdre of the Sorrows* and one
of Brian's most moving and structurally gripping works). A
few composers are born or natural symphonists, some have the
symphony thrust upon them and some, the majority, have
to struggle. It can be said unreservedly that Brian belongs to
the first category. To produce symphonic works he has never
had to compromise the natural bent of his musical thought.

The fact that space has always been necessary to Brian has not always resulted in great length. The 'Gothic' remains alone among his symphonies for size running to unusual length – a length justified in the result, which requires every moment of it. The three instrumental movements are magnificent, but the crown is the great and unique final setting of the *Te Deum*, at the heart of which is a tremendous climax on *Judex crederis esse venturis*, with the interruption of eight distant trumpets and a wailing soprano; it is perhaps surpassed only by the wonderful soft ending for voices alone. The combination of voices and orchestra in this symphony is certainly like nothing else in music, and must be accounted a supreme feat of realized imagination.

The next five symphonies are large, but not so large. The Third, Fourth and Fifth form a connected group; at various points in Brian's symphonic output one finds these groups of symphonies, forming a complete *exposé* of consistent thought. This is also true of Mahler, but it cannot be too strongly maintained that Brian's English character sunders him completely from this Austrian composer. Wherever one turns in these scores one finds new orchestral sounds, organically part of the thought. Consider the superb 'battle' scherzo in the Third symphony, in E minor, composed 1930-31. Here the deployment of sixteen horns in alternating groups of four, and the electrifying sound of two pianos and three timpani on purely melodic matter all result from the nature of the material itself, and produce a movement with a Bruckner-like momentum but utterly independent of any school.

The Third and Fourth, the latter in C sharp minor and following soon after, are purely instrumental. The Fifth, the culmination of this group, is choral – its title is *Das Siegeslied* ('Psalm of Victory') – and was completed in 1933. It is a complete setting of Psalm 68 in the Authorized Version, Psalm 67 in the Douay; Brian appears to have used the Lutheran version, setting the German and making his own English translation. It is in C major and has, entirely in

Brian's own language, a classical, Haydnesque clarity which would seem to go inevitably with the key. That it is one of the greatest choral works in the whole English choral tradition I have not the slightest doubt. It has an astounding variety of expression and it is as masterly in the delicacy of its writing as in the massive treatment of the full resources. There are three linked movements, the first, *Maestoso*, setting verses 1–12, the second, *Lento*, setting verses 13–18 for soprano solo and orchestra, and the third, *Allegro*, verses 19–35.

The Sixth is for solo voice and orchestra, the voice not specified but from compass and emotional range presumably contralto (or possibly baritone). It is a setting of Lord Alfred Douglas's poem, *Wine of Summer*. Composed in 1937, this is the shortest and, in some ways, the most perfectly achieved of these earlier symphonies; the successful solution of a special problem has demanded of him a certain kind of concentration. His handling of the large orchestra, both for its own sake and as accompaniment, ranging from the fullest sound to chamber-musical transparency, is superb. In the vocal part every nuance of the poem is followed yet the result is pure symphonic thought and the voice is at once an interpreter of the words and an instrument of the symphonic orchestra. The Sixth is the last symphony (to date) to employ the human voice. The Seventh, composed, like the *Sinfonia tragica*, in 1948, is again in C major and, different though it is, it has some of the character of the Fifth, perhaps due to the tonality; there is no doubt that Brian is acutely susceptible to key-character. There are three large movements, the first of which opens with imaginative trumpet writing; there is an epilogue called 'Once upon a time', which begins with a reiterated march rhythm on horns and ends with the same for trumpets and horns in the fundamental C major, followed by a sudden magical final chord of A major, scored for strings, bell, trombones and tuba.

Since 1949 Brian has produced a series of short, highly compressed symphonies which still require large orchestras but show that space in music can be achieved by suggestion

rather than bulk. The thought is both terse and expansive;
it finds in each case the form exactly suited to it, eliding ex-
pected connecting links in a way quite unlike Sibelius's. Like
Sibelius, however, he can take sonata style or leave it alone.
He is bound only by essentials. To illustrate this strong and
flexible language, it will serve to examine briefly three symphonies, Nos. 8, 9 and 10. Brian has himself said of these that
they are 'brothers'; they form a definite group though they
stand as separate works.

The Eighth was composed in 1949. It is in B flat minor;
though there are three sections in it, the music is so continuous that it nearly forms a genuine one-movement work. The
orchestra is a large one, including triple woodwind, cor
anglais, bass clarinet, piano, xylophone and glockenspiel
and, apart from the brass, a euphonium which works *à
deux* with a bass tuba. It is this pair of instruments that sets
the atmosphere, and it is noticeable that often in Brian's
orchestral music the bass of the brass is the centre of attention. The symphony is mainly a study in very slow or moder-
ate tempi, a really quick pace appearing only rarely, and in
short bursts. On paper these interjections appear to give a
broken, ejaculatory nature to the music, not evident in performance.

Euphonium, bass tuba and side-drum set off with a favourite rhythm of Brian's:

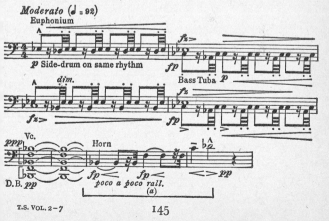

122

The rhythm grows in many ways throughout the work, imparting an ominous funereal atmosphere to the music. In so far as the work has one main theme it is the two parts of Ex. 122; Ex. 122 (*a*) becomes a definite thematic focus as the *cortège* proceeds and grows naturally in the course of a process genuinely symphonic – but remote from the sonata method. Throwing out several themes the opening feels like an introduction to an *Allegro moderato*, apparently the beginning of a main movement. But this is short-lived, lasting only seventeen bars. The *cortège* is resumed and leads to another quick outburst, *Allegro marcia*, and here the 'cellos and basses play a bass theme which is later independently developed:

123

Counterpoint expands and contracts, and the tempo remains fluid as frequently in Brian's later music. After a while, three bassoons dwell on Ex. 122 (*a*), and there follows development of Ex. 123, reduced gradually to a persistent rhythmic influence.

The lamenting first part arrives eventually, via a flute cadenza and a wonderful slow six-eight passage, at the first of two *passacaglia*s. This has an extraordinary theme:

124

Ex. 124 (*b*) develops over Ex. 124 (*a*) (whose rhythm has been already prepared in the trombones) in one of the most astonishing pieces of orchestral sound in my experience. The

whole thing looms like a solid mass until the rhythm of Ex.
124 (*a*) leaves its original shape and pervades the music. There
is an overwhelming climax, and two bars of 'cello recitative
punctuated by the full orchestra lead, through a silent bar
and a reminiscence of the *cortège*, to a second *passacaglia*.
This has a double theme:

and while the music is largely founded on variations of the
lower one (with one variation using the rhythm of the upper
theme) the two themes are combined at the final climax. The
climax is on D minor-major, and reverts immediately to a
short coda, on B flat minor, with reminiscences of the *cortège*, and an ethereal sustained string chord. The final word
is Ex. 122 (a) on the horn, as it was originally heard.

The middle symphony of this triptych, No. 9, was composed in 1951. It has no declared programme. Apart from
the fact that there is no euphonium and no piano, the orchestra is the same as in No. 8, adding an organ in the finale.
There is no mistaking the community of feeling between
these three symphonies. There are also great differences,
particularly in form. Where the Eighth made an extremely
convincing symphonic structure without recourse at any
time to sonata form, the Ninth creates such in both its outer
movements; it is a three-movement work, the movements
played without a break.

I have mentioned the prevalence of march themes in
Mahler (see page 30). It would not be true to say that Brian's

work is dominated by them to the same extent, but he is often drawn to them and they pervade the first movement of this symphony. After a short introduction, *Adagio* becoming *Allegro moderato*, the first movement begins *Allegro vivo* with this theme:

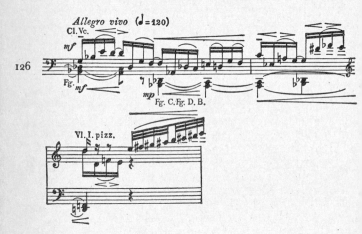

Terse and even cryptic, this idea nevertheless has immense possibilities of expansion and development. It engenders a number of other equally terse themes, making large paragraphs, and takes in material grown from the *Allegro moderato* of the introduction.

A word on Brian's tonality is in place here. He is a strongly tonal composer, but his attitude towards tonality is by no means conventional or incurious. With every new work he explores further, and proves again and again that the limits of tonality cannot easily be defined. Here he begins with a fairly straightforward A minor, but Ex. 126 leans towards flat harmonies which appear to have little or nothing to do with A minor. It is not long, however, before the music explains the apparent contradiction and widens our knowledge of this tonality.

A contemplative and somewhat slower 'second subject' brings with it some beautiful counterpoint but soon gives way to a vigorous development, mainly concentrated on the first group, and it is here especially that the tragic nature of this music is experienced in the accumulation of massive climaxes. No. 8 was concerned with lamentation, No. 9 deals with tragedy. As with Schubert, different though the two composers are, lyrical feeling underlies continuous drama. The recapitulation, exact in the first group (but a semitone higher and emphasizing A minor in a different way), omits the short 'second subject' altogether and sweeps on into a large but concentrated coda. After a climax, this relapses into an elegiac slow movement, cor anglais attended by sombre chords for 'cellos and basses, each divided into three:

127

(Although few composers could be less alike than Havergal Brian and Hans Pfitzner, this movement brings to my mind the equally plaintive slow movement of Pfitzner's fine C major symphony, which also uses the cor anglais.) The brooding contemplation is eventually dispelled by the finale, a vigorous sonata movement with something of the character, though not the actual shape, of a rondo. Ex. 128 is its main theme:

128

Tragedy this work may express, but the finale is informed by a sane and optimistic energy. Hitherto the tonality has been poised round a flickering A minor, gaining steadiness the while. This now proves to be a suspended dominant of D, and the finale asserts and stabilizes D major in a magnificent climactic ending.

The Tenth was composed in 1953–4. It is this time a real single-movement structure, and of a curious kind. The Eighth avoids sonata style; the Ninth embraces it. Now the Tenth glances at it. The euphonium returns and again, with the bass tuba, creates the orchestral atmosphere, but a very different one from that of the Eighth. Wind and thunder machines also appear in the score. The key is an unsettled C minor, which eventually reaches port as C major. But there is no idle or complacent sense of triumph implied in this move. The symphony contains the stormiest music in the three works; from the lamenting *Adagio e solenne* march which opens the work, it gradually gains momentum, resolving the lamentation of No. 8 and the tragic utterance of No. 9. This music is often fiercer in accent than anything in the previous symphonies, but the psychological storm that shapes it gives way at length to a mysterious sense of victory, grim and hard-won, but enduring.

Rhythm of a rugged cast plays a large part in Brian's music and frequently it is rhythm which originates events and themes, often in subtle ways. It is so here, although there is a definite theme at the outset:

The hard-bitten dotted rhythms, so typical of this composer, throw out a 'cello theme which dominates the character of the music for a time, as the speed begins to increase:

130

The music increases in power and stature until at its climax it is thrown back to the opening *Adagio*. Again it speeds up, to a 'second subject':

131

which for a time lives up to the *semplice* with which its composer has marked it. Then it dies out and a muttering fury comes upon the work, *Allegro con fuoco*, constituting a powerful development.

Although the opening bar of Ex. 129 eventually returns and is dwelt upon, there is nothing that can be called a recapitulation in any normal sense of the word. The music explores and probes to the end, finding a goal. New rhythms and new themes are introduced, in predominantly slow tempo with periodic increases; they relate themselves always to what has gone before, but all the time breaking fresh ground. The work ends with a figure of two crotchets and a minim which already suggests the opening of No. 11; each of these later symphonies points beyond itself to the next departure.

No description can hint at the fascinatingly unusual sound

of this music. No one else has done anything remotely like it; it comes from a composer who ponders alone, unruffled by outside disturbances, unconcerned with contemporary trends and fashions. With him, it has always been thus, and so his art is timeless. One feels that a detachment such as this would remain pure if he were to live and compose for another fifty years.*

* Since the Tenth, that is to say between the ages of 78 and 89, Havergal Brian has composed no less than sixteen more symphonies (besides other works, including a Concerto for Orchestra and a 'Cello Concerto), exploring a vein of deep and often enigmatic contemplation with increasing compression of his ideas. Such a phenomenon is unprecedented. At the time of writing, he is still astonishingly vigorous, and anyone who knows him or his work will be surprised if his *oeuvre* is yet complete. Not very long ago I playfully remarked to his wife, 'Keep him alive till the "Gothic" symphony' (to be performed in October 1966). The redoubtable composer was listening; his indignation knew no bounds. 'I'm not going to die – I've just bought a new pair of trousers!' (Ed.)

25

ARNOLD BAX

(1883 – 1953)

David Cox

*

AMONG the definitions of 'romantic' given by the Oxford
Dictionary are the following: 'preferring grandeur or pic-
turesqueness or passion or irregular beauty to finish and
proportion; subordinating whole to parts or form to matter
. . . ' Bax described himself as 'a brazen romantic'; and he
added – 'by which I mean that my music is the expression of
emotional states: I have no interest whatever in sound for
its own sake or in any modernist 'isms or factions.' In his
autobiography, *Farewell, my Youth*, he describes his first
conscious apprehensions of beauty – a vision of the beauty
of the natural world: 'It was the hour of sunset, and as we
stood there, an unimaginable glory of flame developed in
the west so that all the wooded heights seemed on fire.' Soon
after came the sense of sorrow for the mutability of all
things: the regret that a particular day of beauty was passed
beyond recall wrung his heart so cruelly, he tells us, that
he wept bitterly. 'This tenderness of pain, half cruel, half
sweet, is surely an essential quality of the never clearly defined
"romantic mood".'

There we have the key to Bax's world of imagination. The
combination of pantheism and mysticism often finds expression in pages of haunting beauty, such as the *Epilogue* of the
Third symphony. Although there is no specific 'programme' for any of the seven symphonies, their feeling,
their range of moods is similar to the best of the earlier
orchestral works – the tone-poems with definite pictorial
and associative titles, such as *In the Faery Hills*, *The
Garden of Fand*, and *Tintagel*. The first movement of the
First symphony, in fact, had originally been written as a

tone-poem; only later did its symphonic character become apparent.

In form and content, however, the Bax symphonies are by no means vague or inconsequential. Broadly speaking, they are cast in classical mould; but with three movements only, instead of the customary four. The richness, the abundance of invention which they display – therein lies Bax's strength and also his weakness.

For Bax everything came too easily. As a student at the Royal Academy of Music he revealed a natural musicianship and astonishing technical accomplishment. (He was said to be able to play on the piano at sight the most complex orchestral scores.) In composing, the music poured from him, luxuriating in harmonic richness and melodic invention, often over-exuberant, over-elaborated. And from the start he enjoyed independence – freedom to think and write as he wished, freedom to travel as he wished – to Ireland, where he went at the age of nineteen 'in great spiritual excitement', and later to Germany, to Russia, and so on. As a pantheist-mystic by nature he found himself strongly drawn to Celtic life and lore on the one hand, and to Slav traditions on the other. In the same way that Sibelius was inspired by the Finnish sagas (especially the *Kalevala*), so Bax's imagination was fired by Gaelic legends – and by everything connected with the nineteenth century Celtic renaissance. Very early he fell under the spell of W. B. Yeats: ' His was the key that opened the gate of the Celtic wonderland to my wide-eyed youth, and his the finger that pointed to the magic mountain whence I was to dig all that may be of value in my own art.' Bax even stated that the poetry of Yeats always meant more to him than all the music of the centuries. As Philip Heseltine created his *Doppelgänger* 'Peter Warlock', so also did Bax create a second, purely literary personality, his complementary Irish self, 'Dermot O'Byrne', who (as a writer of Irish stories) became a well-known name in Dublin literary circles. This in itself was a remarkable achievement.

Literary images, then, were a tremendously important

stimulus to Bax the musician. And yet, even when the composition is superficially most closely bound to a 'programme' the results are always justifiable in purely musical terms. (The same cannot always be said of the tone-poems of Richard Strauss.) Bax prefaced the score of *The Garden of Fand* with an outline of the Celtic legend that provided the initial stimulus; but he added: 'This tone-poem has no special relation to the events of the legend.' What the composer has in fact done is to create in music the moods of the different parts of the story – with imaginative genius and great technical skill. The wide emotional range, the lyrical and rhapsodic expansion, the highly imaginative portrayal of many different moods – all these tone-poem qualities are transferred to extended treatment and musical development in the series of seven symphonies which began in 1922.

What justifies the name 'symphony' for these works is the fact that different kinds of moods and emotions are vividly brought into contrast and conflict, finally to be resolved in a manner that is personal and also formally satisfying. Basically the language is Wagnerian, with strong Russian influences, from Tchaikovsky to Rimsky-Korsakov and even early Stravinsky. Debussy's colourful world, also, is of great importance. Added to this is the 'Celtic wonderland' influence, expressing itself in harmonic arabesques of sound, exuberance of invention, richness of texture, imagination tending to run riot. The copious and easy flow of ideas in the symphonies has often resulted in music that is episodic in character rather than logically developing. Fluency has frequently taken the place of intense and sustained musical thinking. The result is like an instinctive drama of the emotions rather than a logically sustained argument; but the experience is nevertheless compelling and genuinely symphonic. A tremendous – almost primeval – musical impulse informs these works. The moods range from ferocious defiance to calm resignation, from the feeling of impending disaster to the haunting sense of sadness and regret for things passed beyond recall. The symphonies are often dismissed as amorphous by those who imagine that Bax consists only of

Celtic mistiness and 'atmosphere'. In fact they have considerable strength and frequent astringence; and formally the thematic material is presented with consistency and purpose. There is always great flexibility, but the resulting design is both disciplined and highly original. Most often the basis is sonata form. Indeed, the composer has said that the symphonies deviate little from the lines laid down by the classical composers of the past. The orchestration is a striking and very individual aspect of these works. Although Bax (like Ravel) preferred to compose at the piano (so as to be in direct contact with the material of sound) this did not alter the fact that the orchestral texture was a vital part of the original conception (as the composer's sketches abundantly show).

Bax's First symphony – in E flat – appeared in 1922, and was then found novel and startling. Sibelius had already written five symphonies. The Bax work was considered original enough to be chosen for the 1924 Festival of the International Society for Contemporary Music, held that year in Prague. The tremendous urgency of the work reflects the crisis through which the composer was passing at the time of its composition – a stylistic crisis. Since 1920 he had been dissatisfied with the highly ornamental, over-luxuriant textures of his music, and had rigorously disciplined his style to be more concise, in every way a more direct form of communication. Dedicated to a fellow 'romantic' composer, John Ireland, Bax's First symphony may well be an asserting of a personal and deeply-felt sense of musical values in a musical world which was gradually becoming more and more 'anti-romantic'. The predominant moods of the work are vehement, protesting despair (but never self-pity), phantasmagoric turmoil, brooding tranquillity, nostalgia, and uneasy, unresolved triumph.

132

That fierce opening figure, appearing in many different forms, dominates and unifies the whole work in a manner that one constantly encounters in Bax's symphonies. Finally, it takes the form of a *marcia trionfale*, a peroration suggestive of strength and determination, but overcast with pessimism.

In the Second symphony (1925) – in E minor and C – Bax turns inward. The composer described it as 'catastrophic and oppressive'. Like the other symphonies, it is scored for large orchestra – this time including piano and organ. The four main themes, heard in the introduction, reappear in all the movements; and each movement is rich in other material besides. Although there are rhapsodic and tempestuous sections and much rhythmic vigour in the work, the prevailing feeling is of introspective exploration of an inner world of nightmare and frustration. It is dedicated to Koussevitsky, who conducted the *première* in Boston in 1929.

The score of the Third symphony (1929) gives no mention of key, and the work is, in fact, nomadic in tonality. As before, there is no specific programme; but the composer has acquiesced in the view that he may unconsciously have been influenced by the mood of Northern sagas – but not in the slow movement. This symphony is dedicated to Sir Henry Wood, who first performed it, with tremendous success, at Queen's Hall in 1930, and later in Zurich and in Rome. The Italians hissed it, but the composers Respighi and Casella are said to have been impressed by it. At the 'Proms' it has enjoyed great popularity, but not in recent years. It is the most approachable, the clearest and most consistent in texture, of any of Bax's symphonies; and the third movement ends with an *Epilogue* which is unquestionably one of the composer's finest inspirations.

The first movement opens with a flowing melody for solo bassoon, suggesting the kind of oriental flavour that pervades Rimsky-Korsakov's *Scheherazade*:

This is taken up and developed contrapuntally by other wind instruments, reaches a climax, and subsides. Then, over a recurring figure in 'cellos and double-basses, derived from the opening theme, woodwind and muted bass present the second theme, which is quasi-liturgical in character:

Almost at once the tempo quickens to a dance-like rhythm (of importance later in the movement):

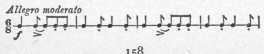

Against this rhythm the strings have a vigorous version of
Ex. 132, and a sombre rising theme is heard in the bass:

136

This leads quickly to *Allegro feroce*, a section the material of
which is based entirely on Exs. 132, 134 and 135, transformed
and developed with pungent rhythmic drive and insistent
purpose to a powerful climax; then subsiding, with the
tempo returning to the initial *Lento moderato*. Muted strings
have a *molto cantabile* passage, apparently derived from Ex. 134,
but lush in harmony, and entirely characteristic of the composer in its mood of wistful, nostalgic tenderness. It begins:

137

The free development of this personal statement is brought
to a climax, and immediately there is a recapitulation – or

rather retrospection – of the main material of the movement, beginning with Ex. 133, now in the violas. The treatment this time throws completely new light on the ideas already stated, and ends in a vigorous coda, based on the rhythmic pattern of Ex. 135.

One thing which this brief description of the first movement shows is Bax's consistent and purposeful use of material in the building-up of a large-scale musical structure. Nothing could be more unrealistic or unfair than to dismiss this music as amorphous.

The second movement of the Third symphony is all based on three thematic ideas. One of these is announced by a solo horn at the beginning:

138

The second important theme is for solo viola, embedded in a *pizzicato* setting: its character is Russian-liturgical in flavour:

139

The first part of the movement consists of various presentations of these two ideas, ending with a richly harmonized version of Ex. 138 for strings, ornamented with arabesques for flute and clarinet, and then a fanfare version of Ex. 139. Now, against chords held by twelve solo strings and a decorative accompaniment for harp and celesta, the horn plays the movement's third main theme, which is akin in spirit to Ex. 139:

mf cantando dolcissimo

140

All this material is then expansively developed, reaching climaxes of passionate intensity, and eventually subsides to final quickly-stated versions of Ex. 139 and Ex. 140. As with the first movement of this symphony, there is nothing here that is diffuse or vague: richness of invention is kept always in strict control, and the orchestral textures are handled with great skill and precision. This movement, perhaps more than any other, makes us aware of the particular quality referred to by Bax himself – the suggestion of 'the tenderness of pain, half cruel, half sweet', and the wistful feeling of regret for things past – the quality which Bax often expresses with such intensity and which shows an important side of his originality.

The last movement begins joyously and robustly, the vitality reminding us of Walton and Bliss. After a rhythmic chordal passage, the first theme, vigorous and *giocoso*, is heard:

(*Moderato*)
Violas & Clarinets

poco f giocoso

141

The mood is mostly virile and restless, with interludes of swaggering confidence, mock-sorrow, and wistful tenderness – and influences ranging from Rimsky-Korsakov (*Russian Easter Festival*) to Gershwin. A climax of crude triumph (derived from Ex. 141) is followed by the remarkably impressive *Epilogue* of unquiet contemplation. The mood is certainly not serenity, but rather that of *omne animal triste* disillusionment after striving and gratification:

142

At the time of the Fourth symphony (1930–31) Bax was apparently trying to avoid writing music that was introspective in character. To this time belongs also the decidedly extrovert *Overture to a Picaresque Comedy*. The Fourth symphony, like the Third, was written mostly in Invernessshire, at Morar and Arisaig, where Bax was accustomed to spend the winter months, surrounded by the bleak, rugged, but inspiring scenery of that part of the west coast of Scotland. Although there is again no programme, the composer has confessed that here the sea was his inspiration – the sea which had also inspired Debussy in *La Mer*, Vaughan Williams in *A Sea Symphony*, and Bax himself in the finest of his tone-poems, *The Garden of Fand*. 'A rough sea at flood-tide on a sunny day', he tells us, is the feeling of the beginning of the first movement. The scoring, for very large orchestra (including organ), is brilliant. The turbulence gives way to many other moods; the movement is cast in flexible sonata form, and the basic material is used consistently with extraordinary variety and subtlety. Then follows a slow movement which is Bax at his most lyrical; it is broad in scope, rich in imaginative detail. And this quiet meditation is followed by an exuberant, brilliant, extrovert finale.

The dedication of the Fifth symphony (1933) is to Jean Sibelius. Here, in contrast to the luxuriance of the Fourth, we have a simplification, even an austerity, and a more fragmentary treatment of material, which seems to confirm a distinct kinship with the great Finnish composer. The music strikes deep; a wide range of feeling is expressed, from profound melancholy to exultation. The contrast in character between this work and the objective 'nature music' of the previous symphony is very striking.

As with the Third symphony, the Sixth (written in 1934 and dedicated to Sir Adrian Boult) represents a peak in Bax's symphonic achievement, and (also like the Third) ends in a magnificent reconciliatory *Epilogue* of great beauty. In the first movement there is a severity, recalling Sibelius, and a daemonic fierceness and turmoil. We are reminded of Bax's First symphony, with its intense four-note motive dominating the opening movement. Here it is a six-note figure which gives unity, and as before the movement is in sonata form and full of dramatic urgency (the more peaceful second subject forming a brief respite). In contrast, the second movement is full of romantic nostalgia, ending with a curious slow march-like section (*Andante con moto*) in six-eight time.

An unusual pattern is adopted in the last movement: Introduction – scherzo and trio – *Epilogue*. Again there is a dominating theme – a six-note figure heard in the clarinet at the beginning of the Introduction. The suspense of this section leads straight into the ferocity of the scherzo, which after a contrasted trio of great charm builds up to a climax of tremendous power and brilliance – a climax of climaxes in Bax's symphonic output. Then, in a striking transition passage, three trumpets (becoming gradually calm and quiet) lead to the *Epilogue* of grave, wistful beauty.

After the satisfying achievement of the Sixth symphony, Bax attempted something different and even more personal in the Seventh (composed in 1939). If the Sixth is the most closely knit, the Seventh is the most relaxed and freely flowering of them all. The first movement, although there are two main themes, is so elaborated with subsidiary material, lyrical and dramatic, that formally it comes near to suggesting free fantasy. The slow movement, pastoral in feeling, with a 'darker' middle section (marked 'In legendary mood') recalls the pre-symphonic Bax. And the last movement, which takes the form of variations, is remarkable because the *ostinato*-like theme and its treatment are unlike anything else in Bax's symphonies:

This theme, after varied and highly personal treatment, broadens finally into the *Epilogue*, more serene than the closing pages of the Third or the Sixth, ending the whole symphonic cycle on a note of profound peace and acceptance. (It is difficult to imagine a less appropriate setting than the New York World Fair for the first performance of this work in 1939.)

Throughout his symphonic output Bax remained 'a brazen Romantic': his music is quite unashamedly the expression of emotional states and the suggestion of a wide range of moods and feelings – though not tied to any extramusical programme. If his works before 1922 suggested the fluent and colourful tone-poet rather than the symphonic architect, this impression was dispelled by the impact of the First symphony, a soundly-constructed large-scale work of tremendous urgency and power. The orchestral colours and textures, also, were masterly and showed great originality. From there on, the seven symphonies of Bax created an imaginative world with its own standard of values – with its challenge to the anti-romantic styles which were becoming more and more widespread and which are now almost universal. Bax is at present out of fashion and neglected. But he found symphonic expression through instinctive musical values, with great artistic sensitivity, formal and technical mastery, and a keen intelligence. A challenge of this sort cannot be indefinitely ignored. With other Romantic works regularly filling such a large proportion of our concert programmes, it is particularly regrettable that Bax's Third symphony, for example, should now be heard so rarely; for here the communication between composer and audience is as clear and vivid as in a symphony of Tchaikovsky.

26

SERGE PROKOFIEV

(1891 – 1953)

Robert Layton

*

GENERALIZATIONS often serve to obscure rather than illuminate the truth, but it is nevertheless true to say that the Russians' genius for ballet has dominated the greater part of their symphonic thinking. The early symphonies of Tchaikovsky offer striking evidence of balletic habits of mind: the slow movement of the first, in G minor, subtitled *Winter Dreams*, is an obvious case in point and so, too, is the main theme of the third, in D, the *Polish*. This is true of the later symphonies as well, for Tchaikovsky never fully succeeded in escaping from the stranglehold that balletic procedures had over his thinking. Even so, they are still marvellous. The Borodin symphonies, too, are episodic in structure though they come closer to organic integration than either Tchaikovsky's or Balakirev's. In a sense, it is arguable that Shostakovich is the first Russian composer of stature to have mastered the art of writing symphonic music, for the first movement of the symphony No. 10 shows indisputable mastery of the processes of organic thinking. At the other extreme, the Stravinsky symphonies are almost wholly balletic; somewhere between the two comes Prokofiev.

As a young man Prokofiev was regarded very much as an *enfant terrible* on the strength of works like the First piano concerto and the *Scythian Suite*; the latter, scored for forces almost as large as those used in *The Rite of Spring*, earned him an altogether undeserved reputation as an iconoclast. In actual fact Prokofiev was at heart far more of a 'traditionalist' than Stravinsky. Throughout his life he was concerned with traditional forms, the sonata, the concerto and the symphony, though, like Stravinsky's, his genius flowered more naturally in the freer forms, such as the ballet and the suite. But whereas Stravinsky, in his quest for ever-changing expressive means, became more cosmopolitan as time went by (without ever losing his highly developed sense of identity), Prokofiev's career after his return to the Soviet Union led him to rest content with the musical language he had developed up to the thirties.

Of all modern composers Prokofiev possessed the richest vein of melodic inspiration and this, combined with his deft and pungent harmonic spicing and his individual sense of orchestral colour, has doubtless won him his wide following with the general public. Works like the 'Classical' symphony, *Peter and the Wolf*, and *Lieutenant Kizhe* are as widely known as they are because of this fresh and vivid melodic invention and the feeling of complete musical spontaneity that informs them.

Prokofiev is said to have kept a notebook always at hand, day and night, in which he jotted down ideas as they occurred to him, and he certainly never allowed any of his (mostly excellent) tunes to go to waste. But in symphonic writing, good lyrical invention is of secondary importance, and it is the hard-hewn pregnant motive capable of giving rise to further musical development that is a basic necessity. Many of Prokofiev's ideas are not wholly symphonic in this sense: this idea, for example, from the Seventh symphony is largely balletic in feeling:

144

It is in fact no surprise to learn that the material of the Fourth symphony (1930) is actually taken from a ballet written at about the same time, *The Prodigal Son*. There is, however, no doubt about either the Fifth or Sixth symphonies: both are true symphonies, even though the degree of organic integration is not comparable, say, to that of a Sibelius symphony.

Prokofiev's first essay as a symphonist, the 'Classical' symphony (1917) falls into a class by itself. It is so well known that description would be supererogatory. Yet at at the same time it is *so* familiar that its perfect proportions, its astonishing mastery of irony, its effervescent high spirits and its striking originality should not go for granted. This is far from being a pastiche, any more than is the brilliantly musical and often highly imaginative *Sinfonietta*, Op. 5 (1909), which in its musical language, its aims and its orchestral outlay, often foreshadows the 'Classical' symphony. It is full of the harmonic sleights of hand and the uninhibited outpouring of melodic ideas that are unmistakably individual. Yet even here, in the opening D major flourish and the main theme that follows it, one detects a strong element of the dance. Prokofiev has harnessed the infectious quality of the ballet to recall the dance-suite origins of the classical symphony. This emerges in all four movements, but nowhere so clearly as in the *Gavotte*, which he later inserted into the first act of *Romeo and Juliet*.

But it is in his middle-period symphonies, No. 2 (1924), No. 3 (1928) and No. 4 (1930) that we find the programmatic element struggling with the symphonic for mastery. In addition to the Russian genius for ballet, Prokofiev inherited the large canvas and elaborate orchestral apparatus of the post-romantic symphony. In his formative years Prokofiev was greatly influenced by his studies with Glière, whose symphonies work on a large time-scale and employ enormous resources. But both those by Glière, and the early symphonies of Miaskovsky which Prokofiev knew and admired, are episodic in design. The smaller scale Miaskovsky symphonies, such as the Fifth, are more organic in conception than the expansive and rhetorical Sixth or the much better known *Ilya Mourametz* symphony of Glière, but there is no doubt that Prokofiev inherited his taste for the opulent orchestral palette from them just as much as from Stravinsky. Although he had a tendency to score thickly throughout his career, nowhere, not even in the

famous *Scythian Suite*, did he surpass the Second symphony in
sheer volume of orchestral sound. The first movement almost gives the impression of being an interminably sustained
fortissimo relieved only by an occasional *forte*. It fully vindi-
cated Prokofiev in his avowed intention to write a work
'made of iron and steel'. In the first movement, at any rate,
it would seem as if Prokofiev were trying to compete in sheer
orchestral violence with the Honegger of *Horace Victorieux*
and the *style mécanique* – and succeeding. Certainly in its
complexity and density of orchestral texture, fecundity of
detail, its bold use of dissonance and its exuberance, it can
challenge comparison with the most audacious scores of the
twenties. The overall impression, however, is far from symphonic. Even the angular opening line with its massive leaps
and its balletic twists and turns suggests a dance of wild
savagery:

145

The composer's own verdict in a letter to Derzhanovsky,
editor of *Muzyka*, which is quoted by Nestyev* is perhaps too
harsh: 'Neither I nor the audience understood anything in
it. It was too thickly woven. There were too many layers of
counterpoint which degenerated into mere figuration.' The
fact of the matter is that although the Second symphony is
hopelessly loose-limbed and totally devoid of any orchestral
self-discipline, there is a great deal of highly imaginative
music in it. This is mostly to be found in the second of the
two movements, a long set of variations, and Prokofiev's
later instinct to revise the symphony is perfectly under-
standable. The orchestral texture in the variations is rich
and luxuriant, and the movement offers many flashes of real

* I. Nestyev, *Prokofiev* (Oxford University Press, 1960), p. 212.

fantasy and poetry. There is frequent resort to *ostinati* and the music is far more diatonic than the first movement: indeed in the opening theme there is almost a hint of the Fourth Symphony, the most diatonic of the seven. There is no denying the eloquence and, indeed, beauty of this theme:

146

Nor is there any doubt about the astonishingly high quality of imagination evinced in the first variation, which opens with this haunting flute *ostinato*:

147

There is an exuberance of detail in the second variation, and the third is an exhilaratingly balletic piece, which suggests that Prokofiev is not wholly in command of his material. For all its incidental beauties, the Second is not a successful symphony, if only because of its lack of cohesion and undisciplined substance. Prokofiev's plans to revise the work, recasting it in three movements, were cut short by his death.

Some of the same criticisms of congested scoring and lack of discipline, episodic rather than symphonic thinking, that can be levelled against the Second apply equally to the Third. Prokofiev made no secret of the fact that this symphony, completed in 1928, was a reworking of material from his opera, *The Flaming Angel,* which he had finished revising some three years before. But the symphony had no greater success in the composer's lifetime than the opera, though it was performed by Monteux, Stokowski, and others. The opera itself had to wait until 1955 for its first stage performance and after its success, the symphony was also revived. It is well known that Prokofiev wished the work to be regarded as wholly independent of the opera and unlike Hindemith in the case of *Mathis der Maler* he did not give the work a title. Nevertheless, the symphonic discipline largely involves the development of ideas especially designed for the purpose and, although there is no reason why the growth of ideas in opera should not be organic (indeed it often is), they are not usually fashioned for this end. Lyrical considerations are uppermost and, as in many Prokofiev operas and ballets, there is no shortage in *The Flaming Angel* of good thematic substance. The opera itself is based on a story by the Russian poet, Valery Bruysov, and is set in sixteenth-century Germany. Its heroine is a young girl, Renata, who sees in her childhood a vision of an angel, Madiel, coming to her and comforting her in moments of trouble. When she is sixteen, she feels the awakening of love for the angel; but he disappears telling her that if she wants to love him as a human being she must meet him in that form. The opera begins with her endeavours to find the mystic visitant incarnate among the men she meets.

The material of the first movement is based on themes associated with Renata, but it is far from integrated in feeling. It is brashly scored and, despite the fact that it goes through the motions of a sonata *Allegro*, it is largely episodic: the coda is undoubtedly the most inspired and imaginative part of the movement, scored with the utmost delicacy of touch and refinement of fantasy. The main idea returns over a gossamer-like texture sustained by a gentle *ostinato* figure. But the slow movement is a far more effective piece as a whole. It derives from the opening of the fifth act when Renata has won through to a certain peace in the atmosphere of the convent. Here is the main idea:

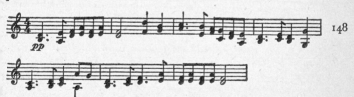

148

This, with its clearly-defined lines, modal in inflection, looks forward to the simplicity of some of his later writing and even foreshadows the direct folk-like simplicity of the lament from *Alexander Nevsky*, though the invention here is less frankly lyrical. But as in so many instances in the middle-period symphonies, argument is sacrificed to description and only a few bars later, a new and obviously descriptive idea is introduced:

149

Although this does not spring spontaneously from the organic fabric of the movement, as is so often the case with Prokofiev, his fantasy is so rich that the intrusion seems wholly justified. The movement is beautifully proportioned, as indeed is the imaginative scherzo, a sinister whirlwind of sound making the most resourceful use of the strings. Prokofiev himself said it was suggested by the finale of the Chopin B flat minor sonata and it certainly has some of the relentless forward drive of that movement. Prokofiev makes the most haunting and poignant reference to one of the most expressive ideas in the first act of the opera to which he also alludes in the finale. This, like the first movement, is grossly overscored and has neither the poise nor the discipline of the inner movements.

Prokofiev seems to have learned from the mistakes of the Second and Third symphonies in at least one respect; for the Fourth symphony (1930) has none of the orchestral extravagance and miscalculation of its immediate predecessors. Whereas the Third drew on comparatively early material (some of the ideas for *The Flaming Angel* date from 1918–19) the Fourth included material from the freshly composed ballet, *The Prodigal Son*. This was commissioned by Diaghilev in 1928 and completed in the fall of that year. The Fourth Symphony was commissioned by Koussevitzky for the fiftieth anniversary of the Boston Symphony Orchestra.

Prokofiev, quite rightly, thought so highly of the material he had used in *The Prodigal Son* that he fashioned no fewer than three other works from it: an orchestral suite, the Fourth symphony, and some of the Op. 52 piano pieces.

The Fourth is less dramatic in character than the Third, and the pastoral element that we encounter in the slow movement of No. 3 emerges as the dominant feature of the first two movements. There is none of the hysterical tension that mars the outer movements of No. 3 or the first movement of No. 2: the atmosphere of the work is far more relaxed and, indeed, one can well imagine some listeners finding the slow movement even a little enervating. The wonderfully gentle opening melody in the first movement is fully characteristic of Prokofiev's harmonic subtlety. Passages from the ballet are, however, transplanted as they stand, not merely in the second and third movements as Prokofiev maintained, but throughout the whole work. The scherzo, for example, opens with this theme, the music of the Temptress in the ballet:

 150

This serves admirably in the context and the music contains all Prokofiev's harmonic spicing and infectious sense of movement. The opening of the finale combines (not wholly successfully) two ideas taken from the ballet, and the last part of the first movement is also directly transposed. The slow movement (which draws most heavily on the ballet) contains some of the most inspired and serene passages that he ever wrote: in them he attains a tranquillity he rarely achieved even in later life. In spite of its immensely attractive material the Fourth remained comparatively unsuccessful in the concert hall, partly, I believe, because there is little symphonic drama in the work. As with Nos. 2 and 3, the musical thinking is loose-limbed and lacking in concentration, and there is an absence of real tonal conflict. A great deal of the symphony takes place in or around C major.

The scherzo is undeniably the most compact and effective of the four movements.

Immediately after finishing work on the Sixth symphony (1947), Prokofiev returned to the Fourth, but in spite of the greater mastery he had acquired, was still unable to fashion the existing material into a more organic whole. Indeed, the revision lengthens all four movements – and the reworking of the bridge passages and development sections in the outer movements seems perfunctory by comparison with the more spontaneous original. All four movements are prefaced by introductions that serve little useful purpose formally; they merely excite impatience for the movement proper to begin. As in the case of the 'cello concerto (1938) which was reworked in the early fifties and published as *Sinfonia Concertante* (1952), there is a tendency to make the argument more readily assimilable by means of repetition. A comparison of the revision and the original of the closing section of the first movement of the symphony is a good instance of this process of simplification. But it would be a pity if, on account of its symphonic failings, the Fourth symphony (whether in its original or revised form) should disappear from the concert hall; it is rich in good musical ideas.

Fourteen years elapsed between the Fourth and Fifth symphonies; during that time Prokofiev had returned to settle in the Soviet Union. There has been a good deal of speculation about the effect of Soviet aesthetic thinking on his artistic development. Whether its effect on his output as a whole was negative or positive, or both, do not concern us here, but that the simplification in his style demanded by the policy-makers did not prevent Prokofiev writing fine music is incontrovertible. The First violin sonata, in F minor, the Second violin concerto, the Sixth and Seventh piano sonatas and the *Alexander Nevsky* Cantata were all written between the Fourth and Fifth symphonies and certainly deserve to rank with the finest pre-Soviet works, the First violin concerto, *Chout*, and the *Scythian Suite* to name only a few. Indeed, of the violin concertos, some critics would, I know, argue that the second is the better of the two.

According to Khachaturyan, Prokofiev once advised him (when writing his famous piano concerto) to 'jot down all the ideas as they occur to you without waiting for the whole thing to mature. Write down individual passages, interesting bits, not necessarily in the correct order. Later on you will use these bricks to build up the whole.' Prokofiev himself certainly often composed on these lines; this explains why his music gives a greater impression of fluency and superabundant invention than it does of organic cohesion. For all we know, the Fifth symphony was probably put together on this principle, though its actual composition took an astonishingly short time, one month during the summer of 1944. But it has a much greater ring of conviction symphonically than its immediate predecessors.

The thematic material in the Fifth symphony is far more integrated than in the three immediately preceding it. The themes not only belong to each other within a single movement, but one feels a closer relationship between material throughout the work. These rhetorical ejaculations which occur either in a *codetta*-like context (in the first case) or simply serve to move the action along at the end of a paragraph (in the case of the finale) bear a far closer relationship to each other than any figures in the middle-period symphonies:

(a) First Movement

(b) Finale

151

Moreover, they perform a definite function in the course of the movement. The first is not lost sight of in either the development or reprise, and the latter plays an important part in generating excitement in the coda of the whole work.

One of the touchstones of the symphony is the fact that insignificant motives that serve a subordinate role in the course of the exposition subsequently turn out to play an unexpected part in the rest of the work. In the early Prokofiev symphonies the subordinate material in the exposition often remains such, but in the Fifth there is much greater economy in this respect. This, for example, is a comparatively minor figure that follows one of the lyrical ideas in the first group and which runs into the first subject itself:

152

This provides the basis for the coda in which the connexion with the first subject is made more overt:

153

The Fifth is, apart from the 'Classical', Prokofiev's most popular symphony. It certainly does not plumb such depths of feeling as the Sixth, though the coda of the slow movement is one of the most magical passages in all Prokofiev. The second movement is probably Prokofiev's most perfectly proportioned scherzo, with an insistent quaver *ostinato* at first mainly on the strings. The melodic line is hard-edged and witty, drawn with great precision and brilliance. The trio section begins with one of Prokofiev's most touching ideas and the accompaniment offers many of the harmonic sleights of hand that Prokofiev delighted in. The slow movement is of great lyrical beauty and contains some impassioned string writing. Notwithstanding the lyricism, much power is generated by a dotted figure first heard in the impressive middle section. The finale is immensely high-spirited and exuberant. Its solemn introduction refers, perhaps satirically, to the opening of the first movement; then an audacious, pert clarinet tune, with accompanying horns, begins the movement proper.

If the middle-period symphonies saw a struggle between Prokofiev's extraordinarily rich and vital imagination and his sense of symphonic discipline, the Fifth is the first large-scale symphony in which he succeeded in imposing symphonic order on his material. The Sixth represents a further step forward. It goes much deeper than any of the others; indeed, it is arguably his finest work and certainly comes nearer to profundity than anything else he ever wrote. It stands apart from the others on several counts. First, the thematic material does not draw attention to itself in any way. Whereas the Fourth and Fifth symphonies (and for that matter the Seventh) open with broad, lyrical ideas, the Sixth begins in a way that leaves no doubt that it is made of sterner stuff. The brass and lower strings spit out a stark, trenchant idea that is highly arresting, so much so that the appearance of the main idea comes as a surprise, gentle, almost seductive:

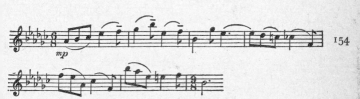 154

Now at first sight this would seem unpromising material for symphonic development, but Prokofiev's mastery as a symphonist can be seen in the way this unlikely 6/8 idea gradually acquires a wiry strength. The trochaic rhythm proves a fertile source of new material. This motive, which crops up immediately after the second subject, obviously arises from it:

 155

The second subject itself is a good example of the reticence of the material, its refusal to draw attention towards itself and away from the symphonic continuity. This is quite unlike the usual Prokofiev second subject with sly, harmonic shifts and fleeting modulations. Instead, the modal flavouring of the theme (as well as its rhythmic plasticity) lends it an almost severe, chant-like character:

156

It is this idea that returns in the tonic, E flat minor, at the very end of the whole work. And by that time it seems to have acquired an air of resignation bordering on despondency. It is as if, after the extrovert breeziness of the finale with its jaunty first subject:

157

and its unflagging sense of movement, Prokofiev had suddenly turned his gaze inwards to reveal an inner life, hitherto concealed. There is, perhaps, a certain bitter flavour about the second subject; and the return to Ex. 156 at the coda, and the explosion that follows it, turns the symphony finally into unmistakable tragedy. The anguished outburst that opens the second movement adds an emotional dimension to his music that one rarely, if ever, encounters in his other work:

It is not too fanciful to suppose that the experience of the war years had something to do with this deepening of Prokofiev's musical imagination, much in the same way as it did with Shostakovich. The greater emotional range explored by the Sixth is reflected in the greater complexity of its organization. Tonally it is far more subtle and carefully thought out than the Fifth, which has a fairly conventional key plan. This is in part due to the fact that it works on a much higher level of dramatic tension. The first movement has an extraordinarily powerful and compelling development section which opens with a surging, insistent Mahlerian theme with modulatory shifts characteristic of Prokofiev, and in the slow building up of tension he shows a masterly control of his material and a magnificent sense of climax.

By the side of the Sixth, the Seventh (1952) is a very lightweight affair, full of charm but much less concentrated in feeling and content. Whether this is due to the philistine onslaught directed against the leading Soviet composers at the 1948 congress presided over by Zhdanov or Prokofiev's failing powers it is difficult to say. Prokofiev suffered a fall in 1949 which impaired his health. Delightful though many of the symphony's ideas are, and although the opening is eloquent and the inner movements have a fund of balletic charm, the work lacks the weight of its immediate predecessors. Whether or not Zhdanov's strictures carried any real weight, Prokofiev does seem to have lowered his critical sights in his attempt to broaden his appeal. This would account for the lapse into banality in the second group of the first movement, a theme which he later recalls in the finale, and which is a good example of the uncertainty of aim which informs the work. But this immensely likeable symphony, for all its shortcomings, shows that even at his weakest, and it is a decidedly weaker work than Nos. 1, 4, and 5, not to mention No. 6, Prokofiev's was a mind so musical, so fertile, interesting and spontaneous that he never lost his power to fascinate.

27

EDMUND RUBBRA

(b. 1901)

AND

MICHAEL TIPPETT

(b. 1905)

Harold Truscott

*

RUBBRA and Tippett have shared certain formative influences; each however has produced his own individual result. Both have shown a great interest in Elizabethan religious and secular vocal music and the monodic music of the seventeenth century. To this Rubbra adds a strong influence from his teachers, Holst and R. O. Morris, and from Vaughan Williams, although he has never shown in his own music the slightest desire to use folksong material or style.

A strong religious belief, intellectual rather than emotional, has perhaps had the most influence of all upon Rubbra's music. This has shown itself from the beginning in a fondness for setting the words of mystical poets such as Henry Vaughan and John Donne. The general leaning towards the motet and madrigal has had a considerable influence on Rubbra's music as a whole, instrumental as well as vocal. Early works such as the *Fantasy* for two violins and piano (one of the finest of his compositions to this day), by expanding ideas of the same type as may be found in the shorter unaccompanied choral works, show the fitness of his naturally vocal invention for extended development. An occasional leaning towards impressionism (he greatly admires Ravel) resulted curiously in superficial impressionistic effects producing an entirely unimpressionistic sound, because he could not disregard his desire for cogent musical form and shape.

However, the potentiality of his music for growth to great stature became more and more apparent through such works as the *Fantasy* already mentioned (which is not a fantasy), the first string quartet, in F minor, Op. 35, and the *Sinfonia Concertante* for piano and orchestra, a magnificent piece of integrated musical thinking with a fugal finale dedicated to Holst.

It was inevitable that such a musical nature should come eventually to the symphony, and this he did in 1936, when he began his First. It is a fine work, although it will probably never be a popular one. (Rubbra's symphonies have not so far been given the chance to show whether or not they *can* be popular, their public and broadcast performances being miserably few; and it is one of the great musical disgraces of our time that only one (No. 5) has ever been recorded.) The difficulty with the First symphony is that it demands enormous concentration in listening and that its orchestration is persistently thick and without relief. The latter is partly true of the Second also. Much has been written of the complete lack of a sense of orchestral colour in these works, and the problem has been dismissed as a similar one to that of Brahms. But the fault is not the same. Brahms has a tremendous sense of orchestral colour, *for his own music*, and against these first two symphonies of Rubbra he appears as a brilliant master of the orchestra. But Rubbra had shown, in earlier works, that he *had* a true orchestral sense: the *Sinfonia Concertante* is one example. Why, then, was it so devastatingly absent from his First symphony? I think the answer lies in the nature of the music. Here is the opening of the first movement:

Allegro moderato e tempestuoso (♩ = 92)

159

This – the germ from which everything else in the movement grows – is the upper line of a choir of brass and is partly

mirrored by the bass. The whole movement is a contrapuntal exploration of the possibilities of Ex. 159 and subsidiary
themes are simply part of the general growth. The attempt
to find 'second subjects' and comment on their lack of contrast, is futile. Rubbra is not writing a sonata movement. I
find the sound of this music satisfactory, but it is not primarily an orchestral sound at all, and I think one must forget the orchestra and colour and concentrate on line-
development and the immense satisfaction that this can
bring. I believe that Rubbra has written a movement (much
as Bach did in the Art of Fugue) which was initially conceived as music without a particular medium, or which
requires a medium we have not got, and that he has written
it for orchestra as the only existing substitute. He has, indeed,
revised the scoring of both the first two symphonies, but the
recalcitrant element is in the music and no scoring would
remove it. Once this is understood, stumbling-blocks *are*
removed.

Rubbra was only too aware of the problem and in his
later symphonies he has tamed his music to a point where the
orchestra is felt, as it is in Brahms, to be the proper medium.
He will never have Mahler's orchestral sense, but a Rubbra
symphony scored in Mahler's manner would be ridiculous.
In his Third and Fourth symphonies he wrote one near and
one actual masterpiece. There are no finer symphonic ideas
in the whole range of English (and much Continental) symphonic writing than the opening passages of these two
works, shown in Exs. 160 and 161 respectively, and in each
case the ideas are developed at the same standard:

160

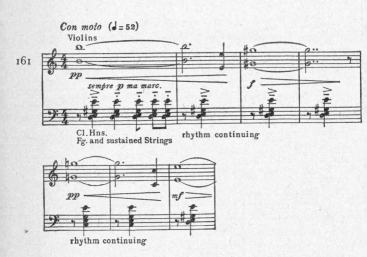

The Third is more nearly a sonata work than the first two symphonies. The growth of the horn figure (*a*) has a real sense of sonata drama about it, as the movement progresses with a gradual increase of tempo characteristic of Rubbra's thinking. Development is constant but so allied with shifting orchestral timbres that there is no sense of over-complication. His orchestra is noticeably smaller than in the first two symphonies, being classical, if one allows trombones. This first movement produces two magnificent climactic ideas, one quiet, the other loud:

184

162

163

Ex. 163 gives the music tremendous impetus at just the right moment. Each exists at its finest level as a result of its context.

Rubbra's second movements are generally of a lighter nature. He has a way, as in this work, of writing a movement fascinating for the play of light and shade around a single theme. I can find only two faults in this symphony. Both the beautiful slow movement and the fugue which ends the final set of variations seem to be cut short at points where more could be said.

The Fourth is a masterpiece. Its opening, Ex. 161, is superb and its promise is realized at every stage of the work. Its contrapuntal growth amalgamates successfully with a real sonata sense. And it is here combined with a feeling for sensuous colour which removes the last possible obstacle to this rare and rich symphonic thinking – here quite as dependent upon a dramatic sense of tonality as the classical or romantic symphony.

The later symphonies to No. 7 (the last so far) have kept

up this successful solution of a definite problem, although none surpasses or even quite equals the magnificent Fourth. The Fifth has a wonderful second movement with a characteristic main theme:

164

Here the feeling is happy but serious. There is much that is child-like in Rubbra's music, and this is one of its finest qualities.

Despite Tippett's occasional unpracticality in instrumental writing, he is less problematical than Rubbra. Both composers are notable for an absence of display in their approach to composition: indeed, this has been a fundamental stumbling-block in the way of understanding Rubbra's music. But there is a surface liveliness in Tippett's music which makes him easier to get on with. In such works as the *Fantasia on a theme of Handel* for piano and orchestra, the concerto for double string orchestra and the second string quartet he has made manifest his preoccupation with beautiful sonorities, contrapuntal line and rhythmic complexity. The latter is the fruit of his love for the masterpieces of Elizabethan vocal and instrumental music, and it can be carried too far. In some of Tippett's music I think it is.

He has written so far only two symphonies, but it was almost as inevitable as it was for Rubbra that he should come to this style. Neither of the two existing works is perfect and I feel that he has not yet made his most determined onslaught on the symphony. Of the two I think there can be no question that the First is the finer. Composed in 1945 on a large scale, there is no basic orchestral problem here as there is with Rubbra. In a very definite A major, its first movement integrates a number of different ideas in a strong sonata style. Its opening:

165

sets out two of these: the figure of descending fourths and the cross-rhythm theme in the bass. These are rhythmically at odds and much of the movement is concerned with working out the conflict thus produced, as well as co-ordinating other themes which grow from these two. The whole is governed by a real sense of dramatic tonality and the type of rhythmic freedom Tippett has learned from the sixteenth century composers.

The slow movement, is, I think, the most beautiful Tippett has written, characteristically setting out two rhythms on which to base its contemplation:

166

The third movement, a *presto* scherzo in spirit although not in name, contains some splendid themes; it is sometimes overloaded, especially in the woodwind, much as the music of Vaughan Williams and Walton is at times. The string writing in the trio section is beautiful, and a wonderful contrast. Tippett caps these three movements with a finale in which march themes and fanfares work out a splendid culmination to this pageant-like drama, but it ends mysteriously.

The Second symphony (1957) shows some gain in clarity of thought and orchestration (though it is very difficult to play). While being a highly enjoyable work, it does not carry Tippett's symphonic growth any further; it is perhaps a little too defiantly in C major, and too content with material which exists more to provide interesting rhythmic patterns than for its own sake:

167

Ex. 167 is its beginning. The manipulation of the opening rhythm and the semi-quaver theme set against it arouses only detached admiration. In spite of this criticism the work leaves most contemporary symphonies asleep at the post: it is only by the standard that Tippett has himself set that one can criticize it. And the slow movement has some writing as fine as he has ever conceived, notably this *Molto tranquillo* passage:

168

28

WILLIAM WALTON

(b. 1902)

David Cox

*

WILLIAM WALTON began like a seventh member of *Les Six*. The style was markedly continental, pointed with wit and satire, bursting with exuberance. Nothing folky. No shadow of Vaughan Williams. If *Façade* recalled *Les Six*, the rhythmic complexities of *Portsmouth Point* (1925) suggested a strong influence of Stravinsky and of jazz. Rhythmically, not musically. Already Walton was beginning to discover his own highly individual musical personality – a progress which continued in the *Sinfonia concertante* and in the viola concerto, where one saw the influence of Prokofiev and Hindemith and where cunning and ingenuity were now blended with a romantic melancholy and depth of thought, in a wholly original manner. The dramatic realism and explosive vitality of *Belshazzar's Feast* (1931) brought something new to English oratorio, and the composer's range of expression was considerably extended. In the symphony in B flat minor (1933–4) self-realization was completed – and the first movement in particular remains today Walton's finest and most characteristic achievement.

Walton composes slowly and laboriously. The final impression of technical brilliance has been built up gradually in each work, with difficulty. Every work – every phrase of every work – is a careful and penetrating self-discovery. In the process, the influences – be they Elgar, Sibelius, or Stravinsky – have become so transformed and integrated that they are no longer identifiable, but have become part of a style which is genuinely of the twentieth century and at the same time a completely sincere personal utterance.

Such is the symphony No. 1 in B flat minor. It was the composer's deliberate intention to write 'absolute music' on a large scale, but he was antipathetic to the prolixity of the late nineteenth-century symphony, favouring more the Beethoven form. As with Sibelius, every bar is necessary and to the point. This symphony is highly organized, but in quite a different way from the classical method. There are groups of interrelated themes in place of contrasted first and second subjects. Sometimes these themes are linked by the pattern of the accompaniment, sometimes by a rhythmic characteristic. There is no mere repetition: the themes are constantly appearing in altered forms, but are always identifiable, even when new intervals are introduced into them. Another marked characteristic is a clear-headed use of tonal ambiguity, including a mixing of major and minor, which leads to pungent results, harmonically and melodically. Most typical of all is the use of pedal-points and very slow-moving bass parts, giving a sense of tonal anchorage and of purpose to the often very dissonant contrapuntal textures which are found above. Interest is usually contrapuntal rather than harmonic. (Sometimes the impression brings to mind seventeenth-century counterpoint against a slow-moving *cantus firmus*.) In the instrumentation of this many-voiced music Walton mixes his tone-colours in a manner somewhat similar to Elgar. The orchestral textures often suffer from over-thickness. This applies to parts of the First symphony. But the actual forces employed are not specially large: the orthodox 'full orchestra', with the addition of only a third trumpet and a second timpanist.

The first two movements were completed in (for Walton) a fairly short time. The slow movement came slowly. Then there was a pause: Walton found it very difficult to write something which satisfactorily rounded off the symphony. (The first performance of the work in fact took place with three movements only.)

The first movement, *Allegro assai*, begins *pianissimo*, but with a tremendous vitality and intensity which is sustained throughout. At the very opening a group of several thematic ideas are presented, over a drum roll on B flat:

These motives are developed in many different ways. The oboe figure, centring round D flat, is particularly important and eventually dominates the whole movement. Highly characteristic of the composer is the arabesque-like figure near the end of the oboe melody (as quoted above). So too is the vital rhythmic ingredient provided by the second violins – the same rhythmic idea that eventually brings the movement to a fierce conclusion. The importance of the interval of the seventh – to Walton, and to this movement – is brought out by two thematic ideas which form the basis of later developments. One is an augmented version of the figure in the bass at bar 12 of Ex. 169; the other is also closely related.

170

The first theme of the second subject group bears a strong relationship to the oboe theme quoted in Ex. 169 – with the arabesque-like figure turned upside down:

171

This whole movement is a rich organic growth, relentless and logical, rising to tremendous climaxes. There are two quiet *meno mosso* sections, but viewed as a whole the complex development increases steadily in violence and tension, leading finally to a telescoped recapitulation and coda.

After the high tension and rhythmic vigour in the first movement, the fierceness is continued in the scherzo, which is marked *Presto con malizia*. Here the most striking features are the great rhythmic and dynamic variety and the many shades of 'malice', from snarling contempt to sinister vindictiveness. The scoring is brilliantly effective, with quite individual touches – a gruff, syncopated theme in thirds low down in the bass strings; a savage *marcatissimo* unison theme.

The angular rhythms, the bars of irregular length – recalling Stravinsky – eventually give way to a sudden breathless, obsessive rhythmic pattern (nine bars before figure 68 in the score) which must have been suggested by a similar passage of *Le Sacre du Printemps* (in the 'Dance of the Chosen Virgin'). Gradually this obsessive rhythm takes possession of the whole orchestra. There is no customary trio section to provide respite.

The slow movement bears the indication *Andante, con malincolia* ('melancholy': the Italian word should be *malinconia*). Lyrical and contemplative in character, the movement is full of an unsatisfied melancholy, a wistful and haunting beauty. From the first quiet statement on the flute, over a pedal note of C sharp, there is a continuous melodic and contrapuntal growth, the themes changing shape as they proceed – elaborating gradually to a tragic climax. At the end of the movement there is a return to the mood of its opening section, with a brief echo of the plangent flute melody. We find thematic affinities with the first movement, emphasizing the unified nature of the symphony as a whole. And besides the examples of pedal notes used as tonal anchors, there are many other fingerprints of the composer in evidence during this movement – such as dissonant contrapuntal passages resolving into unisons, and the constant liking for tonal ambiguity.

The finale, as already stated, was completed some time later and with difficulty. It is far less intense in feeling than the previous movements – at least until the coda – and in itself this would not necessarily be a disadvantage. But whether it is sufficiently strong to provide a satisfying conclusion after the tremendous first movement, the savage scherzo and the deeply probing slow movement, is a matter of opinion. The mood suggests an aspiring, rhetorical affirmation, a 'massive hope', which does not quite ring true – and there is too superficial a jauntiness in the fugal section. The issues already expounded are bigger than this, and fulfilment is not found in a ceremonial *maestoso*. . . . But this is a question of personal reaction: one must listen and decide for oneself.

Certainly the more extrovert character of the finale contrasts strikingly with the rest of the work, and throws into relief the renewed tension that comes with the *coda*. The movement is divided into distinct sections: first, the fanfare-like *maestoso* prologue, rooted again in B flat (the previous two movements have gone to remote tonalities); then there is a vigorous section marked *brioso ed ardentemente*, where short

pungent phrases are developed in irregular rhythms, in a
manner recalling *Belshazzar's Feast.* Abruptly this breaks
off, and a fiery fugue subject is announced, full of Walton
fingerpints:

172

It is developed in *fugato* style, freely, in 3/4 time – with a
quiet, contrasted interlude; then building to a climax, and
leading to a *vivacissimo* section in 3/8 time. Here, in scherzo
form, all the previous material of the movement is developed, ingeniously and extensively. A tremendous climax is
reached, and all the percussion (including six timpani, with
two timpanists) enter, *fortissimo*, leading to the epilogue;
this brings back the *maestoso* theme and, with references to
earlier material, sums up the whole work in an exultant
peroration.

During the past forty years, Walton has always been very
much aware of the changing musical climate, but has always
had the strength of character to develop along his own lines.
The First symphony, in the nineteen-thirties, represented an
important and positive statement of faith at a time when
traditional values were being discarded and 'symphony'
had been abandoned by the anti-romantic composers.
Walton gave us a work full of dramatic contrast and tension
– always in purely musical terms. This, and the demonic
rhythmic energy, make the symphony quite shattering in its
impact. And from the point of view of structure, it is one of
the soundest and most impressive pieces of musical archi-
tecture of our times.

Nothing that Walton has written since has had the same degree of compulsive intensity. Lyrically and harmonically, his style has widened but not gone deeper. There is more flexibility; and everything is more relaxed. He knows well the serial techniques of the present, but is indifferent to fashion and chooses his own course with an integrity that one cannot but admire. The relaxed form of utterance, however, brings a feeling of disappointment. The Second symphony, written a quarter of a century after the First (in response to a commission by the Royal Liverpool Philharmonic Orchestra) is more a *divertimento* than a symphony. Like No. 1, however, it is highly personal, unmistakably Walton throughout. The fingerprints are there, but musically the work is thin in content – though enjoyable and highly accomplished.

A larger orchestra is employed this time, comprising triple woodwind, the usual brass and strings, timpani, piano, celesta, two harps, and the now fashionable vibraphone, in addition to the more usual percussion instruments. In the first movement, we find a two-subject contrast. The themes are akin, both being based on the characteristic leaping major seventh. The contrast is between the moods of restless brilliance and *grazioso* wistfulness. Harmonic ambiguity, so typical of Walton's style, pervades the movement, and the zestful scoring often brings to mind his *Scapino* overture. An elegiac slow movement follows – a lyrical meditation, expanding to a strikingly dramatic (almost operatic) climax. And the three-movement work ends with a *Passacaglia*, the theme of which includes all the twelve semitones of the octave:

173

The first three notes form the chord of G minor, the key of the opening movement. Walton's use of this twelve-note theme in the succeeding variations is ingenious and sardonically unserial! The variations are short – ten in number – with considerable contrasts in mood. The final brilliant *fugato* and coda lead to an unequivocal chord of G major, many times reiterated by the full orchestra, and the work ends with a flashing reference to the opening theme of the first movement. Here is enshrined the spirit of relaxed enjoyment.

29

DMITRI SHOSTAKOVICH

(b. 1906)

Robert Layton

*

SHOSTAKOVICH was something of a sensation from the very
first; indeed, this is hardly surprising, for the First symphony
is a remarkable work by any standards and a truly astonishing achievement for a youth of nineteen. But since its first
performance in 1926 a good deal of the interest that has been
focused on him has been of a quasi-political rather than
purely musical nature. The *Lady Macbeth* affair brought up
the thorny problem of the relationship between the artist
and the State, though criticism of the Soviet attitude to the
arts was considerably softened during the Anglo-Soviet
honeymoon of 1941–5. At the time the epic war symphonies
evoked romantic images of a steel-helmeted, fire-fighting
composer inspired to heights of militant rhetoric by the common struggle against Nazism. Patriotic clouds obscured
musical judgements in all but a few and the immediate post-
war years saw a decline of interest in his work. In the fifties
the picture of the patriot-composer was replaced by that of a
different kind; the soulful, sensitive, somewhat neurotic
introvert quailing under the whiplash of Zhdanov's philistine musical philosophy. The more liberal artistic policy
that followed the death of Stalin, the so-called 'thaw', and
the publication of works like the Tenth symphony, the
violin concerto, and the Fifth quartet filled in and broad-
ened the picture; and now, in the sixties, Shostakovich has
emerged as a kind of symphonic father-figure and has almost
(but not quite) come to occupy the pedestal from which
Sibelius has just been toppled by the mighty young scholar-
critics of the New Musical Journalism.

There can, of course, be no serious contention that Shostakovich is of comparable stature, for Sibelius's roots go back to the classical symphony and his profoundly original sense of form and command of the processes of organic thinking betoken the great symphonist. Moreover, the interest in Sibelius has never been of the merely topical kind which has befallen Shostakovich, largely because Finnish society differs less from our own than Russian. In a sense much of the topical interest is justified, for Shostakovich is a documentary composer far more bound up with his time than say, Miaskovsky, Prokofiev, or any other of his Soviet contemporaries. In this lies both his strength and his weakness. Even his most fanatical admirer will concede that only a handful of Shostakovich's works are independent of time in the sense that those of Sibelius or Debussy are.

Yet because the experience Shostakovich communicates is deeply felt and his involvement whole-hearted, he succeeds in his best work in transcending the topical. While he fails in the eloquent and moving Eighth symphony (the second of the three wartime symphonies), because of documentary involvement, he succeeds in the Tenth in universalizing the experience.

Shostakovich's view of the symphony is frankly Mahlerian: no experience is excluded; the symphony contains the whole world with all its contradictions. At their best the symphonies have the epic panoramic sweep of the great Russian novelists. The brashness, bombast, and vulgarity that one encounters (even in the finest) are part of the Mahlerian inheritance. The lofty feelings and the sense of spiritual desolation that one meets in the slow movement of the Fifth, the bitter pessimism of the searching *Largo* that opens the Sixth, rub shoulders with the brutality of the third movement of the Eighth or the flippant, almost schoolboy, humour of the Ninth. Certainly, it is difficult to reconcile the concentration of mood and thought in the first movement of the Tenth with the un-self-critical doodling in the recitative passages that mar the Seventh and Eighth or the rabble-rousing patriotic hack-work of the Third and Twelfth. Some of these contradictions might possibly be explained in terms of the pressures brought to bear on Shostakovich by the society in which he lives. The vapid and feeble cantata, *The Song of the Forests*, written in response to the 1948 conference of Soviet composers is an instance in point. But others, I believe, are as much a part of his individual make-up as they are of many other Russian artists both in this century and the last. The crudeness and repetition that we find in the symphonies portraying the 1905 and 1917 revolutions are as deliberate here as they are in Eisenstein. They must be accepted as part of the whole personality.

In comparing the symphonic achievement of Prokofiev and Shostakovich one cannot escape the conclusion that Shostakovich is more uneven. Prokofiev is himself far from even, but in terms of pure musicianship he is undoubtedly the finer composer. And yet Shostakovich's ultimate achievement seems to me to be greater: for Prokofiev explores a world with well-defined bounds beyond which he rarely strays. Within these limits he moves with the greatest degree of assurance, having at his command a rich vein of melody (hardly surpassed in the present century), a well stocked and refined imagination, and immense musical resource. Yet except in the Sixth symphony, where he comes nearest to profundity, he never matches the Shostakovich of the Tenth in depth or range of feeling. Shostakovich goes much further than Prokofiev in his sense of compassion and his capacity for suffering. There seems to be a greater awareness of the whole tragedy of the human condition. Much the same is true at the other end of the scale: Prokofiev hardly ever sinks to the hair-raising banalities that ruin the finale of the Shostakovich Eleventh or practically the whole of the Twelfth. But that Shostakovich is prepared to take the risks of a bigger emotional canvas with its attendant glories and miseries can be seen already in the First symphony (1925).

The slow movement of the First shows us an imagination and a degree of compassion that go far beyond youthful insight. One has only to compare this with the First symphony of Glazunov, written when he was fifteen, for the full force of the achievement to become apparent. The young Glazunov was immensely musical and articulate, yet in human terms the promise shown by the two composers was never commensurate. The Glazunov was modelled on the musical procedures of the nationalists, whereas Shostakovich shows much greater inner resource. Although he reveals a considerable debt to the Russian tradition, the formative influences in his style are *not* the most interesting thing about the work. What is important is that it communicates a vital spiritual experience.

This slow movement gives a good foretaste of the way in which Shostakovich's thematic invention is indivisible from the harmonic context. The main theme, for instance, hardly makes sense divorced from its harmonic support. Cover up the bass stave and the angularity of the line seems meaningless; yet read them together and its expressive, poignant quality makes its intended impact:

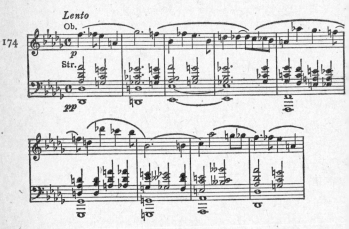

Shostakovich's vein of introspection is part of the Tchaikovskian legacy, as is his penchant for the autobiographical cross-reference that we find in the later works, and particularly in the Eighth quartet. Certainly the second group of the first movement of this symphony has the balletic quality

DMITRI SHOSTAKOVICH

of some Tchaikovsky, though it has a rather dry, ironic flavour. The very opening with its preponderance of fourths has Hindemithian overtones and the symphony was written, as Gerald Abraham has reminded us,* at a time when Soviet musical life was most responsive to outside penetration. Hindemith was invited to Leningrad during the twenties and his music, along with that of Berg, Schreker, Křenek, and Stravinsky, was known there. There is, too, in the First symphony a more subtle relationship between the main ideas than there is in the works immediately following it, though the thinking is more episodic than organic. There are, of course, some miscalculations: the proportions are not always perfectly judged. Climaxes are often too hastily arrived at. But Shostakovich's flair for orchestration is already evident though some of the credit for his immense expertise in this direction may well be due to his teacher at the Conservatoire, Maximilian Steinberg.

There can be no doubting the genius of this First symphony and the astonishing maturity of its young composer. Hence, one can well understand the disappointment which greeted some of the later works. The immediate success of the work placed Shostakovich in the position of being Russia's leading composer of the younger generation and, in a sense, the spokesman of the revolution. He was only eleven when the revolution took place, so that he was the first Soviet composer of international standing whose formative years had been spent under the new régime. Accordingly Shostakovich applied himself to revolutionary themes with some enthusiasm, and if in the pursuit of the *proletkult* he became occasionally bombastic or over-emphatic he was not alone in this.

Both the Second and Third symphonies are in one movement and both make use of choral support. The Second (1927), completed two years after the First and subtitled *Dedication to October*, is by far the more interesting of the two. The opening for strings alone is dark and impressive and

* Gerald Abraham, *Eight Soviet Composers* (Oxford University Press, 1942).

from its complex texture this trumpet motive appears. In its angularity it shows an obvious kinship with the First symphony:

It is clear that Hindemith and Prokofiev are still models. There are plenty of dotted-quaver semi-quaver patterns that in their angularity of line show an interest in the former composer; and the string *glissandi* (at Fig. 44 in the score) against a complex woodwind texture suggest Prokofiev.

The solo violin passage (at Fig. 30) suggests a developing sense of humour inspired, perhaps, by Stravinsky's example. The norm of dissonance is higher in the Second symphony than in either the First or the Third, as this passage from No. 2 shows:

There is, of course, a good deal of rhetoric and the final chorus has a modal, folk-like flavour but it all adds up to something far more substantial than the Third symphony (1929). Like the Second, the Third is little known in this country though it was performed in the thirties under the direction of Sir Henry Wood. It includes a choral setting of a banal poem, *On the First of May*, and it is this that serves as a sub-title. The Third bears much the same relation to a symphony as a poster does to a work of art. There is no attempt to develop thematic material and little or no sense of forward movement. For the most part development is replaced, as it is in the first movement of the 'Leningrad' symphony, by rhetorical gestures, recitative, and repetitive rhythmic patterns. One passage with its wide leaps is worth quoting as it looks forward to the war symphonies and the absence of an inner part *continuo* support recalls late Mahler:

177

If the Third is cliché-ridden, bombastic and irretrievably banal, the Fourth (1935–6) is a very different proposition indeed. Although something of the improvisatory quality of its predecessor still remains, there is far more concentration in this and a much greater, though still sporadic, sense of continuity. At the time of its completion Shostakovich was in disfavour with the authorities. The *Lady Macbeth* affair was at its height and the composer withdrew the work after it had gone into rehearsal. Naturally it has aroused a good deal of curiosity and although it was published in a two-piano reduction not long after the war, it was not until recently that it was first performed. Its first performance outside

Russia took place at the 1962 Edinburgh Festival. It is a much bigger work than its predecessors (it takes about an hour) and in idiom it is probably the most exploratory of all the Shostakovich symphonies. It evokes a world totally unlike that of anything he had written before and marks a definite extension of his creative personality. Its first movement literally teems with ideas: its mood is turbulent, the lines angular, and the norm of dissonance considerably higher than in the other symphonies. Much of the movement is frankly rhetorical and there is frequent resort to *ostinati* to maintain the impetus. Although the movement is not welded into a coherent symphonic whole, it is distinguished by extraordinary richness of detail and flashes of real vision.

The second of the three movements, a scherzo, is one of Shostakovich's most effective and well-knit pieces. It begins innocently enough but its insistent rhythms soon lend the music a dark, menacing quality. Although it has, at a superficial level, the facility of the scherzo of the 'Leningrad', there is something far more relentless about this movement. Its acid, bitter flavouring is part of the process of digesting the influences of Mahler and Prokofiev, both of whom loom large in all three movements. It is the finale that seems to me to strike at a far deeper level than the other movements both in range and complexity of feeling and quality of imagination. Its fantastically evocative coda and powerful, brooding atmosphere leave no doubt in the mind that this symphony records a tragic spiritual experience. It is not possible to see this symphony in its proper perspective as yet: if, for example, Sibelius had withheld his Fourth symphony until the end of his life, it would take some time before the process of assimilation had worked and enabled us to see his whole symphonic development in its true light. Shostakovich's Fourth is without any shadow of doubt a vital link in the chain of his symphonic development and it certainly throws new light on the achievement of No. 5. (There is even a Mahleresque anticipation of the main subject of the first movement of the Fifth.)

The Fifth (1937) represents a definite advance along the
road to symphonic mastery. The canvas is not overladen
with interesting detail, as in the Fourth, and there is a
greater harmony between means and ends, form and content. The tonal plan is far more classical and the music is
frankly diatonic. The opening material appears unpromising at first sight but it contains the seeds of genuine symphonic growth and is fashioned with much greater discipline. The parts seem to belong much more to each other
and to the whole than was the case in the Fourth. There are,
indeed, obvious references in the finale to earlier material
but there are many more subtle allusions besides. Much the
finest movement is the eloquent *Largo*: it breathes purer air
than any of Shostakovich's earlier symphonies. Perhaps
because its musical language is less complex, it can explore
with greater directness of utterance a world of feeling that
ranges from a serene detachment in the face of sorrow to a
downright expression of grief. The writing is wonderfully
sustained: it sounds as if it were written at white heat and it
is no surprise to learn that it was in fact composed in the
short space of three days. The level of inspiration is high and
the use of thin textures lends it a sense of great space. This is
the kind of writing I mean:

178

The second flute entry, incidentally, alludes to the first subject of the first movement, though the listener is not made conscious of it.

The development section of the first movement is another matter. Here there is a much greater sense of contrivance, though the movement as a whole is a fine one. The coda is extremely poetic and the exposition has a classical restraint and purposeful sense of movement. The second group is another instance of an extremely spacious deployment of parts; and, incidentally, like the slow movement of the First symphony, this theme, with its extraordinary wide leaps, makes no sense divorced from its harmonic context. The scherzo is wholly successful and extremely exhilarating: the trio makes almost sarcastic reference to Mahler's mannerisms.

The Fifth is a major achievement, but it is a pity that its popularity has overshadowed the excellence of the Sixth (1939). Shostakovich had originally planned as his Sixth symphony, a choral setting of Mayakovsky's *Ode to Lenin* but in the event discarded the idea in favour of a wholly orchestral work. Much the weightiest of the three movements is the opening *Largo*. Practically all the material of the movement is concentrated in the trenchant, eloquent opening paragraphs which have a tremendous sweep and a dark, tragic intensity:

206

Here in this movement there is further evidence of Shostakovich's developing feeling for pure line. After the opening there is a long threnody-like passage beginning with strings in which Shostakovich reverses the order in which the material was stated. The first two bars are prefaced by the phrase (*b*). Later the rise and fall of the minor third (*a*) is transformed into a new idea. This is one of Shostakovich's most powerful and moving works; the writing conveys utter desolation and loneliness.

The second movement, too, is one of his most inventive pieces full of exuberance and irony. But its brilliant surface hides considerable delicacy of feeling which emerges at the end of the movement: the coda is shot through with a touch of melancholy, a nostalgic longing for a playful innocence that has been lost. Shostakovich was thirty-three when he finished this symphony, and by now the earlier influences of Prokofiev and Hindemith have been fully assimilated. This idea with the spiky leaps of a minor ninth, obviously inherited from Prokofiev, is treated in an original way; note, too, the fourths in the last three bars:

180

After the brooding depths of the *Largo* and the eminently successful scherzo, the finale seems on the face of it to offer little more than a return to the shallow humour of *The Golden Age* or *Lady Macbeth* from which one of its themes is taken. But there is much more to it than this. It is far more unified than the finale of the Fifth, and because of its greater concentration and drive as well as the context in which it appears, its vulgarity and mordant humour acquire another dimension. It is in fact a bold stroke of daring on Shostakovich's part to marry such apparently incongruous worlds as those of the first and third movements.

Of the three wartime symphonies conceived as a trilogy, it is the 'Leningrad', his Seventh (1941), that has come in for the most savage critical mauling. Its seventy minutes inspired Ernest Newman's quip that to find its place on the musical map one should look along the seventieth degree of longitude and the last degree of platitude. Its exploitation for propaganda purposes during the war may account for at least some of its neglect since. The notoriety of the first movement may account for the rest. It is here that Shostakovich replaces the development section with a theme which he reiterates some dozen times and which is designed to represent the approach of the Nazi invaders. Whereas in the Eighth symphony (and for that matter the slow movement of the 'Leningrad' itself), Shostakovich comes nearer to universalizing the bitter suffering of war, this naïve stroke of pictorialism reduces the Seventh to the impotence of topical art. (I have not been able to trace a public performance of this symphony since the war; nor has it been broadcast, though recordings have recently appeared.)

For it to disappear permanently from the repertory would be a grave misfortune however, for it contains some fine music. The exposition of the first movement is informed by a seriousness of purpose and quality of inspiration that is inferior only to the very best Shostakovich and the return of the first subject in the reprise has a touching simplicity. The long bassoon recitative in the restatement is a blemish. One can only deplore Shostakovich's propensity for instrumental recitative, for it disfigures the first movement of the Eighth symphony, as well as other works such as the Second quartet, written at about the same time.

The two inner movements are fortunately not flawed in the same way as the first. The scherzo is an excellent piece with an attractive and wholly characteristic idea:

181

The contrasting motif is a gentle, plaintive oboe melody with a delicate, almost obsessive, accompaniment. The mood, apart from one outburst of violence, is pastoral and contemplative. The slow movement has the ring of genuine feeling about it. With its noble, chorale-like woodwind writing, interspersed with impassioned string recitatives, it comes closer to religious feeling than any other Shostakovich movement. In spite of the despair of some passages, the movement as a whole communicates a sense of belief in positive human values. The writing is episodic, as is that of the finale, the coda of which reverts to the bombast of the Fifth symphony's closing pages.

The Eighth symphony (1943) is only slightly shorter than the Seventh but it is free from its worst excesses. Despite the tranquillity of the coda the overall impression left by the work is one of profound pessimism. The very opening recalls the Fifth: this, too, began with a pregnant string motif which settled down to make way for a more serene, spacious idea. The main idea of the first movement strikes an immediate note of anguish:

182

Later in the course of the movement this theme is brutalized in a way that leaves no doubts about the programmatic implications of the music:

The Eighth is another instance of Shostakovich's practice of beginning with an *Adagio*, spacious in design, and combining the inward-looking function of the slow movement with the structural outlay of a sonata-movement. This movement is both long and unremitting in its sheer intensity of feeling.* The balance is restored by two fast movements. Shostakovich seems to have favoured the five-movement plan at this time, for both this and the Ninth symphony (1945), as well as the piano quintet (1940) and the Third quartet (1946), are in five movements. The humour of the second movement strikes a somewhat hollow note nowadays, but the hard, metallic third movement with its relentless *ostinato*-rhythm and explosive *sforzandi* is brilliantly exciting. The *Passacaglia* that follows drains to the bitter dregs the sorrows and despair of the war years and although the (somewhat uneven) finale wins through to a peaceful, haunting close, it is the peace of exhaustion and resignation rather than real tranquillity of spirit. The Eighth symphony is not a perfect work of art, though it contains all the raw materials of one. It is an impassioned protest against war. But it is not a work in which the composer evinces complete mastery of his material.

The Eighth was not the kind of patriotic rallying-point that the 'Leningrad' had been and it met with comparatively little success at the time, both in Russia and abroad. Nor, for that matter, did the Ninth symphony, in E flat, the final

* Koussevitzky went so far as to call this a movement 'which by the power of its human emotion surpasses everything else created in our time'.

part of the trilogy, fare better. Shostakovich's sense of humour has often created difficulties, and the idea of a Ninth
symphony being short, lightweight, and even frankly comic
strained the official sense of humour.* Reactions abroad were
also divided and those who do not share the composer's
very individual sense of humour tend to dismiss the Ninth
altogether. For others it ranks as one of his most delightful
works. The opening theme sets the tone admirably; it is crisp,
compact and ironic:

184

The movement is extremely concise: it has in fact been
called Haydnesque though it is a good deal shorter than the
average first movement of Haydn's later symphonies and its
humour far broader. The second subject has almost something of the circus about it. Its entries later in the movement
are prepared by a trombone whose abortive attempts to
establish the new key in the least appropriate places provide
excellent comic effects. But below the surface there is a sense
of relentless movement as if the comedy provided a distrac-
tion for events working at a deeper level whose shape is never
clearly defined. This deeper side of the work emerges in the
slow movement, a tender, reflective piece tinged with pathos.
Its tranquillity seems often endangered and is finally disturbed towards the end of the movement by an anguished
outburst that fleetingly recalls the earlier war symphonies.
As in the Eighth, the last three movements are played without a break and in all of them there seems a good deal of self-
parody. The finale, for example, refers obliquely to a leading motif from the First symphony, while the brilliant

* For a full account of criticism of this and the Eighth symphony at the
1948 Congress of Soviet Composers presided over by Zhdanov, see
Alexander Werth's *Musical Uproar in Moscow* (London, 1949).

scherzo often seems to parody the corresponding movement of the Sixth. The Mahlerian trumpet tune in the trio section of this movement (and what a good tune it is!) recalls a similar passage in the middle movement of the Eighth. One wonders whether in the finale the parody is confined to Shostakovich himself. I have a strong suspicion that Khachaturyan is the target five bars after Fig. 96 in the score. In no other frankly humorous work, however, is Shostakovich's sense of timing more sure than in this symphony. The fourth movement, for example, consists of an expressive bassoon recitative over sustained chords. It is as if he were mocking his own predilection for this device until we suspect the mock solemnity to cloak an element of real seriousness. Before the suspicion has removed this ambiguity, the finale upbraids us with its trivial, brainless and completely disarming tune. Not even in *The Golden Age* and the concerto for piano, trumpet, and strings does Shostakovich succeed in producing a more entertaining and witty score than he does here.

There is no doubt that this score came as a shock to Soviet audiences. As Rabinovich[*] says: 'We were prepared to listen to a new monumental musical fresco, something that we had the right to expect from the author of the Seventh and Eighth symphonies, especially at a time when the Soviet people and the whole world were still full of the recent victory over Fascism. But we heard something quite different, something that at first astounded us by its unexpectedness.' However, Nestyev wrote that the work 'charmed the listener with such perfect form that it seemed as though every sound had been exactly matched and that every tinge of colour and every secondary tone subordinated to a sapient purposefulness'.

Shostakovich was still in his thirties when he wrote the Ninth and the view that he had not wholly lived up to the promise of his First symphony was still prevalent, at least in this country. Certainly none of his symphonies up to this

[*] See Dmitry Rabinovich, *Shostakovich* (London, 1959) p. 99.

time are absolutely flawless if judged by the Olympian standards of the great symphonists, though there is no doubt that they offer ample evidence of symphonic genius. The Tenth symphony (1953) changed this. The troubled post-war years brought greater depth and imaginative vision as well as greater mastery and control over his materials. The violin concerto, written before the Fourth quartet (1949) but withheld until after the appearance of the Tenth symphony, as well as the superb Fifth quartet (1951), mark an enormous step forward in his creative development. The slow movement of the Fifth quartet has a greater serenity and depth than anything else Shostakovich had written up to that time. But the Tenth symphony is undoubtedly his masterpiece. In common with many composers, Tchaikovsky among them, Shostakovich found difficulty in writing a wholly successful finale. Even as fine a symphony as the Fifth lacks a finale that measures up to the quality of invention and feeling in the other movements, particularly in the *Largo*. It is as if Shostakovich is consciously writing down at this point, coarsening his palette and rendering his voice more strident so as to make sure of its impact. Discounting the less ambitious Ninth, the finale of the Tenth is the first in the symphonies to achieve real unity. It meets the traditional classical requirement for the finale to be positive in outlook without compromising the integrity of the symphony as a whole. There is no need for the optimism encouraged by Soviet critical opinion to be synonymous with the emptiness one finds in the Second and Fourth symphonies of Kabalevsky or the First of Khrennikov, for this lacks neither depth nor pathos. There is a good deal of both behind the innocent, childlike façade presented by the main theme:

185

213

This darker side emerges in the tragic outburst towards the end of the work, a gesture perhaps inspired by the example of Prokofiev's Sixth symphony:*

186

This motif is directly related to the opening material of the movement from which Ex. 185 itself grows. On closer study it will be found that the material of this symphony is far more integrated than in any other Shostakovich work. The entry of Ex. 186 is prepared by an accompaniment based on the motif D, E flat, C, B (in German D, S = Ess, C, H, and representing the composer's own name): this plays an enormous part in the *Allegretto*. The D, S, C, H tag is used in many of his best works including the Fifth quartet, the violin and 'cello concertos, and in the obviously autobiographical Eighth quartet.

The scherzo is a *tour de force* of invention and its resources of energy seem limitless. Its opening idea, incidentally, is anticipated in the second movement of the Third quartet but there its energy is soon dissipated: here it is self-renewing. If in contrapuntal ingenuity this movement is not the equal of the scherzo of the violin concerto, its vitality is far more explosive and what it lacks in length, it makes up for in density and power. The immense force mobilized by this highly concentrated movement is probably the best way of dealing with the issues raised in the opening movement, which enshrines the core of the whole work. It is as deeply-felt and as self-revealing an utterance as the first movement of the Eighth; but here the experience has undergone a more thorough-going process of symphonic distillation and its argument is far more cogent and compelling. The symphonic processes seem at perfect harmony with the material with which they work and the music grows right from the opening bars:

* Prokofiev had died only a few months before the composition of this symphony.

Although the material of the symphony has a less highly defined rhythmic profile than that of its immediate predecessors, there is no spare flesh on it. The issues are too serious for empty rhetoric or any device that may divert attention from the argument. Each idea as it is presented comes to play a vital part in the organism as a whole. In it Shostakovich handles his materials with an economy he has only subsequently achieved in the magnificent 'cello concerto (1959) and it is in this exercise of true symphonic discipline that he removes the experience from the private world to the universal. The balance, not always perfect in earlier works, between the part and the whole is struck here: the whole is indivisible, more than the sum of its parts rather than less. The moving coda shows just how deep are his reserves of human compassion.

After the achievement of the Tenth, the Eleventh and Twelfth represent a lowering of the symphonic sights. There is in the Eleventh (1956) none of the density of the Tenth either in its concentration of material or intensity of feeling. Both the Eleventh and Twelfth (1961) are inspired by the events of recent Russian history, the former by the abortive 1905 rebellion and the latter by the 1917 October Revolution. Thus they are programmatic in intention and programmatic rather than symphonic considerations dictate their development. If some stretches of the Twelfth sound like an overblown film score this is partly the reason. The programmatic and the symphonic have struggled for mastery in some of Shostakovich's earlier symphonies but the use of non-symphonic material in the form of revolutionary songs represents an additional handicap to the organic integration of the work. The Eleventh must be regarded as a vast and often impressive tapestry into which material of considerable imagination has been woven. But it lacks the cohesion of the Tenth; an interesting detail will linger in the memory and the impression it leaves will be far stronger than that left by the work as a whole.

The opening idea of the first movement is undoubtedly a case in point. These icy sounds which are recalled in the course of subsequent movements are indeed highly evocative:

188

Yet the movement as a whole is static and repetitive. The revolutionary songs themselves are wholly absorbed into the bloodstream of Shostakovich's own musical personality. Even the incongruous melody (given out by two flutes at Fig. 8 in the score) with vague overtones of *Rigoletto* acquires a Shostakovichian mask, though it is in the slow movement that his identification with them is most complete. The second movement makes its impact largely by insisting relentlessly on a rhythmic pattern and by so doing securing a powerful cumulative effect. Far too much of the work, however, is centred around its tonic, G minor. It must be conceded that Shostakovich's use of tonality in this work is primitive by comparison with his finest work. Even the Twelfth symphony is more cogently laid out on the tonal plane, although its material is far less interesting.

The Twelfth seems to traverse much the same ground as its predecessor; the same old revolutionaries are there making much the same speeches as they did in 1905! The work never really lives up to the promise of the opening although the slow movement has some fine things in it.

Whether the Thirteenth symphony (1962) or its successor (on which the composer is now working) will be found to continue the inner searchings of the Tenth symphony or follow the descriptive, overtly propagandist functionalism of the Third and Twelfth or the compact, hard-hitting logic of the 'cello concerto, only time will tell. The First symphony showed his genius and the Tenth showed it capable of fulfilment and self-renewal.

30

MARTINŮ AND
THE CZECH TRADITION

Robert Layton

*

SINCE Dvořák and Smetana, only two Czech composers
have established themselves in the international repertoire,
Janáček and Martinů. Both of them are in a sense post-
nationalist in outlook. Janáček, with his acute ear for the in-
flexions of human speech, almost recalls the way in which
Mussorgsky mirrored the spirit of the Russian language in
his songs and operas, while Martinů with his frank and
diatonic melodic style shows a distinct awareness of the folk
elements which form part of the musical personality of both
Dvořák and Smetana. This is seen at its most obvious in his
cantata, *A Bouquet of Flowers* (1937), based on Czech folk
poetry and one of his most successful choral works. Martinů
also evinces a feeling for nature as powerful as that of any of
his countrymen only excepting Janáček. In an opera like
The Cunning Little Vixen Janáček shows a much greater identification with the natural world but he rarely, if ever, thought
in terms of long sustained paragraphs and his operas
(and much of his other music) are finely-wrought mosaics
made up of intensely imaginative but molecular segments.
The very nature of his inspiration precluded a symphonic
issue.

Martinů's awareness of nature, however, takes second
place to his sense of tradition. The Czech symphony has a
distinguished lineage whose roots go back to the Mannheim
school, and represents the intermingling of many styles.
Some of the freshness and sense of freedom that one feels
about Dvořák's woodwind writing (and Martinů's, for that
matter) may well be inherited from the outdoor serenade
music of eighteenth-century Czech masters like Krommer

Kramář. Dvořák's own development, his gradual assimilation of the influence of Wagner (the slow movement of the
D minor symphony, No. 4, shows how large this shadow
loomed) and Brahms, show how the Czechs, though foster-
ing their own national folk idiom, have never fallen into
insularity. Their geographical proximity to Vienna hardly
permits them to. The Czech symphonists active in the first
decade or so of the present century certainly responded to
Vienna, to Mahler, Wagner, and Richard Strauss, as much
as they did to Dvořák. And just as Fibich, for example,
responded to the Leipzig school and to Smetana and Dvořák
in about equal measure, so composers like Suk, Josef
Bohuslav Foerster, and Novák compounded their own blend
of Czech nationalism and Viennese tradition.

The immediate heirs of Dvořák's mantle were Josef
Bohuslav Foerster (1859–1951) and Josef Suk (1874–1935).
Of Foerster's five symphonies it is probably the Fourth, in C
minor, that is best known outside Czechoslovakia. In a good
deal of his orchestral music Foerster freely employs the lush
palette of Straussian romanticism and in, for example,
Cyrano de Bergerac there is a self-indulgence that recalls
Bantock in this country or a composer like Rangström in
Sweden. Yet his Fourth symphony contains music of genuine
nobility and restraint. Its first movement attains a natural
dignity of utterance although the extensive use of the pedal
point and the building-up of climaxes which are left, as it
were, in mid-air point to an admiration for Bruckner, though
the influence is not wholly assimilated. Apart from the somewhat calculated symmetry of its phrase lengths there is much
to admire in the scherzo, where the debt to Dvořák is more
obvious, for this is a delicately-wrought and inventive piece
with an individual flavour of its own. There is a tendency to
sprawl in the expansive slow movement and it is here and
in the finale that the slightly self-conscious 'Edwardian'
rectitude of the music makes itself felt. Foerster's personality
assumes a certain pallor when it is placed alongside the
more vigorous and full-blooded imagination of Novák
(1870–1949) who possessed a greater sense of continuity

and a richer fantasy. Novák's contribution to Czech music lies mostly in his chamber music and in the impressive cantata, *The Storm*, and thus lies outside the scope of this volume.

Suk, like Novák, was a pupil of Dvořák and subsequently married his daughter, Otilia. Although his reputation rests largely on his smaller instrumental pieces, there is no doubt that in the *Asrael* symphony, his second, he speaks in accents far more personal, richer in feeling and intensity than in any of his other works. *Asrael* is the Angel of Death and the symphony was begun in 1904 shortly after Dvořák's death, but during its composition, only a year later in fact, Suk suffered another bereavement in the loss of his wife. He poured all his grief into the symphony and the work is one of rare vision and compelling power. In its organization it owes a good deal to the 'cyclic' principle fashionable at the end of the nineteenth century, the material with which the work opens being recalled during the course of the other movements. In Suk's case, however, this is far from the perfunctory gesture at unity that we find in many of his contemporaries (in, say, Glière's *Ilya Mourametz* symphony) and the basic material, which, incidentally, includes a theme from an earlier work, *Raduz and Mahulena*, is integrated into the whole with considerable imaginative resource. Occasionally, it is true, a thematic cross-reference can seem obtrusive, as it does in the finale, but for the most part Suk handles this basic material with considerable mastery. His canvas is a large one: the symphony plays for just under an hour and this, together with the 'introverted' character of much of the music, suggests more than a passing acquaintance with both Mahler and Liszt. The scherzo, the centrepiece of the five movements, is vividly Mahlerian though in the slow movements Suk's use of chromatic harmony, individual though it is, shows a stronger debt ultimately to Liszt. One of the main motifs of the introduction is a good example of the way in which he has absorbed Liszt and Mahler into his own blood-stream, as it were, and this has given life to a highly personal expressive language:

189

Although the work is programmatic, no knowledge of this is necessary for the music to make its full impact. The sense of numbness in face of grief would, I think, be conveyed whether one knew its history or not. On the other hand a good deal of the music, and in particular the scherzo and finale, is vigorous, fiery, and exciting. However, Suk is at his most characteristic in the more contemplative music of the fourth movement. This haunting phrase is worth quoting as it shows both his strength and weakness. The high quality of its inspiration is clear at the opening of the oboe phrase with its accompanying poetic murmur from the strings. Yet Suk often gives the impression of over-sweetness: the 'cello line is characteristic of late romantic thinking with its inability to resist excess of detail:

190

The *Asrael* symphony has not yet received its proper due outside Czechoslovakia. It is more than a moving human document: it shows an imagination of considerable power and individuality. Certainly no symphony of international stature appeared in the decade or two immediately following it. Neither Pavel Borkevec (b. 1894), a fastidious craftsman, nor Jaroslav Ridký (1897–1956), who wrote no fewer than seven symphonies, command anything like the sharply-defined musical personality of Bohuslav Martinů (1890–1959).

Martinů first made his name in the twenties with works like *Revue de cuisine* and *La Bagarre* which are scarcely, if at all, representative of the mature composer. Like many prolific artists his output is uneven and, as with Hindemith, what appears as an individual fingerprint in his finest music seems in his feeblest a tiresome mannerism. His 'sprung' rhythms are an instance in point: in the Fifth symphony (1946) they seem an integral part of the forward-surge of the line but occasionally they may appear an elaborate mechanism for charging a line which is otherwise deficient in interest and vitality.

By the thirties Martinů's musical personality had stabilized itself. The formal precision of eighteenth-century musical procedures clearly fascinated him and in works like the *Concerto grosso* (1938) and the charming *Sinfonietta giocosa* for piano and orchestra (1940) his delight in 'neo-classicism' can be seen at its most obvious. It was not until the forties, while he was living in exile in America, that he turned to the symphony. He wrote five symphonies in rapid succession, the First appearing in 1942 and the others at annual intervals until the Fifth (1946). The Sixth, *Fantasies symphoniques*, followed in 1953. If Martinů looks back beyond Dvořák to the Czech masters of the eighteenth century in much of his orchestral music, his symphonies remain, as we might expect, untouched by the nineteenth-century Viennese masters. The Martinů symphonies have a family likeness so strong that superficial critics might mistake it for uniformity of character. Common factors serve to obscure important differences. In a sense each of the symphonies is concerned with different aspects of much the same world and as that world becomes more familiar, so the differences become the more readily apparent.

Some of the common features are immediately striking. Each symphony lasts about half an hour or less and after No. 1 no formal innovations occur. The symphonies are scored for much the same forces (all except the Sixth include a piano) and in their treatment of the orchestra do not greatly differ from one another. Only the Sixth stands apart in its hedonistic delight in orchestral virtuosity and brilliant colouring. Here the orchestral effects are vivid to an extent hardly surpassed in any other Martinů work. Martinů draws a highly individual sound from his orchestra and secures an effect of great clarity even when the score abounds in octave doublings. He often thickens his texture in this way: yet though the outlines are softened, the overall sound remains admirably clean. Writing of his First symphony, Virgil Thomson said:

The shining sounds of it sing as well as shine; the instrumental complication is a part of the musical conception, not an icing laid over it. Personal, indeed, is the delicate but vigorous rhythmic animation, the singing (rather than dynamic) syncopation that permeates the work. Personal and individual, too, is the whole orchestral sound of it, the acoustical superstructure that shimmers consistently.

These words could apply equally well to the glowing, luminous climax of the Fifth symphony, and in fact to all of the Martinů symphonies.

Martinů's melodic style is highly personal and accordingly one can trace common melodic habits of mind. He often begins a movement with a small rhythmic cell or a pregnant thematic germ from which grow the ensuing paragraphs. The beginning of the Third symphony and that of the finale of the Fifth are charged by the same three-note figure:

Yet the character of the ensuing music could hardly be more dissimilar. In the Third symphony this serves as a springboard for a turbulent *Allegro* with the characteristic interplay of 6/8 and 3/4 and a rhythmic tenacity that recalls the masterly double concerto (1938). In the Fifth it is interwoven into some sustained lyrical writing for strings that is as eloquent as the Third symphony is tense.

Similarly, this segment from the scherzo of the Fourth symphony:

is embedded in the triumphant, surging tune in the finale of the Fifth:

Yet this kind of melodic thinking, borne along as Virgil Thomson put it by this 'singing syncopation', is mobilized in quite different contexts. The scherzo of the Fourth symphony pulsates with a vibrant, relentless rhythm which has none of the lyrical radiance of the finale of No. 5. Indeed, it is in the trio section of the same scherzo, a gentle, pastoral theme, quite unlike Ex. 193 in character, that a greater resemblance is felt.

194

Both have a predominantly singing quality: both lines constantly avoid definite cadence points: both rely on the strong rhythmic structure of the tune.

Quite often Martinů concentrates his melodic activity within a comparatively small compass, say a fourth, before he bursts into larger, stronger leaps. Much of the tensile quality of his lines derives from the alternation between two notes, throwing all the interest on the rhythmic interplay between 6/8 and 3/4 or other devices of syncopation. This eloquent theme from the Sixth symphony shows the above characteristics as well as the muscular strength of his melodic thinking and the length at which he can sustain one unbroken idea:

195

Of the six, the Second symphony is perhaps the most relaxed in mood. It is largely pastoral in feeling and from the
very beginning its ideas open out in a wholly unforced
manner. The first subject sounds characteristically easy-
going though the cohesive forces just below the surface work
so as to impose a well-knit structural pattern on the apparently discursive course taken by the music. There is little
of the tension that one finds in the Third symphony, which
is much weightier. The second movement of No. 2 seems to
cast a backward glance over its shoulder at the slow dance
movements of Dvořák; there is the same directness of
speech and the pastoral atmosphere is almost wholly un-
disturbed by hints of urban sophistication:

196

The same is true of the other two movements, both of which
are short and quick. The finale has much the same kind of
buoyancy that one finds in the corresponding movement of
the Third piano concerto (1948).

The next symphony has a bigger emotional canvas and
has nothing of the Second's dance-like character. Indeed it
has something of the dark serious purposefulness of the
double concerto (1938). The opening movement is finely
sustained and builds up with an inexorable sense of impetus.
It is admirably counterbalanced by the slow movement
which has scoring of great transparency; it seems almost
luminous at times, while the string writing is of great
eloquence:

197

Any work of art is a considered reaction, as it were, to the artist's experience of life and the value of the work must be assessed in relation to the positiveness of the reaction. There is no doubt that Martinů's work is largely positive in feeling. The last three symphonies represent an advance on the first three not because they are more positive or considered, but simply because his greater experience in symphonic thinking enabled him to move with greater assurance in a wider dimension. The Fourth symphony is not content with the relaxed, easy-going mood of the Second: it radiates a positive state of happiness and exhilaration and calls on new reserves of energy. Its texture is far from thin (for Martinů is never wholly free from the charge of overscoring) yet it seems to have a glowing, incandescent quality that conveys a feeling of great light. The scherzo is a *tour de force* of sheer kinetic power: its sense of movement is both relentless and irresistible. Martinů achieves this by various devices one of which is combining brilliant rhythmic patterns and small energetic motives (Ex. 192 is one) with a purposeful sense of harmonic progression. The sustained woodwind writing over the relentless string rhythm between Figs. 8 and 10 in the score is an instance of this skill in mobilizing a sense of propulsion. The slow movement is perhaps the least successful of the four, for there are lush overtones that seem out of keeping with the far from self-indulgent character of the other three.

The Fifth is the last of the purely 'abstract' symphonies: while the Sixth is not overtly programmatic, it does bear the subtitle *Fantasies symphoniques*, and at one point towards the end of his life Martinů decided not to number it among the symphonies. Martinů has an almost classical view of the limits imposed by the symphonic discipline. In a sense the Fifth is the most classical and perfectly balanced of the symphonies: the perspectives are precisely judged and the control over detail and its relation to the work as a whole is complete; there is no trace of the slight sentimentality that clouds the slow movement of the Fourth. It is filled with the life-enhancing power we find in his very best work and its statement is wholly affirmative.

The Fourth and the Sixth symphonies open up new worlds of sound: the Fifth consolidates territory already won and is less exploratory than either. Both the Fourth and Fifth have recourse to direct sectional repetition. This way of treating material argues an approach to form which has its origins in the eighteenth century dance suite: it is certainly far removed from the post-Beethoven concept of the symphony in which material constantly evolves and assumes new forms and meanings. The Sixth symphony is far more concerned with a constant growth of the melodic line than its immediate predecessor. Though on first sight it appears to be more episodic, in fact Martinů never really abandons the thread of the argument. He appears to only because the detail in the musical landscape this work unfolds is richer in colouring and immediate in impact. At times the *Fantasies symphoniques* has the visionary quality, the enhanced awareness of colour, the vivid contrasts and more brilliant hues that are said to come from taking mescalin: certainly there is a proliferation of textures, exotic foliage and vibrant, pulsating sounds that have no parallel in the earlier symphonies. But for all the absorption in the new microcosm he has unfolded – the opening of the second movement unleashes an extraordinarily imaginative, insect-like teeming activity – there is still the sense of great space. Some of the orchestral effects cast a backward glance at *Le Sacre*, but this music is non-episodic and the world it evokes has nothing in common with that of Stravinsky's ballet. The material of the symphony bears on closer examination much greater kinship than one first imagines: these two ideas (the first from the first movement, Fig. 3 in the score, and the second from the finale) appear in different contexts and perform different functions, but have a close relationship:

198

It has been argued that Martinů was content with his discoveries, that he made little effort to expand the frontiers of his world of experience. Up to a point this is true, for he did repeat himself in many of his works. But the finest music in these symphonies glows with an inner warmth and love of life, inimitably expressed.

31

VAGN HOLMBOE AND THE
LATER SCANDINAVIANS

Robert Layton

*

IT is the most difficult thing in the world to write in the immediate shadow of a giant. The nineteenth century was dogged by Beethoven's achievement, so much so that even as late as Brahms there was a feeling that the resources of the symphony had been exhausted, that Beethoven had said all that was to be said. Similarly, in Scandinavia, late as it was on the musical scene, the towering figure of Sibelius was a forbidding and intimidating phenomenon. Sibelius was so highly personal a composer and so original a symphonist that to surrender to his influence almost sapped the vital springs of an independent musical personality. Like Debussy he is either inimitable or only too superficially imitable: those who were influenced produced a pale reflection of the 'outer' vestigial personality. The mannerisms were reproduced in a composer like Madetoja, for example, but the inner processes of his musical thinking were but dimly apprehended.

Perhaps because his musical language is less profoundly idiosyncratic than Sibelius's and his involvement with regional landscape less intense, Carl Nielsen would seem, superficially at least, a more fruitful influence. Yet though Nielsen is undoubtedly more European and, on the face of it, life-giving, it is paradoxical that the finest living Scandinavian symphonist, the Danish composer, Vagn Holmboe, owes more to Sibelius and at a profound, indeed almost hidden, level, than he does to his great countryman. This influence does not make itself felt at the superficial level of idiom. When it does, as in the Third and Fourth symphonies of the Swedish composer, Dag Wirén (b. 1905), it is immediately discernible. But in studying the later Holmboe symphonies it becomes clear that the lessons of Sibelius have been understood, and in his concentration on the principle of metamorphosis he comes far nearer to the Sibelian ideal than Wirén.

Holmboe was born in 1909 and after completing his studies in Copenhagen with Knud Jeppesen, he studied for a time in Berlin under Ernst Toch and later on in Rumania, where he came into contact with Balkan folk music. This (with the music of Bartók) was rapidly assimilated into the composer's own individual expressive language. Another powerful stimulus was the Danish musical tradition which had been so richly fertilized by the work of Carl Nielsen: Holmboe certainly inherits from the Danish master some of his most endearing characteristics: a lively imagination, and an alert, inquiring mind full of vitality. He is an extremely prolific composer, and has written eight symphonies; at the time of writing he is working on a ninth. Holmboe is particularly attracted to the chamber orchestra: he has written at least twelve chamber concertos and an extremely fine symphony for chamber orchestra (Op. 53).

In whatever genre, Holmboe's work shows him to be the possessor of an austere and often angular melodic style which makes free use of diatonic melodic patterns. There is no lack of contrapuntal interest and although some of his music wears a somewhat severe countenance (for he does not attempt to compromise his individuality for the sake of easy accessibility) he never courts obscurity for its own sake. It is, however, in his symphonies that his real stature clearly emerges. His First symphony (1935) is scored for a modest ensemble of chamber proportions and a second followed three years later. The Third and Fourth symphonies, subtitled respectively *Sinfonia rustica* and *Sinfonia sacra*, are war works, both dating from 1941. The Fourth is a choral work and it is worth noting *en passant* that Holmboe has a real feeling for choral writing. He avoids lines of great angularity and produces a smooth, flowing texture, rich in contrapuntal artifice yet wholly spontaneous in feeling.

It is however the Fifth symphony (1944) which the composer himself regards as the turning point in his career as a symphonist. It is in this work that he achieves a mature and fully integrated symphonic style. Its vital, urgent opening has distinct overtones of Stravinsky:

199

But this first movement has the feel of a genuine symphony. It moves forward with unrelenting logic and maintains its trenchant impact and its unflagging sense of direction to the very end. Much of Holmboe's linear thinking has a modal flavour about it and a good deal of the harmonic tension in his music derives from clashes of lines in a polymodal context. Formally this movement breaks no new ground though one cannot but admire the resourceful use Holmboe makes of the rhythmic figure (marked 'x') during the course of the movement. The second movement is more obviously pastoral in character: the expressive woodwind writing is characteristically pellucid and the contrapuntal interest often considerable. The exuberant and high-spirited finale, effective though it is, is more conventional in utterance than the other two movements.

The Sixth (1947) is a dark, sombre symphony which opens with a long, brooding line in which the interval of a fourth plays a dominant role:

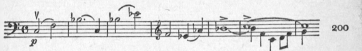

200

Later on, by a process of metamorphosis, this becomes:

201

This interest in metamorphosis is the very stuff of organic thinking and Holmboe's capacity for organic thought is the hallmark of a true symphonist. The Sixth symphony is a big work and like Nielsen's Fifth, is in two movements; there is, incidentally, an oblique reference to the Nielsen symphony in the *poco inquieto* section of the first movement at Fig. 4. The opening pages generate a polyphony that is both powerful and eloquent and the coda of the whole work is individual and moving. However, the work is far less compact in design than the impressive Seventh (1950), a one movement work about twenty-five minutes in length. From the very opening this is music of unmistakable urgency:

202

From this terse, pregnant utterance, powerfully arresting and immediately compelling, there follows this idea which is given to the violas:

203

There is some highly explosive orchestral writing before another idea, obviously related to the above, grows out of the texture:

204

This theme is subject to constant shifts of emphasis and subtle changes but it turns out to be one of the leading characters in the drama. The structure of the work is highly interesting, in four quite definite sections linked by three interludes, scored with the utmost translucence and clarity. The opening section, based on the foregoing material, is highly concentrated and never relaxes its sense of forward thrust. Ex. 204 undergoes extensive treatment before the opening idea is restated: the initial note is omitted at one point (five bars before Fig. 4 in the score) and it gives rise to this sort of transformation:

205

At the climax of the first section the main ideas are drawn together (Exs. 202 and 204 are heard simultaneously) and the music gradually moves towards the slow section. This has a characteristic intensity and has long, flowing lines that at times recall the Sixth symphony. But for all their angularity these are beautifully supple and expressive and never for one moment does Holmboe lose sight of the sense of

forward movement that distinguishes him. Here is the main
idea of this section:

206

After the sustained and thoughtful slow section in which the
colours are, on the whole, dark and forbidding, the luminous
scoring of the second *intermedia* makes an excellent contrast.
It links the slow section to the brilliant, indeed mercurial,
scherzo: this is scored with an icy precision. In saying this
I must add that this does not hold true of the climax of the
scherzo, which seems to me overscored. After the scherzo
has got under way Holmboe returns to some of the early
substance of the work (Exs. 204 and 205) before the final
intermedia and the highly-charged coda which ends the
symphony.

But describing the general outline of the Seventh
symphony or its closely integrated thematic structure
(which would need far more music examples) can give little
idea of its character. It is immensely powerful music, as
dense in concentration as it is clinically precise in its cal-
culation of sonority. Of all Holmboe's symphonies it is the
most intensely personal up to this time. It makes no con-
cession to sensuous gratification but has an inner strength,
muscularity of rhythm, a distinction of ideas and continuity
of invention that mark it out from the general run of post-
war symphonies.

The Seventh was first heard in Denmark in 1951 and had
its *première* abroad at the I.S.C.M. Festival at Baden-
Baden in 1953: the Eighth, however, has not yet been performed outside Scandinavia. Subtitled *Sinfonia boreale* (1951–
52), it is a much more expansive work designed on an altogether larger canvas than its predecessor. It consists of four
movements which are not linked together. The most deeply
felt of them is the slow movement which, with its plaintive
woodwind cries, shares the same elegiac* feeling that one

* The work is in fact inscribed *In memoriam Herbert Häffner*.

235

finds in the corresponding movements of the later Shostakovich symphonies. Here is the opening:

The 'cello and double-bass line is very characteristic: a
similar idea punctuates the main idea of the slow section of
the Seventh symphony. As in all the Holmboe symphonies,
irrespective of their proportions, the music grows consistently
from its initial germ material. The Eighth opens with a
simple idea on bass clarinet over a pedal point on double-
basses:

In itself this may seem a commonplace musical utterance
but it generates a torrent of activity. Much of the substance
of the movement derives from this: the three notes B, E, and
F appear in various guises and a good deal of the subsidiary
thematic material grows out of it, including this idea:

In this massive symphony everything springs from a genuine
musical impulse and there is an overwhelming feeling that
the musical processes that take place are inevitable steps in
the working-out of the drama. In a way the experience can
be likened to a journey; the sense of forward movement is
inexorable, the feeling of purpose is firm, yet the wealth of
detail *en route* renders it unpredictable.

Holmboe's music has a certain reserve. Its impact is not
always immediate because he makes no compromise whatever with current fashions. He relies on the cumulative
effect of a work rather than on isolated details of colour and
texture. The Seventh and Eighth symphonies have both a
continuity of thought and an elevation of feeling unlikely to
appeal to the vitiated palate. At a time when fragmentation
rather than continuity is in vogue and the appetite for colour
and 'exciting' textures more or less insatiable, Holmboe's
qualities are likely to be passed over. The pontifical teenage
mandarins of the New Musical Establishment are more
readily excited by a few empty gestures from a composer
bursting with personality but with little to say in terms of
pure music than they are with a more reticent personality
who can argue in cogent musical terms but who does not
readily surrender his secrets.

One of the reasons why the Holmboe symphonies are
successful as symphonies is to be found in the quality of the
thematic ideas. There are many Scandinavian composers
who are far better melodists: among them Wirén, Rosenberg and Saeverud, but the secret of symphonic writing lies
in the ability to evolve long-term thinking from non-lyrical
ideas. The basic idea, for example, in Holmboe's chamber
symphony (Op. 53) written in 1951 between the Seventh
the Eighth symphonies, is not in itself distinguished, rather
the contrary:

Yet it is by its enormously resourceful and imaginative treatment in ever-changing contexts that this material acquires such variety of emphasis. Hence, at each playing this score reveals something new that had escaped one's attention before. The scoring for single woodwind, horns, trumpets, timpani, and strings is beautifully spacious: the most individual sonorities being produced by the most simple and economical of means. The third movement is a model of euphonious woodwind writing and the cool but luminous quality of the writing for upper strings and woodwind is haunting.

Holmboe scores over his contemporaries by the compactness of his thinking and the stability of his musical personality: he is the only living Scandinavian symphonist who has never compromised his integrity. He has followed his own star and has remained unresponsive to the fashionable changes in the stylistic barometer that have affected, for instance, the Swedish composer Blomdahl.

Both Hilding Rosenberg (Sweden) and Niels Viggo Bentzon (Denmark) have flirted with the twelve-tone technique for a time and though both have eminently distinctive personalities neither has the capacity to think as succinctly as does Holmboe.

Niels Viggo Bentzon comes from a highly musical family and is related to the nineteenth-century Danish composer, J.P.E.Hartmann (1805–1900). Like Holmboe he studied in Copenhagen under Jeppesen; unlike his countryman, he took little interest in folk music either in Denmark or abroad. An immensely prolific and gifted composer, he is rarely happy unless he is writing or performing his music and his creative energy seems almost limitless. During his twenties the music of Hindemith made a considerable impact on him, though it never exercised too cramping an influence on his imagination. Bentzon has no fewer than nine symphonies to his credit and he also makes extensive use of thematic metamorphosis. Indeed the Fourth symphony is entitled *Metamorphoses*, though the transformation of ideas often takes place at a more primitive level than in a Holmboe symphony. *Metamorphoses* contains music of remarkable imaginative power but, despite its composer's ingenuity, the work lacks the cohesive force so necessary in symphonic writing. It sprawls, and its substance lacks density; no amount of derivation of themes can disguise this. That Bentzon has an individual approach to form, however, and is well able to concentrate his material on a somewhat smaller scale, emerges in the fine third piano sonata, the first movement of which offers an interesting and convincing working-out of some fascinating musical material within the broad framework of sonata form.

Of the Swedish symphonists after Berwald and Stenhammar, the most commanding figure is surely Hilding Rosenberg (b. 1892). He, too, is a prolific composer with an enormous amount of orchestral and chamber music to his credit. Like most Scandinavian composers he came for a time under the spell of Sibelius and the Finnish master's imprint makes itself felt in many of his early scores (a good example is the *Interlude* from the suite, *Journey to America*, drawn from his opera of the same name). On the other hand we find that Rosenberg yields to the fascination of Schoenberg's experiments in his early chamber symphony (1923), an indication of his eclectic style and wide sympathies. This diversity of style can be traced throughout his creative career and is indicative of his inquiring mind, keenly conscious of the various cross-currents of contemporary music. Rosenberg has never closed his mind to any of these, which is not the same as saying that he has uncritically embraced every fashionable fad from central Europe, as have some of the younger Swedes. Notwithstanding his receptivity to new ideas he has an undeniably individual outlook.

Although they are not so concentrated as Holmboe's, the Rosenberg symphonies contain some very fine music. Like many other Swedish composers, including Dag Wirén and Lars-Erik Larsson, he has a highly developed feeling for nature: his musical equipment also comprises an enormous facility and a fastidious craftsmanship. His Second symphony (*Sinfonia grave*) dates from the early thirties and brought him to the threshold of his artistic maturity, but it is the Third (1939) that has established itself more securely in the repertoire, at least in Sweden. It originally bore the subtitle *The Four Ages of Man*, but Rosenberg subsequently revised the work, cutting out a fugal section from the scherzo and also withdrawing the title. In spite of its programme (which drew on Romain Rolland's *Jean Christophe*) the work stands firmly on its own feet as music. In the first movement we can see that Rosenberg has not altogether been unaffected by the angularity of Hindemith, for the interval of a fourth plays quite a part in his linear thinking. Yet the opening idea is both individual and informed by a sense of purpose:

211

Despite the fact that a twelve-note row is at once followed by its inversion, the movement is strongly tonal. It generates some writing of real eloquence and expressive power: the writing for strings is particularly impressive. The second group, too long, alas, to quote here, is one of Rosenberg's most exquisite inspirations. Its delicate colourings and beautiful transparent scoring reveal a vein of poetry that by far surpasses that of his contemporaries. The theme itself is full of a tender, sorrowful lyricism that breathes the air of gentle melancholy characteristic of so much Swedish art. The first movement of this symphony is an impressive achievement by any standards and Rosenberg's invention shows an imagination and poetic vision of undoubted quality. The second is a contemplative, ruminative movement with a tendency towards diffuseness but of very great beauty. Least successful, perhaps, is the scherzo, which has a relentless sense of momentum but suffers from monotony of texture. The finale, however, matches the first two movements and sounds a note of genuine nobility.

The Fourth symphony (1940) is subtitled *The Revelation of St John the Divine* and like its successor, No. 5 (1944), is a choral work. The Fourth offers a splendid example of Rosenberg's diversity of style: much of the choral writing is firmly wedded to tradition and is smooth and gentle in its contours and even austere in utterance. But Rosenberg does not make the mistake of so many of his younger contemporaries in writing vocal music that is excessively angular and obviously instrumental in conception. The orchestral writing, on the other hand, makes free use of dissonance and is far less restrained. Both the Fourth and Fifth are much larger than their immediate neighbours. More unified in style and containing moments of real serenity, is the Fifth symphony. Much of its invention is simple and diatonic: yet in terms of sheer euphony and richness and fantasy it must be classed among his finest achievements. Its successor, No. 6 (1951), is wholly instrumental and on a smaller scale. The writing is often episodic but much of the music moves on a high level of inspiration. Both the Third and Sixth symphonies deserve a firmer place in the repertory than they now hold, for Rosenberg speaks with an individual voice.

Although Dag Wirén has probably more spontaneous musicality and a well-stocked fantasy he is not quite as successful as a symphonist. His classical leanings emerge clearly in Symphony No. 3 (1943–4) which gained numerous hearings in this country immediately after the war. The first two movements in the Third symphony correspond very much to the first and second groups in a sonata movement, while the finale fulfils the function of developing the previous material and drawing its threads together. However, Wirén's phrase structure is somewhat limited in the sense that he rarely builds up long, flowing lines and has little of the rhythmic flexibility or rhetorical command of Rosenberg. His Fourth symphony (1951–2) is to all intents and purposes monothematic, though the germ-idea does not prove itself of sufficient seminal power to fertilize the whole growth. Much the same criticisms can be levelled against the short-breathed phrase-structures of the stimulating Norwegian composer Harald Saeverud who has written nine symphonies. The Sixth, *Sinfonia dolorosa*, is even shorter than Wirén's Fourth, but its impact is greatly diminished by the same musical flaws. Yet these are both serious attempts to wrestle with the symphonic problem.

32

THE SYMPHONY IN AMERICA

Peter Jona Korn

*

AFTER the Second World War, America's leading symphony orchestras, already well known internationally through their recordings and broadcasts, embarked on concert tours all over the world. In general, these tours were not very much different from similar ones by leading orchestras of Europe. In either case, repertory works by the great German, French, Russian and Italian composers were heard, and it remained largely a personal matter whether one liked the Boston Symphony's Brahms better than that of the Berlin Philharmonic, or whether the Philadelphia Orchestra's Debussy seemed more impressive than that of Amsterdam's Concertgebouw. Moreover, such preference depended as much, if not more, on the conductor's conception, since the technical virtuosity of all these orchestras was beyond question. If anything was proved by these tours, it was the fact that America's great orchestras play music of European composers every bit as well as leading orchestras the whole world over.

But there was one great difference: while European orchestras found it natural to build each of their 'export' programmes around a major composition of one of their compatriots, the American orchestras did no such thing. When an American work was played at all – by no means always the case! – it was usually a curtain raiser, seldom longer than a few minutes. To feature a full-fledged American symphony as the major work of an evening was an exception rather than the rule. Consequently, listeners may have concluded that America has few really important symphonic composers, and that these 'specialize' in overtures, essays for orchestra, and similarly brief programme dividends.

243

Nothing could be further from the truth. In fact, the symphony has special appeal for the American composer and a virtual renaissance of the symphony has taken place in America precisely at the moment when a generation of European composers has rejected it, at least temporarily. A reason for this lies in the American character, which is marked by generosity, often to a fault, by a decided flair for the dramatic, by a preference for sharp contrasts and by a leaning to over-statement. The *al fresco* character of a true symphonic style is better suited to these attitudes, which in turn are a reflection of the wide, spacious character of a typical American landscape, than, for instance, chamber music, which tends to place greater emphasis on detail.

Most American symphonies are contemporary works. Hardly any significant American symphony is more than thirty years old, and few of them can be considered firmly established in the symphonic repertory. America's entire history of serious music, her entire symphonic tradition, is part of this century, more specifically the last four decades. America's 'good' composers are practically all alive. To be sure, a few composers lived in America during the nineteenth century. Some of them even wrote symphonies. These followed the established romantic pattern so closely as to be virtually indistinguishable from works of lesser European composers. American composers went unnoticed, unless they went to Europe, as did Edward MacDowell. America's first major composer, he owed his initial success to Franz Liszt and the influential German publishing house of Breitkopf and Härtel.

The first composer of note to attempt a break with European tradition and to envisage a kind of music that could be classified and identified as American was Charles Ives, considered by many to be the only outstanding composer America has produced. Arnold Schoenberg, almost his exact contemporary (both were born in 1874; Schoenberg died in 1951, Ives in 1954), made the following statement after he had settled in America: 'There is a great man living in this country, a composer. He has solved the problem how to preserve one's self and to learn. He responds to neglect by contempt. He is not forced to accept praise or blame. His name is Ives.' This pronouncement provides, if nothing else, a revealing glimpse of Schoenberg's own attitude toward the world around him. It tells us, in fact, more about Schoenberg than about the man who is the object of his praise. But it is fair to assume that a common bond between these two composers did indeed exist, and that Schoenberg's respect for Ives was fully reciprocated. Both men reacted to the problems and challenges facing a composer of their generation in a similar manner. Both broke with tradition, though Schoenberg had shown a marked degree of technical mastery within that tradition, and Ives had not. Moreover, Schoenberg had evolved one particular method, which he believed to be the solution to his problem, and he followed this method consistently. Ives, on the other hand, experimented seemingly without aim, here tinkering with fractional intervals (intervals smaller than a half-tone), there exploiting the possibilities of diatonic melodies juxtaposed against sharply dissonant harmonies, or the effectiveness of tone-clusters.

Far too much has been made of the fact that Ives was the first to try out these and many other new devices, years ahead of Schoenberg, Haba or Cowell. In our time, when the preoccupation with new devices has become all important to a point where the quality of the music itself is no longer a criterion for its evaluation, this is not particularly surprising. In view of that, Leonard Bernstein's proclamation that Ives is 'our first really great composer – our Washington, Lincoln and Jefferson of music' should be taken with more than a grain of salt. Regarded as a belated recognition of a creative personality who was all but totally ignored during his lifetime, such a dictum is heart-warming. As a *bona fide* evaluation of Ives the composer it is, unfortunately, a gross exaggeration. Charles Ives can be called many things: a symbol of America's fight for cultural independence, a man of profound integrity and untiring devotion to his own ideals, a non-conformist who went his own way at all times and at all cost; but by no stretch of imagination can he be called a great composer. He was, in fact, not even a very good one.

Surely it is no accident that even during the 1930s, when America became increasingly composer-conscious, and the names of Roy Harris, Aaron Copland and Samuel Barber became internationally known, Ives remained in obscurity. The Second symphony, a major work that poses no problems either to the performer or to the listener, was not played until 1952, fifty years after it had been completed. The Fourth symphony, regarded as a key work by Ives enthusiasts who know the manuscript, has yet to be heard, or even published in its entirety.* This symphony is reputed to be so difficult as to be virtually unperformable. There are today, however, music festivals and concert series specializing in the performance of unperformable music, with limitless rehearsal time and lavish funds available; still, nothing has been done to bring about a performance of this work, and it can only be assumed that even Ives's enthusiastic supporters feel his cause is better served by the mysticism surrounding a significant final symphony that has never been heard, than by its actual performance. This is consistent with the fact that it is always Ives's role as a 'pioneer', never the quality of the music itself, on which the claim to his greatness as a composer is based. But a composer must always be judged on the merit of his works, never on his attitudes or intentions. To have done something 'first' means very little; to have done it 'best', a great deal.

The quality of Ives's music is, to say the least, highly inconsistent. He mixes many techniques, and he masters none. The Second symphony, for instance, can be classified as a typical work of the late romantic period, entirely appropriate for a symphony written at the turn of the century. Interjected into the thematic material are snatches of Americana, ranging from the barn-dance favourite 'Turkey

* It has now been performed. (Ed.)

in the Straw' and the patriotic 'Columbia the Gem of the Ocean' to military bugle calls. Here as in other works, this technique represents Ives's desire to break away from the European tradition and write 'American' music. To term this approach eclectic would be correct, but it would say very little, inasmuch as every composer since Bach has been in some measure an eclectic. What separates the good eclectic from the bad one is that the former is able to forge divergent stylistic elements into a language of his very own, and that Ives was never able to do. A telling example of this lack of amalgamation so typical of Ives are the three final measures of the Second symphony: at first the opening bar of 'Columbia' is heard; then a trumpet blows 'reveille', which leads to what should be the final F major chord – instead, Ives ends with a wild atonal chord, reminiscent of the final chord of Mozart's 'Musical Joke':

212

But a blotch of 'wrong notes' is not very funny, not even in Mozart's otherwise delightfully clever work, and in a late romantic symphony it is downright silly. One of the chief drawbacks of the Second symphony is its heavy-handed orchestration, a fault Ives was able to avoid in his Third symphony, which is scored for small orchestra. Excepting the Second, this is the only numbered symphony to be recorded (Ives also wrote a 'Holiday' symphony and an incomplete 'Universe' symphony) and it is much the better work of the two. In contrast to the boisterous quality of the earlier work, the Third is predominantly lyrical in quality, as exemplified by the opening theme:

A much shorter piece, it is less verbose and repetitious, considerably more integrated in structure and texture, and while hardly justifying any of the superlatives that have surrounded the composer's name in recent years, it is a pleasant enough work to merit an occasional hearing.

After the First World War, as the creative span of Charles Ives's life was nearing its end, a new, vigorous and enterprising generation of American composers emerged, a generation that set out to do precisely what Ives had projected: to write serious music which was characteristically American. Many of these composers went about it in a rather unusual way: they went to Paris to study composition with Nadia Boulanger, who idolized the Russian Stravinsky and was otherwise a thoroughgoing exponent of the French point of view. Considering the rather low esteem in which the symphonic tradition, which was essentially German, was held in the musical Paris of the 1920s, it is even more astonishing that one of Mme Boulanger's favourite students should go on to become America's major symphonist: Roy Harris (b. 1898), whose musical development centres around the symphony, and whose every creative period culminates in one or more works in that form.

Initial performances of the first Harris symphony to be heard, the 'Symphony 1933' (a Symphony No. 1, written in 1928, has never been performed), instantly revealed that here was a composer with a true flair for the symphonic, and later works have, of course, confirmed this impression. Harris's symphonic style can be summed up in a key phrase: dramatic simplicity. This holds true for virtually

all aspects of Harris's symphonic idiom: thematic statements that are precise and therefore easily retained;
harmonic patterns that are predominantly chordal, rather
than the incidental result of counterpoint, with shifting
triads as a base; counterpoint more sparingly used than is
usual in most contemporary music, and never designed to
replace musical development; and above all, a love for the
sound of the orchestra as a body, with a decided partiality
to the sound of strings and open brasses, rather than as an
assembly of many solo players.

At the same time, Harris's language is perhaps more
characteristically American than that of any other symphonic composer; it is American music as Brahms is German, Debussy French or Vaughan Williams English, not
because of an occasional use of folk material, but because of
an inherent national flavour that defies definition.

All of these attributes are combined in a rarely-achieved
degree of concentration and balance in his best known work,
the Third symphony, which has become firmly established
in the symphonic repertory. Serge Koussevitzky, prior to the
world *premiére* by the Boston Symphony in 1940, called it
'the first great symphony by an American composer', and
the special pedestal this work has occupied ever since has
borne out his evaluation.

Like two other pivotal works, the 'Symphony 1933' and
the Seventh (1954), the Third is cast in a one-movement
form, consisting of various shorter sections, none of which
constitutes a movement in itself. The work opens with a
long chant by the 'cellos, with the violas sustaining the final
note of each phrase:

Con moto (84 M.M)

214

Neither this opening section, nor any of the following ones, has a second theme, the thematic contrast being provided by the development from one section to another, rather than within the individual sections.

The symphony's most famous theme, one of the best known in American music, is the subject of the fugal section:

One of Harris's favourite devices, a technique of alternating major and minor thirds, often in parallel motion, later combines with a development of the fugal subject's first motive to provide one of the symphony's finest moments:

Nothing could emphasize Roy Harris's acknowledged debt to the grand symphonic tradition more fittingly than the coda, a glorious chant in which the brasses dominate, set over a pedal point on the note D in the timpani:

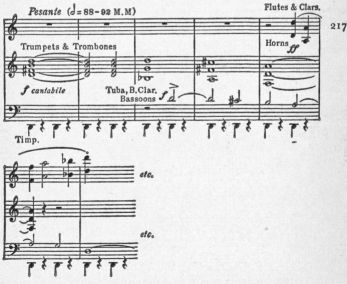

251

one of the most stirring endings of any symphony written in our time.

It is sometimes maintained that, in his subsequent symphonies, Harris has done nothing essentially new, that he has in effect merely re-written the Third. As a statement of fact there is a grain of truth in this; as a criticism, there is not: each new symphony represents a further step in his development, which can be described as a gradual, continuous growth, rather than a succession of different phases, a description that fits another famous graduate from the ranks of Mme Boulanger's American pupils, Aaron Copland (b. 1900).

Apart from their teacher, these two men, who have become the two outstanding exponents of what could be called the 'American School', have little else in common. Harris's development moves in one continuous line, while that of Copland can be divided into successive periods, each of them emphasizing another aspect of the composer's many-sided talent, and revealing a different influence that stimulated his creativity at a particular time. Copland himself has stated that his three symphonies are respectively representative of his work in the 1920s, the Thirties and the Forties, and this statement may serve to explain what importance the symphonies have within his collective work.

For Roy Harris, the symphony is the lifeblood of his creativity; works in other forms, no matter what their individual significance, are relegated to a place of secondary importance. In other words, Harris is first and foremost, and in the truest sense of the word, a symphonist.

Copland is not; for him, the symphony is of marginal importance; it becomes a symphonic restatement of what he has expressed, in different media, during a preceding period. This is especially true of his last symphony, designated as No. 3. (Though it is, like the Third symphony by Harris, actually No. 4, if an early 'Dance' symphony is included in the count.) The Third symphony was written from 1944 to 1946, and should be viewed as the culmination of one of Copland's most important periods, which was marked by his interest in American folklore and by a sharp turn to utmost simplicity. His three great American dance scores, *Billy the Kid*, *Rodeo* and *Appalachian Spring*, were written during that period, and the style of these and other works composed in the years before and during the Second World War finds its symphonic expression in the Third symphony. *Appalachian Spring* in particular is closely akin to the Third – there is a likeness of texture, of orchestral timbre between these two works, as evidenced by the symphony's opening theme:

218

This work, as all of the music of that period, is especially intriguing in its lightly textured, transparent passages, the most ingratiating single feature of the composer's style. A fine example is the beginning of the coda of the last movement:

which leads to the final recurrence of the symphony's principal subject (Ex. 218).

If transparency is Copland's strong point, he is least successful with massive sounds. His orchestral *tutti*, the backbone of a symphonic idiom, have a tendency to sound strident rather than full, noisy rather than powerful. Tragedy, drama, pathos, basic attributes of a symphonic language, are foreign to his nature. His great love is the dance, a love that is wholly requited. This is probably the main reason why the Third symphony, in spite of its many moments of enchantment, has not become nearly as popular as the three dance scores.

The pronounced tendencies of Copland on the one hand, and Harris on the other, are neatly blended in the personality of yet another Boulanger pupil: Walter Piston (b. 1894). Equally successful as the composer of seven symphonies as with his immensely popular ballet *The Incredible Flutist*, Piston is without question America's most mature composer. This maturity is reflected in the consistently high level of his output – there is virtually no such thing as 'bad Piston'. He is a composer of *moderation*, in the most positive sense of the word – moderation that is the result of discipline and control; not of limitation, except those limitations he imposes on himself. With a sure instinct he avoids extremes; his basic approach in matters of form, of melody or harmony and of instrumentation, is traditional. There is no particular device or innovation associated with his name or identified with his work. It is the absence of anything unusual rather than its presence that characterizes his style, which except for a bit of Americana in *The Incredible Flutist*, is not so pronouncedly American as that of Harris or Copland.

If any one element can be said to dominate in so well-balanced a style, it is the lyrical, as illustrated by the gently flowing nature of the opening measures of the Fourth symphony:

220

Walter Piston has never been the subject of heated controversy, and never will be. He has established a reputation as a good, solid craftsman who turns out one splendid work after another. He has no passionate detractors nor adulating disciples. There is, in other words, nothing extraordinary about him – except, perhaps, the strong possibility that his symphonies may well turn out to be the most durable written in America today.

Another composer who, like Piston, has seven symphonies to his credit is William Schuman (b. 1910), leading younger representative of the American School. In Schuman's music the influence of his teacher, Roy Harris, is unmistakable, but this is true only for certain technical aspects, rather than for the character of the music itself. In contrast to Harris, who prefers the rich, glowing sonorities of brasses and strings in lower registers, Schuman's orchestral palette is dominated by bright, piercing colours, with a decided partiality to trumpets and high violins. He has an affinity for sharply clashing sonorities, although his basic harmonic structures are entirely tonal. He is a brilliant orchestrator, a knowledgeable composer completely in command of every aspect of contemporary technique. Withal, there is a certain synthetic quality about his music, outside the realm of verbal definition; it leaves an impression of having been conceived in a spirit of emotional detachment, it is a music of symphonic gestures rather than of symphonic content. Something that is often said – incorrectly – of Walter Piston is true for William Schuman: he is the prototype of an academic composer.

At least three other symphonists of the Harris-Copland generation must be mentioned here: America's most prolific writer of symphonies, Henry Cowell (b. 1897), who, at the time of writing, has completed his fifteenth; Ernst Bacon (b. 1898), the author of four works in this form; and the self-styled 'bad boy of music', George Antheil (1900–59), who produced six symphonies.

While the formulation of an American idiom in symphonic music became a major goal for many a composer, there were others who remained aloof from such efforts. This was true in particular for those who sensed that the price a contemporary composer must pay for ignoring or rejecting his roots in the immediate past (for the American, this meant the romantic tradition of Europe) was to accept a degree of rootlessness, with the resulting limitation of his range of expression.

A major figure with strong ties to the romantic tradition is Samuel Barber (b. 1910); he is also, potentially, a symphonist of major importance, though this potential has yet to be realized. Barber's First symphony remains, next to the Third symphony of Harris, the most important single symphony by an American composer. But while the Harris work, the product of a mature man of forty, is entirely integrated into this composer's steady evolution of a symphonic style, Barber's First, written at the age of twenty-five, remains a one-shot affair, a flash of brilliance he never again equalled, at least not in the symphonic field.

Structurally there is a definite resemblance, in design as well as proportion, between these two one-movement works. But while the Harris is epic in conception, the Barber is a cyclic symphony, in which the principal motive of the opening theme:

221

is brought back, in altered form, at two strategic points: first, as the theme of a scherzo section:

222

and later as the subject of a *passacaglia*:

The academic designation of Barber's style is 'neo-romantic'. This is a somewhat superficial classification, based entirely on the viewpoint that his language represents no radical break with that of the recent past. But if Barber's manner of handling melody and harmony, if his use of the orchestra is correctly identified as an outgrowth of nine-teenth-century tradition, it should also be recognized that in matters of form his ability to condense and to telescope, his ingenuity in developing ideas of great emotional impact in a highly concentrated manner is anything but romantic in attitude. Barber is a very difficult composer to classify, and that may be taken as a clue to his considerable stature.

His Second symphony, written while in service in the U.S. Air Force during the Second World War, does not fulfil the promise of the First. The successful one-movement structure of the earlier work is abandoned in favour of the more conventional three-movement design. There are some fine passages in the first movement, especially the captivating second theme:

but much of the two subsequent movements sounds lab-
oured, even contrived, in a degree that is unusual for the
music of this gifted composer.

Two other notable traditionalists, each with five symphonies to his credit, are Howard Hanson (b. 1896), whose
Second ('Romantic') symphony was very much in vogue
for a good many years, and Paul Creston (b. 1906), equally
successful with his Second symphony, which has become
one of the few symphonies firmly entrenched in the repertory of American orchestras. Both men represent a type of
creative artist rare in our time: one who is completely unconcerned about new systems, techniques or aesthetic
approaches, at least in so far as they relate to his own
creativity. This non-conformist attitude has enabled Paul
Creston and Howard Hanson to remain, at all times, true
to their own impulses, thereby assuring their public, as well
as themselves, of the complete honesty of every note they
write.

All of the composers discussed thus far, those rooted in
the European tradition as well as those laying the foundations for a new American one, have – as symphonists – one
thing in common: they are firmly committed to tonality.
The harmonic structure of their symphonies is based on the
traditional concept of key relations. In some cases, as in
Copland's Second ('Short') symphony, this concept may
stretch pretty far. But neither this nor any other work of

these composers is atonal, either in a free sense, or within the strict discipline of the twelve-tone technique.

Only two of America's established composers have written symphonies that go beyond the limit of what can be recognized as tonal music: Wallingford Riegger (1885–1961) and Roger Sessions (b. 1896). Sessions, one of America's most respected teachers of composition, has been a dominant influence on a number of younger composers, and some of these have built impressive reputations of their own. Yet none of them became symphonists; they are best known for their works in other media, primarily chamber music. Surely this is no mere circumstance; atonal music has the ability to command only an extremely limited span of attention, a fact that was well recognized by that paragon of atonal brevity, Anton Webern. In larger forms, and when a full orchestra is employed, the spineless quality of music that renounces the binding attribute of tonal centres becomes only too apparent.

Wallingford Riegger, who was strongly attracted to the clashing sonorities resulting from atonal writing, as well as to themes consisting of twelve-tone rows, tried in his Fourth and last symphony to explore the possibilities of playing off simple diatonic material, such as the opening theme:

225

against sharply dissonant textures, entirely atonal in function and character.

Roger Sessions, as if to emphasize that it is not 'atonal' music, uses key signatures throughout his Second symphony. This serves no practical purpose except to make it even more difficult for the performer to grapple with a score that is fiendishly difficult to begin with, as evidenced by the viola theme of the *Adagio*:

226

A minute analysis of this symphony will no doubt confirm the existence of carefully submerged tonal centres, to which these key signatures have reference. The same kind of analysis would bring forth very similar results with any given score of Schoenberg or – much more so – Berg or Dalla-piccola, none of whom uses key signatures. Atonal music is, after all, nothing else but tonal music in which the tonal functions occur and permute in the shortest possible space of time.

But the listening ear is not concerned with such theoretical considerations: what it hears, when listening to the Second symphony by Sessions, is atonal music. Taken on these terms, this work is certainly among the best atonal sym-phonies written in America, or for that matter, anywhere else. Schoenberg's influence is obvious, but Sessions avoids Schoenberg's unfortunate habit of cross-breeding a multi-tude of constantly changing rhythmical patterns which, far from providing contrast, actually result in a sort of rhyth-mical mush. Moreover, Sessions has a much better ear for effective sound combinations, and a gift for orchestral colour that recalls Alban Berg. Nevertheless, the predominant impression of the Second symphony (and more so of the much weaker Third) is one of restlessness, of nervous tension, conjuring up the image of the 'tortured composer' who is himself sorely in need of consolation, rather than having the ability to console.

In the symphonies of America's younger generation of composers, strong tendencies towards either nationalism or traditionalism become less pronounced. It might be said that an amalgamation of these tendencies is taking place. This generation (composers born during and after the First World War) is separated from the middle generation of Barber and Schuman by an American composer of Armenian extraction, Alan Hovhaness (b. 1911), whose production of symphonies rivals that of Henry Cowell: at the last count, Hovhaness had arrived at number thirteen. His style is a peculiar fusion of basic diatonic material, stated in the simplest terms possible, with oriental elements which are a dominating factor in his music.

It is debatable whether or not Leonard Bernstein (b. 1918) can rightfully be called a symphonist; both his symphonies cross over into the realm of programme music. This is less true of his First symphony, 'Jeremiah', the first major orchestral work to reveal the creative potential of America's most versatile musical personality. But it is certainly true of his Second symphony, 'The Age of Anxiety', based on a poem by W. H. Auden, a work that is not only programmatic enough to qualify for the designation of symphonic poem, but one that also uses an *obligato* piano to such an extent that – programme or no – it sounds more like a piano concerto than a symphony. Both works, however, are highly stimulating, imaginative compositions, and in particular 'Jeremiah' deserves to be performed much more widely than is presently the case.

America's outstanding younger symphonist is Peter Mennin (b. 1923), who wrote six symphonies before the age of thirty-five. Mennin's idiom abounds in rich chordal texture, colourful in its carefully planned sonorities, as in the following passage from the introduction to the first movement of the Sixth symphony:

227

Other young Americans whose symphonies have been performed by major orchestras include David Diamond, who heads the list with a total of eight symphonies; Vincent Persichetti and Meyer Kuperman, who have written four symphonies each; Roger Goeb, Alexei Haieff, Peter Jona Korn and Robert Ward, each with three symphonies; and Easley Blackwood, Ellis Kohs, Robert Kurka, Benjamin Lees, George Rochberg and Robert Starer, all authors of two symphonies.

Ernst Toch (b. 1887) is, in the strictest sense, not an American; but every one of his four symphonies was written long after he had become an integral part of the American musical scene, and if any one country has the right to claim him it is the United States where he made his home after 1934.

As a symphonist, Toch constitutes a unique case in the annals of musical history. Occasionally composers have waited until late in life to produce a single symphony, as for instance Franck or Kodaly. But no composer has ever written his First symphony after he reached sixty, and then gone on to write three more symphonies within a total period of eight years.

Three of the four Toch symphonies are linked by dedication to persons whose life and thought had a profound meaning for him. Thus, the First is dedicated to 'Joseph (Seppl) Fuchs, the faithful friend of early school days' – a self-explanatory dedication, in its obvious association with the composer's own youth. The Second and Fourth symphonies are dedicated respectively to a man and a woman who, to Ernst Toch, represent the highest degree of sainthood attainable in a human being: Albert Schweitzer's name graces the title page of the Second, while the Fourth, most intimate of the four symphonies, is dedicated 'to the memory of a beloved friend, Marian MacDowell', widow of Edward MacDowell. But what about the Third? It carries no dedication, beyond an acknowledgement that it was commissioned by the American-Jewish Tercentenary Committee of Chicago 1954. Perhaps the motto that precedes it will provide a clue. It is a passage from Goethe's *The Sorrows of Young Werther* and reads: 'Indeed am I a wanderer, a pilgrim on the earth – but what else are you?' Toch relates that he read Goethe's novel as a soldier during the First World War, and that this book is closely associated with his emotions during that time. But beyond that, perhaps unconsciously, these words define his own fate, as well as that of millions who became 'wanderers' in the course of wars and persecutions in our time, and in the light of this interpretation the Third symphony assumes a quasi-autobiographical aspect that virtually rules out a more specific dedication.

The two preceding symphonies also carry mottos, the First a quotation from Luther: 'And be the world full of devils . . .'; and the Second the verse: 'I will not let thee go, except thou bless me.' (Genesis XXXII, 26.) No motto precedes the Fourth, but a speaker recites two tributes to

Marian MacDowell, written by Toch himself, between the movements of the three-part work. The literary element, whether in the form of the spoken word or as a motto, adds a further dimension to Toch's musical message; it is not to be mistaken for the central idea of a programme. What Toch expresses verbally concerns only the spirit of his symphonies.

Toch's idiom has, at all times, been highly chromatic; but he has discovered the secret of achieving a perfect equilibrium between chromatic and diatonic material, without transmitting a feeling of stylistic schizophrenia. A simple C major *cantilena*, such as the following theme from the scherzo of his Second symphony, is characteristically Toch to anybody even superficially acquainted with his idiom:

228

How strikingly this contrasts against the opening subject of the same movement:

229

etc.

Yet there is no change of style, of character, or even of mood as Toch progresses from the chromatic quality of one section to the diatonic structure of the next. The magnitude of his personality unites widely divergent techniques into a coherent musical language that is unmistakably his own.

Toch's originality in the use of the orchestra is second to none; he is fond of delicate textures, sometimes achieved by the multiple subdivision of violins, as in the second movement of the Third symphony. But the impact of an orchestral *tutti* is equally important to him, and his mastery in extending the orchestra's range of sound to its very limit is evident from the final pages of each of the first three symphonies.

Toch is just as apt to confine himself to a comparatively small complement of conventional instruments (for instance in the Fourth symphony) as he is ready to demand specially manufactured instruments when his inner ear calls for them, as he did in the Third. It is a telling commentary on the state of music in our time that this requirement, motivated entirely by the artistic considerations of a superior creative mind, met with so much resistance that conventional instruments had to be substituted when the score was published, while other composers, whose creativity does not extend beyond an interest in sound experiments, often are provided with specially built facilities and substantial funds to carry out their ideas.

Ernst Toch's late style is a synthesis of various earlier periods in his development, which, however, all grew from a deep understanding of musical culture in Western civilization. This kind of synthesis occurs every so often in the history of music. Such a fusion must, of necessity, transcend national boundaries; the symphonies of Ernst Toch, Austrian-born world citizen of American nationality, serve as a reminder that the significant music of an era is not national, but cosmopolitan in character.*

* Ernst Toch died on 1 October 1964, having in the meantime composed another three symphonies. (Ed.)

33
PROSPECT AND PERSPECTIVE
Hugh Ottaway

*

'The glamour of the anarchist and the mystery of the sphinx have begun to pall, and we are faced with the unenviable task of making constructive effort and plain statement appear interesting.'

CONSTANT LAMBERT, *Music Ho!* (1934)

'After all, Europe will have to abandon itself.'

JOHN CAGE (1962)

THE immediate prospect has many grim features. It is hard to name one symphony by a composer under fifty that looks like entering the repertoire, even for a season. The aspiring young symphonist, baffled by the problems of tradition and innovation, may well decide that he, too, will have to abandon himself. The odds are heavily against him: on the one hand, he experiences the burden of some two hundred years of symphonic history; on the other, an *avant-garde* that is not only anti-symphonic but overtly nihilistic. In the concert hall he has to compete with Haydn and Mozart, Beethoven and Brahms, Mahler and Sibelius. . . . At Darmstadt, Warsaw or Palermo he finds 'constructive effort and plain statement' held up to ridicule: the non-artistic gestures of that veteran 'dada-ist' John Cage, at one time located on the luniest of fringes, have become increasingly 'central' and representative. It looks like the end of the road. And the lesson to be drawn from Lambert's shrewd analysis is not that we have been here before but that the road has been suspect for a good many years.

Few would dispute that a crisis exists. Some musicians who less than ten years ago expressed enthusiasm for the festivals of modern music now recoil perplexed. A broadcast discussion* between two young composers, Alexander Goehr

* Recorded by the B.B.C. in June 1963 and broadcast in the Third Programme.

and Gunther Schuller, proved most revealing: their subject was the American musical scene, but much of what they said concerned their own disenchantment with the European *avant-garde*. For them, it seems, the spell was broken by 'the John Cage philosophy'. 'What bothers me,' said Gunther Schuller, 'is that there are so many young composers, and I met them in every country I visited, who reject totally the very idea of wishing to be connected to a previous tradition: I mean, they want to have a complete break-off point.' Significantly, both speakers fell back to Schoenberg. Again, that ardent Schoenbergian Hans Keller – assisted by his *alter ego* Piotr Zak! – has demonstrated that a valid distinction between bad art and non-art can no longer be made. The critics who commented on Zak's *Mobile** were mostly disposed to take it seriously rather than dismiss it as nonsense or suspect a hoax.

Discussion of these questions tends to have an all-too-limited perspective; 'classical' pitch-serialism is invariably the vanishing point. A great deal is said about a 'crisis in communication', but the underlying crisis of community, already implicit in the music of the second Viennese school, passes unremarked. It is generally assumed that Schoenberg stands above the present controversy; as Gunther Schuller put it, 'if Schoenberg is restored to his rightful position as the most important innovator of our century, then I think this situation will greatly improve'. And yet, ironically, it was Schoenberg who first made possible the systematic fragmentation of musical language. Athematicism, 'the discovery of the single note', and other forms of fragmentation were able to enter by the front door – i.e., in the name of structural consistency. Clearly, the discussion cries out for a deeper perspective and a wider frame of reference. Both may be found in the symphonic mainstream of European musical experience.

---

* There is no such composer or composition. The 'work' consisted of Keller and an assistant improvising freely with a battery of percussion instruments – and an 'electronic' background to lend authenticity (Third Programme, 1961).

It is worth recalling that the early symphony, especially at Mannheim in the 1750s and 1760s, was the embodiment of far-reaching changes in musical expression. Designed to appeal to a new and growing public, it broke with the past by creating a language of dynamic contrasts: musical form, hitherto purely spatial (architectural) in conception, now became a dramatic principle of construction capable of harnessing a variety of tonal and thematic tensions and of resolving them into a higher unity. Fundamental to this revolution was a new kind of musical movement based upon a dynamic sense of tonality. That it *was* a revolution can be shown at a number of levels, but there was nothing approaching 'a complete break-off point'. On the contrary, it can equally be shown that the new formal principles, as consolidated by Haydn and Mozart, were derived from the old, and that the impulse behind them, far from being one of abandonment, was essentially positive.

Such far-reaching changes do not occur in isolation. Nothing that is human is self-contained: a new kind of musical movement implies a new kind of attitude to experience and cannot be accounted for purely in terms of musical materials. The rise of the symphony, and of the entire sonata outlook, was neither fortuitous nor inevitable, neither a whim of fashionable taste nor a compulsive working out of tonal forces. Indeed, the classical symphony was a hard-won achievement, an outstanding creation of what is conveniently called the Age of Enlightenment or Age of Reason. No doubt we should beware of labels such as these – the eighteenth century witnessed much that was unenlightened and irrational – yet they serve to represent a stream of thought and feeling which we recognize as vital to the period. And vital for us, too, unless we subscribe to something like 'the John Cage philosophy'.* For despite the voices of the

* The very antithesis of the Enlightenment: 'He looks with a sort of wonder on things just because they exist or happen; his attitude to the world is one of perpetual, child-like amazement; he seems content to observe things, without any desire to change or influence them.' Michael Parsons, *John Cage* (*New Left Review*, No. 23, Jan.–Feb. 1964).

'disillusioned', the Enlightenment remains the watershed of our twentieth-century hopes and aspirations: as E. J. Hobsbawm has remarked, 'all progressive, rationalist and humanist ideologies are implied in it, and indeed came out of it'.* No matter how utopian, naïve or mechanistic some aspects of the Enlightenment may have been, considered as a whole it is a landmark of the greatest significance, an affirmation of man's ability to master his environment, both natural and social. Sonata dynamism, with its active, purposive enlargement of tonality, exactly mirrors this expanded view of human potentiality. Perhaps no other age has devised a form of musical imagery at once so precise and so susceptible of development.

To speak of the Enlightenment's 'discovery of man' is scarcely an exaggeration, for the new humanism differed from the old in many important respects. In particular, it was less abstract, for it was based on tangible, if sometimes erroneous, scientific progress, and it was latently democratic. The democratization of music is inseparable from the early history of the symphony. The classical symphony is a public statement, in a way that is true of little, if any, previous music; neither ceremonial nor ritualistic, it celebrates a new scale of human values and a new social vision. In this respect, Beethoven's symphonies differ from Haydn's in degree rather than in kind. Beethoven's assertion of the individual will is an exhortation to the world at large – 'O ye millions, I embrace ye!' – and his public is ideally the whole of mankind. However 'anarchic' he may have seemed to some of his contemporaries – Goethe, for instance – Beethoven's colossal tonal structures and their relation to tradition are ample evidence that he, too, believed in civilization. But for him the vision of the Enlightenment implied a conscious remaking of society, a liberation of the human spirit through heroic endeavour: in his symphonies, especially the 'Eroica' and Nos. 5, 7 and 9, sonata dynamism

* See *The Age of Revolution* (Weidenfeld and Nicholson, 1962): a stimulating discussion of the 'dual revolution' – the French and the Industrial – and of its ramifications down to 1848.

is potently transformed by the 'romantic' virtue of enthusiasm.

Romanticism was both an extension of the Enlightenment and a reaction against it. While it opened up a new world of subjective expression and so enriched the content of humanism, it also tended towards mystification and the cult of the sublime. As disillusionment set in – a disillusionment that was only too widespread after the Liberal *débâcle* of 1848–9 – romanticism became a refuge, increasingly remote from social reality, and artistic aspiration assumed the character of a solitary quest: 'the artist and his soul' seemed the one enduring theme. What Ernst Fischer calls 'the celebration of the individual's absolute uniqueness, the unbounded Byronic subjectivism'* is undoubtedly the highest common factor in this very complex situation. So far as music is concerned, it was decisive. The search for an ever greater degree of harmonic expressiveness, often in a programmatic context, not only weakened the feeling for the larger aspects of tonality but undermined the kind of structure that had been based upon it. Fittingly, it was Wagner, the supreme romantic egoist, who formulated 'the art of transition' and 'endless melody' as new principles of expression.† And it is significant that neither of the greatest symphonists from the Wagnerian epoch – Brahms and Bruckner – was a typical romantic. For all his pessimism and romantic melancholy, Brahms believed passionately in an objective musical structure; and Bruckner's symphonies, despite the attentions they received from the Wagnerites, have the kind of objectivity one associates with the religious composers of a much earlier period.

If Bruckner is felt to stand *above* the struggle, this is because his religious view of the world was entirely innocent and free from self-consciousness. Not surprisingly, he has had no true successor. By the end of the century, the

* Ernst Fischer, *The Necessity of Art* (Pelican Books, 1963).

† Though it was not his fault that his own supreme mastery of tonality was not grasped by those of his successors in whom the weakening is manifest.

humanist disenchantment had deepened into an acute sense of alienation. As artists became more and more absorbed in the 'sublimity' of their own subjective experience, so their hold on reality became more precarious: the romantic ego, now turned in upon itself, sought fulfilment in a pseudo-religious ecstasy (Scriabin), a contemplative hedonism (Delius), or a world of pure sense-experience (Debussy). It is a pointer to Mahler's stature that, for him, no such 'solution' would do. Though essentially a victim of the same situation – who more so? – Mahler strove for a comprehensive vision, at once humanistic and religious, that would meet humanity's needs as well as his own. His 'world-saving' subjectivism stands as a monument at the brink of the abyss.

Mahler was the last major symphonist in the Viennese tradition, and the very precariousness of his position may well explain his peculiar fascination for many of us today. Humanistic march themes figure prominently in his imagery, but more often than not these have a heavy, funereal tread, even a spectral, nightmarish quality; and sometimes in his later music the harmonic texture tends to disintegrate in a way that reaches out towards Schoenberg. Mahler's doom-laden suspensions and the agony of Schoenberg's 'twelve unresolved *appoggiaturas*' are, of course, intimately related, only Schoenberg made a virtue of the kind of experience which Mahler had struggled to keep at bay. As romantic individualism entered its ultimate, agoraphobic phase, new expressive principles again emerged: 'endless melody' was translated into the endless permutation of pitch-serialism, and the possibility of purposeful tonal activity – the mainspring of humanist expression – was consciously rejected. Not only atonality but its necessary concomitant, a new kind of musical movement – fundamentally static, however hectic its condition – was now established.

Such frenzied immobility is an apt musical image for those twentieth-century spirits who are overwhelmed by the implications of living. Only in violence can such extreme subjective tensions find release: from Schoenberg (via Webern) to Karlheinz Stockhausen is surely an inevitable and compulsive progression, both musically and psychologically. In its destructive irrationality Stockhausen's music is, almost literally, alienation gone mad. That some musicians give it positive value in terms of 'the abnegation of harmonic consciousness' and 'the desire to "begin again" *ab ovo*' – the Cage philosophy, in fact – is indicative of the extent to which the humanistic vision, and with it the symphonic aim, has been renounced. The unsymphonic symphonies of a relative conservative like Hans Werner Henze provide corroborative evidence – from the other side, so to speak.

The talk of '*ab ovo*-ism' may sound revolutionary and attractive, but in the world as we know it this is simply one more evasion of reality. We can no more 'begin again', in the sense of 'a complete break-off point', than withdraw to prepared positions. As Deryck Cooke has reminded us – in a piece on Mahler, interestingly enough – 'we of the twentieth century, discouraged though we may be, are still committed to the heavy responsibility handed on to us by the nineteenth – that of trying to better the conditions and the quality of human life throughout the world; and we have no other spiritual capital to draw on than the philosophy of humanism. To turn back to outgrown religious dogmas, or to fall back on a cynical nihilism and hedonism – two attitudes which are indeed all too widespread – is a declaration of spiritual bankruptcy.'* What makes this commitment so acute is the knowledge that now, for the first time, we have the technological resources capable of bringing many of the hopes of the Enlightenment within our reach, and also – need it be said? – the means of accomplishing our total destruction. We must face the fact that man's irrationality *may* have the last word; the imagery of violent fragmentation could be only too prophetic. But however overwhelming and impersonal the forces against us may appear, they are not superhuman; our fate, unlike our music, is not 'pre-

* 'The Word and the Deed': see *The Listener*, 2 July 1964.

determined'. To say that in the end *it is up to us* may sound pathetically naïve: the individual's sense of helplessness is too deeply rooted, its expression too authentic, to be simply shaken off like a touch of the shivers. Even so, for the artist these five monosyllables hold a special kind of truth. I am reminded of Rudolph Reti's words: 'We will never be able to change reality as long as we cannot change our dreams'.* To submit to the prevailing trend – and much that passes for protest, pity and compassion is really a submission – is so much easier than to affirm a large, constructive vision of the future; and yet, 'discouraged though we may be', are our imaginations so impoverished that this hopeful alternative must seem beyond our grasp? Here, of course, the cynics shake their heads and mutter 'shallow optimism'. But the cynics have a vested interest in misinterpreting constructive effort; they may even recognize that a return to humanism is more demanding, more revolutionary, than all the 'break-off points' imaginable.

This is not a plea for further ventures in neo-classicism or neo-romanticism: would-be solutions on the purely stylistic level only confuse the issue. It is a plea for a genuine re-engagement with the humanist tradition. What does this entail? First, of course, the right sort of vision, clear-headed and unsentimental, and a refusal to be side-tracked by private cults and 'isms'. Next, an ability to learn from the past in the way that Mozart (after 1780) learnt from J. S. Bach, the later Sibelius from Palestrina, and Rubbra from the madrigal composers – to cite only three very different examples. In effect, a composer 'chooses' his influences according to his needs, and where the influence is right the outcome is not pastiche or any other form of imitation but the absorption of some expressive principle. The most pressing need today is surely the recovery of a sense of musical movement capable of sustaining a coherent and dynamic structure. This is fundamental and brings us face to face with the question of tonality. Here the basic choice

* *Tonality – Atonality – Pantonality* (Rockliff, 1958).

is really very simple: to recognize the existence of tonality and to try to use it in new and positive ways, or to exclude what is still the most life-enhancing dimension of musical expression. As the Editor has remarked in his Introduction to Volume One, 'the human sense of tonality has many times been modified, but cannot be abolished. To attempt this is to cease to be comprehensive, to be narrowly exclusive.'

Equally important is a desire to make contact with the vast potential audience of the 1960s. This is not a matter of 'writing down' or of aiming at a familiar response, but rather one of utilizing forms of musical imagery that are rooted in the common experience of our age. The creative reappraisal which the American Aaron Copland made around 1934 – one is tempted to call it Copland's New Deal – is closely relevant to this discussion. During the years 1930–33 Copland had turned more and more to a 'special public' and his work had become increasingly esoteric. His dissatisfaction with such a course was, he says, 'a recrudescence of my old interest in making a connexion between music and the life about me'. Nearly twenty years later he wrote these reflections:

One of the primary problems for the composer in an industrial society like that of America is to achieve integration, to find justification for the life of art in the life about him. I must believe in the ultimate good of the world and of life as I live it in order to create a work of art. Negative emotions cannot produce art; positive emotions bespeak an emotion about something. I cannot imagine an art work without implied convictions; and that is true also for music, the most abstract of the arts.

It is this need for a positive philosophy which is a little frightening in the world as we know it. You cannot make art out of fear and suspicion; you can make it only out of affirmative beliefs. This sense of affirmation can be had only in part from one's inner being; for the rest it must be continually reactivated by a creative and yea-saying atmosphere in the life about one. The artist should feel himself affirmed and buoyed up by his community. . . .*

* *Music and Imagination* (Oxford, 1952).

Clearly, for Copland the composer's relationship with his community is the crux of the creative problem. What this meant to him in his most fruitful period can be seen from a study of the Third symphony (1946) and from a comparison of the symphony with the deeply alienated piano variations (1930).

Some, no doubt, will consider it perverse to end with a reference to Copland's Third symphony. True, this composer is neither a born symphonist nor the heir to a symphonic tradition; his imagination is much inclined towards a terse, epigrammatic mode of expression. But this is precisely the point. The fact that a composer such as Copland, as he enlarged and opened out his vision, sought fulfilment in a large-scale symphonic work is not the least of answers to those who say the form is 'worn out'. In reality a form does not wear out, for it has no physical existence; so long as there are artists prepared to grapple with experience, not merely to reflect it, the idea of the symphony – dynamic, constructive, expansive – will remain a great creative challenge.

INDEX

Abraham, Gerald, 201
Alkan, 47, 102
Antheil, George, 256
Arnold, Malcolm, 13
Auden, W. H., 262

Bach, Johann Sebastian, 12, 133, 183, 275
Bacon, Ernst, 256
Balakirev, Mily, 166
Bantock, Granville, 93, 141, 219
Barber, Samuel, 246, 257ff., 262
Bartók, Bela, 113, 114, 231
Bax, Arnold, 121, 153ff.
Beethoven, Ludwig van, 10, 12, 16, 22, 32, 35, 38, 42, 48, 53, 54, 55, 71, 89, 90, 92, 94, 120, 132, 190, 228, 230, 268, 271
Bentzon, Niels Viggo, 238ff.
Berg, Alban, 201, 261
Berlioz, Hector, 16, 17, 18, 104, 141
Bernstein, Leonard, 245, 262
Berwald, Franz, 239
Bizet, Georges, 104
Blackwood, Easley, 263
Blake, William, 119
Bliss, Arthur, 161
Blomdahl, Karl-Birger, 238
Borodin, Alexander, 52, 129, 130, 166
Boughton, Rutland, 141
Boulanger, Nadia, 248, 252, 254
Boult, Adrian, 124, 163
Borkevec, Pavel, 222
Brahms, Johannes, 21, 52, 55, 56, 91, 132, 141, 182, 219, 230, 249, 268, 272
Brian, Havergal, 140ff.
Britten, Benjamin, 13

Bruckner, Anton, 34, 39, 48, 51, 90, 132, 133, 143, 272
Bruysov, Valery, 171
Bunyan, John, 121
Butterworth, George, 116

Cage, John, 268, 269, 270, 274
Cairns, David, 104
Carner, Mosco, 15
Casella, Alfredo, 157
Chausson, Ernest, 104
Chopin, Frédéric, 172
Conrad, Joseph, 98
Cooke, Deryck, 44, 274
Copland, Aaron, 246, 252ff., 255, 259, 276ff.
Cowell, Henry, 245, 256, 262
Cox, David, 15ff., 114ff., 153ff., 189ff.
Creston, Paul, 259

Dallapiccola, Luigi, 261
Debussy, Claude, 9, 104, 114, 118, 142, 155, 162, 198, 230, 249, 273
Delibes, Léo, 18
Delius, Frederick, 273
Dent, Edward J., 19
Diaghilev, Serge, 172
Donne, John, 181
Douglas, Alfred, 144
Dukas, Paul, 104
Dussek, Jan Ladislav, 90
Dvořák, Antonín, 52, 56, 218, 219, 220, 222, 226

Edward VII, 22, 25
Eisenstein, Sergei, 199
Elgar, Edward, 15ff. 116, 126, 141, 189, 190

Fauré, Gabriel, 104
Fibich, Zdenek, 219
Fischer, Ernst, 272
Foerster, J. B., 219
Franck, César, 104, 264
Frankel, Benjamin, 13
Fricker, Peter Racine, 13

Gairdner, Temple, 23
George V, 22
Gershwin, George, 161
Glazunov, Alexander, 199, 200
Glière, Reinhold, 168, 220
Gordon, General, 20, 21
Goeb, Roger, 263
Goehr, Alexander, 268
Goethe, Johann Wolfgang von, 264, 271
Gounod, Charles, 16
Gray, Cecil, 99
Grimm (brothers), 31

Haba, Alois, 245
Haieff, Alexei, 263
Handel, George Frederick, 12
Hanson, Howard, 259
Harris, Roy, 246, 248ff., 252, 255, 257
Hartmann, J. P. E., 238
Harty, Hamilton, 15
Haydn, Joseph, 35, 53, 97, 144, 211, 268, 270
Henze, Hans Werner, 274
Heseltine, Philip (Peter Warlock), 154
Hill, Ralph, 128
Hindemith, Paul, 9, 12–13, 170, 189, 201, 202, 207, 222, 239, 240
Hobsbawm, E. J., 271
Holbrooke, Joseph, 141
Holmboe, Vagn, 230ff., 239, 240
Holst, Gustav, 114, 125, 181, 182
Honegger, Arthur, 169
Housman, A. E., 65
Hovhaness, Alan, 262

Indy, Vincent d', 104, 106
Ireland, John, 156
Ives, Charles, 244ff.

Jaeger, A. J. ('Nimrod'), 20
James, Henry, 41
Janáček, Leos, 218
Jeppesen, Knud, 231, 238

Kabalevsky, Dmitri, 213
Keller, Hans, 9, 269
Khachaturian, Aram, 175, 212
Khrennikov, Tikhon, 213
Kipling, Rudyard, 16
Klopstock, Friedrich, 39
Kodály, Zoltan, 114, 264
Kohs, Ellis, 263
Korn, Peter Jona, 243ff., 263
Koussevitsky, Serge, 104, 157, 172, 210, 249
Křenek, Ernst, 201
Krommer (Kramař), Franz, 218
Kuperman, Meyer, 263
Kurka, Robert, 263

Lalo, Édouard, 104
Lambert, Constant, 268
Larsson, Lars-Erik, 240
Layton, Robert, 166ff., 197ff., 218ff., 230ff.
Lees, Benjamin, 263
Liszt, Franz, 16, 26, 220, 244
Luther, Martin, 264

MacDowell, Edward, 244, 264
MacDowell, Marion, 264
Madetoja, Leevi, 230
Mahler, Gustav, 13, 15, 29ff., 53, 141, 142, 143, 147, 179, 183, 198, 203, 204, 206, 212, 219, 220, 268, 273, 274
Maine, Basil, 22, 26
Manduell, John, 104ff.
Martinů, Bohuslav, 218ff.
Mayakovsky, Vladimir, 206
Mellers, Wilfrid, 55
Mendelssohn, Felix, 16

Mennin, Peter, 262–3
Meyerbeer, Giacomo, 18
Miaskovsky, Nicolas, 168, 198
Monteux, Pierre, 170
Morris, R. O., 181
Mozart, Wolfgang Amadeus, 32, 35, 38, 53, 71, 96, 247, 268, 270, 275

Newman, Ernest, 15, 208
Nielsen, Carl, 46, 52ff., 93, 230, 231, 233
Novák, Vitězslav, 219, 220

Ottaway, Hugh, 52ff., 268ff.

Palestrina, Giovanni Pierluigi da, 81, 82, 275
Pannain, Guido, 127
Parry, Hubert, 114, 115, 141
Persichetti, Vincent, 263
Petersen, Frede Schandorf, 61
Pfitzner, Hans, 149
Piston, Walter, 254ff.
Prokofiev, Serge, 126, 166ff., 189, 198, 199, 202, 204, 207, 214
Puccini, Giacomo, 126
Purcell, Henry, 114

Rabinovich, Dmitry, 212
Rachmaninoff, Sergei, 128ff.
Rangström, Ture, 219
Ravel, Maurice, 104, 156, 181
Rawsthorne, Alan, 13
Reed, W. H., 28
Reger, Max, 132, 133, 135
Respighi, Ottorino, 157
Reti, Rudolph, 275
Riegger, Wallingford, 260
Richter, Hans, 15, 16, 20, 22
Ridký, Jaroslav, 220
Rimsky-Korsakov, Nicholas, 155, 157
Rochberg, George, 263
Rolland, Romain, 240
Rosenberg, Hilding, 237, 238, 239ff.

Roussel, Albert, 104ff.
Rubbra, Edmund, 181ff., 186, 275

Saeverud, Harald, 237, 242
Saint-Saëns, Camille, 104
Sammartini, Giuseppe, 37, 40, 47
Satie, Erik, 114
Schmidt, Franz, 132ff.
Schoenberg, Arnold, 10, 13, 239, 244, 245, 261, 269, 273, 274
Schreker, Franz, 201
Schubert, Franz, 32, 38, 96, 97, 98, 100, 126, 134, 137, 149
Schuller, Gunther, 269
Schuman, William, 256, 262
Schumann, Robert, 16, 94, 97
Schweitzer, Albert, 264
Scriabin, Alexander, 273
Searle, Humphrey, 13
Sessions, Roger, 260ff.
Shelley, Percy Bysshe, 22, 23, 142
Shostakovich, Dmitri, 13, 126, 166, 179, 197ff.
Sibelius, Jean, 12, 20, 32, 44, 45, 52, 55, 80ff., 121, 132, 145, 154, 163, 167, 189, 190, 197, 198, 204, 230, 231, 239, 268, 275
Simpson, Robert, 9ff., 56, 57, 59, 128ff., 152, 276
Smetana, Bedrich, 52, 218, 219
Spohr, Ludwig, 16
Stanford, Charles, 141
Starer, Robert, 263
Steinberg, Maximilian, 201
Stenhammar, Wilhelm, 239
Stockhausen, Karlheinz, 274
Stokowski, Leopold, 59, 170, 246
Strauss, Richard, 16, 17, 141, 155, 219
Stravinsky, Igor, 9, 11–12, 13, 113, 155, 166, 167, 168, 189, 192, 201, 202, 228, 232, 248
Suk, Josef, 219, 220–22

Synge, J. M., 142

Tallis, Thomas, 126
Tchaikovsky, Peter Ilich, 129, 130, 155, 165, 166, 200, 201, 213
Tennyson, Alfred, 26, 116
Thomson, Virgil, 223, 224
Tippett, Michael, 181, 186ff.
Toch, Ernst, 231, 263ff.
Törne, Bengt de, 94
Tovey, Donald, 140
Truscott, Harold, 29ff., 53, 132ff., 140ff., 181ff.
Turner, W. H., 15

Vaughan, Henry, 181
Vaughan Williams, Ralph, 114ff., 132, 162, 188, 189, 249
Verdi, Giuseppe, 216

Wagner, Richard, 16, 18, 19, 54, 114, 155, 219, 272
Walton, William, 161, 188, 189ff.
Ward, Robert, 263
Warlock, Peter. See Heseltine
Webern, Anton, 274
Werth, Alexander, 211
Whitman, Walt, 115
Wirén, Dag, 230, 231, 237, 240, 241-2
Wolff, Albert, 110
Wood, Henry, 15, 140, 142, 157, 203
Wordsworth, William (composer), 14

Yeats, W. B., 154

Zak, Piotr, 269
Zhdanov, 179, 197, 211

*Some other books published by Penguins
are described on the following pages*

INTRODUCING MUSIC
Ottó Károlyi

Some acquaintance with the grammar and vocabulary of music – enough to understand the language without speaking it – greatly broadens the pleasure of hearing it.

Introducing Music at long last makes the attempt to convey the elements of the art to music-lovers with no technical knowledge. Setting out from the relatively open ground of tones, pitches, timbres, sharps, flats, bars and keys, Ottó Károlyi is able to conduct the reader out into the more exciting territory of dominant sevenths and symphonic structure. His text is clearly signposted by musical examples and illustrations of instruments described, and no intelligent reader should have any difficulty in following the path. On arrival at the end, in place of being confused by the technicalities of a programme note, he should be within reach of following the music in a score.

THE PELICAN HISTORY
OF MUSIC

Edited by Alec Robertson and Denis Stevens

The concert-goer and music-lover anxious to discover some of the hidden wealth of musical history will find in this series of three volumes an account of many kinds of music: primitive and non-Western, liturgical, medieval, renaissance, baroque, classical, romantic, and modern. Although there is some technical analysis, the authors and editors have concentrated on fitting music into its proper frame, whether ecclesiastical, courtly, or popular.

Each musical epoch is discussed by an expert who considers the music at its face value, instead of thinking of it merely as a link in a chain of development ending in the music of Beethoven or Boulez. The reader can therefore come to understand musical trends and styles both within and without the normal orbit of concerts and opera, and will be able to enjoy unfamiliar music as well as the accepted classics.

A special feature of each volume is the group of illustrations that have been chosen to set the scene rather than to illustrate any specific points in the text.

CHAMBER MUSIC

Edited by Alec Robertson

Chamber music has frequently and rightly been described as the music of friends, in allusion to the intimate team work the playing of it involves and its special character. The term itself covers a huge field of beautiful, and still far too little known, music, the exact limits of which are undefined. For the purpose of this book, a companion volume to *The Concerto* and *The Symphony*, it is taken to range from duet works to octets, and to cover the time from the early eighteenth century to the present day. Haydn is given pride of place as having developed the string quartet, the central medium of chamber music, to a wonderful peak of perfection. Chapters follow on the various kinds of chamber music by Mozart, Beethoven, Schubert, and many others up to Bartók, whose six string quartets are considered to be in the great classical line. The remaining composers are grouped together according to their countries of origin.

'Much valuable guidance in its prescribed field' – *The Times Literary Supplement*

The companion to this volume

THE SYMPHONY VOLUME 1
HAYDN TO DVORAK
Edited by Robert Simpson

THE PENGUIN GUIDE TO
BARGAIN RECORDS
Edward Greenfield, Ivan March, and Denis Stevens

'Comprehensive and reliable guide to the enormous number of LPs of classical music now retailing at about a guinea (in some cases as cheaply as 12s 6d or 10s). You can build up an exciting record collection at about half the normal price with this handy little volume to refer to' – *Observer*

'Genuine bargains are distinguished from what is merely cheap' – *Guardian*

'It would be hard to find better or more simply presented advice than Messrs Greenfield, March, and Stevens give us here' – *Musical Times*